RESTORING HONOR TO PUBLIC SCHOOLS

A Teacher's Vision for American Education

William E. Smith

ROWMAN & LITTLEFIELD EDUCATION
Lanham • New York • Toronto • Plymouth, UK

Published in the United States of America
by Rowman & Littlefield Education
A Division of Rowman & Littlefield Publishers, Inc.
A wholly owned subsidary of The Rowman & Littlefield Publishing
Group, Inc.
4501 Forbes Boulevard, Suite 200, Lanham, Maryland 20706
www.rowmaneducation.com

Estover Road
Plymouth PL6 7PY
United Kingdom

British Library Cataloguing in Publication Information Available

Library of Congress Cataloging-in-Publication Data

Smith, William E., 1950–
  Restoring honor to public schools : a teacher's vision for American
education / William E. Smith.
     p. cm.
  Includes bibliographical references.
  ISBN-13: 978-1-57886-928-2 (cloth : alk. paper)
  ISBN-10: 1-57886-928-5 (cloth : alk. paper)
  ISBN-13: 978-1-57886-929-9 (pbk. : alk. paper)
  ISBN-10: 1-57886-929-3 (pbk. : alk. paper)
  ISBN-10: 1-57886-930-7 (electronic)
  ISBN-13: 978-1-57886-930-5 (electronic)
  1. Public schools—United States. 2. Educational accountability—
United States. 3. Education and state—United States. 4. Educational
change—United States. I. Title.
  LA217.2.S62 2009
  370.973—dc2   2008034469

♾™ The paper used in this publication meets the minimum requirements of
American National Standard for Information Sciences—Permanence of Paper for
Printed Library Materials, ANSI/NISO Z39.48-1992.

Contents

Foreword

THIS IS ONE BEAUTIFUL BOOK. I considered other adjectives such as *powerful* and *compelling* and *commanding*, and they all fit, but *beautiful* is best. The book seems to me a variation on a Tralfamadorian novel. Tralfamadore is a planet invented by Kurt Vonnegut in the novel *Slaughterhouse Five*. As Vonnegut explains, Tralfamadorian novels are slim volumes of messages that Tralfamadorians can read simultaneously. "There isn't any particular relationship between the messages except that the author has chosen them carefully so that when viewed simultaneously they produce an image that is beautiful, surprising, and deep."[1]

I call this book a variation on the Tralfamadorian novel because there are relationships among the messages, but they are no less deep for that. You can't see all the messages simultaneously, but I doubt you'll put the book down for long.

For anyone who has been tracking school reform for a while, there is nothing especially new in any one of the messages, but they are delivered with an originality that impresses and inspires, and clarifies. For example, as you near the end of the book, it hits you that among American public education's worst enemies are present and former secretaries of education: Bennett, Alexander, Paige, and Spellings. Paige's notorious comment calling the NEA a terrorist organization is mentioned, but, although Bennett is taken to task, one of his worst statements is not: As head of the Federal

Communications Commission, Reed Hundt went to former Secretary Bennett and asked him to support legislation that would
bring Internet infrastructure to both public and private schools.
According to Hundt, "He told me he would not help, because he
did not want public schools to obtain new funding, new capability,
new tools for success. He wanted them, he said, to fail so that they
could be replaced with vouchers, charter schools, religious
schools, and other forms of private education."[2]

Imagine a secretary of defense saying something similar about
the military. Smith weaves together many instances of how politicians and the media repeatedly scorn public education. It's the old
Nazi trick—tell a lie often enough and people will come to believe
it. The good news is, parents don't, at least not yet. But Smith wor-
ries about the consequences for the kids. Although he has no data,
nor do I, Smith thinks "it just doesn't seem likely that students will
achieve as much academically if they're continually hearing that
their schools stink."

Part of the beauty of the book is Smith's interweaving of anecdote and data. He has thirty years of experience as teacher at various levels and as principal. So he has lots of anecdotes and a compelling writing style to make them stick. He's a born storyteller. But
often after telling a story he brings in the numbers, the statistics
from the research literature to back up the story's point (one is
tempted to call it a moral). It is a powerful technique. He tells of a
student who brought a gun to school and uses that as a springboard
to talk about all the things kids bring to school from their lives outside it. From his exposition you see clearly the absurdity of No
Child Left Behind's "schools-can-do-it-all" assumption.

But often the stories alone can make the point because Smith
is such a powerful storyteller, usually recounting his own experiences. Smith tells of his impoverished school in the Lowcountry of
South Carolina. You start to sweat from the heat and humidity just
from the description. His school has no air conditioning. The other
schools in the district do, but only because the parents have bought
window units. His kids' parents can't possibly afford to do the same.
When he requests additional funding from the superintendent, the
super tells him the district treats all schools equally. Smith finally

makes a plea to the board and gets his funding. His point, though, is that equal does not always mean fair.

His imaginary conversation between a teacher and her students as she tries to get them to do their best on the National Assessment of Educational Progress (NAEP) is nothing short of hilarious, largely because it rings so true. I once asserted to Archie Lapointe, then the executive director of NAEP, that NAEP systematically underestimated achievement because kids didn't take it seriously. Archie replied, "Yes, our hardest problem in NAEP is keeping them awake during the test." When a district I worked in tried out NAEP items in some middle schools, half the teachers reported they had trouble keeping the kids on task. Smith makes the equally valid point that NAEP is not the kind of test kids expect, especially during these times of hyperemphasis on state tests. Nor are TIMSS, PISA, or PIRLS.

His story of a Committee for Educational Excellence would be equally funny if it didn't concern important outcomes and if it didn't show, as Smith's stories often show, the operation of Campbell's law. Campbell's law states, "The more any quantitative social indicator is used for social decision making, the more subject it will be to corruption pressures and the more apt it will be to distort and corrupt the social processes it is intended to monitor." NCLB, anyone?

And that's a major point Smith repeats: Our education reforms have corrupted education. Keep in mind that *reform* does not mean *improve* but only *reshape*. In the matter of high-stakes tests, Smith says this gives rise to the illusion of reform success and, as test scores climb, to the illusion of educational excellence. But, because the reforms are enacted by people who don't understand education, and because the schools are hyperfocused on the tests, not on moving beyond them, the illusion of success is soon followed by the illusion of educational failure.

Smith closes with steps we can take to elevate the discourse about education. Because I've been tracking—and trying to counter—the debased discourse for almost twenty years, as recently as a year ago I would have been wont to dismiss these, saying, "It will not happen." And it is true that outfits like Alliance for Excellent Education and

Edin08 continue to demean schools. Fear China, fear India. More math, more science. That's all there is to it.

But there are hopeful signs today. People are once again writing about education and democracy. I am particularly encouraged by the loose, ideologically diverse coalition known as the Broader Bolder Approach to Education (www.boldapproach.org). So far as I know, the Broader Bolder group does not assign books as a teacher might. If it did, though, *Restoring Honor to Public Schools* might very well top the list.

Gerald Bracey
Independent Researcher/Writer
Alexandria, Virginia

---

[1] Vonnegut, K. (1968) *Slaughterhouse Five*. New York: Dell. The wording here is slightly altered from the original which reads, "There isn't any particular relationship between all the messages, except that the author has chosen them carefully, so that, when seen all at once, they produce an image of life that is beautiful and surprising and deep" (p. 88).

[2] This piece by Reed Hundt can be found at www.susanohanian.org/outrage_fetch.php?id=351. It was retrieved on November 7, 2008.

Introduction

THE IMAGE OF BOBBY COULD HAVE BEEN LIFTED from a Norman Rockwell painting. He is lanky and freckle-faced and is wearing hand-me-down overalls with a plain white shirt. A cowlick protrudes from his tousled hair as he turns and rises after acknowledgment from Schoolmarm Andrews. As he slowly straightens his slender frame and stands erect to the left of his desk, he smiles shyly and answers her question about the cost of farm supplies from the local general store.

Bobby and the other boys in the class sit two abreast on the right side of the room, separated by a wide aisle from the girls, who are similarly arranged on the left. The shortest children sit in the front, followed in order by successively taller students. A pot-bellied stove partly obstructs the aisle near the middle of the classroom, and the morning sun filters into the otherwise dimly lit schoolhouse from windows on both sides, providing light that hardly seems adequate for the work of the schoolmarm and her students.

Green paint that has been subtly darkened by the passage of time covers the wide wooden planks that form the ceiling and walls—except, that is, for the boards that extend along the front and sides of the room at the children's eye level. These have been painted black and serve as a crude chalkboard that is covered with carefully written arithmetic problems, penmanship lessons, and traditional maxims for daily living.

Pigtails tied with ribbons rest on the shoulders of most of the girls. Almost all are attired in homemade print dresses, and a few wear matching bonnets. As the schoolmarm conducts the morning's arithmetic lesson, Adam fidgets with the suspenders that seem to press a little too tightly across his plaid shirt. Jeremy and Billy, the shortest boys in the class, sit in the front row, both in white T-shirts, the toes of their dark shoes barely reaching the floor as they swing their legs with the nervous impulsivity of fourth grade males.

When Schoolmarm Andrews calls for volunteers to "cipher" problems on the blackboard, every student strains upward with a raised hand. The four girls and three boys who are selected scramble excitedly to the front, grapple briefly for short pieces of chalk, and enthusiastically begin their computations.

As the children complete the arithmetic lesson, and I sit in the back of the room on a salvaged oak church pew, no amount of effort could possibly enable me to suppress the exhilaration I have been feeling since we arrived this morning to participate in the living history of a one-room schoolhouse. My fourth grade students will spend the entire day reliving an earlier era in American history—ciphering on the blackboard and on individual slate boards, writing with quill pens, playing at recess with hoops and other antique toys, competing in a traditional spelling bee, and eating authentically prepared lunches brought from their homes in pails and baskets.

As the hours speed by, I delight in my students' learning and joy of discovery. Our classroom studies and simulations of life in nineteenth-century America gave the children a glimpse into that earlier era, but this reenactment of education in the 1890s provides them with a level of understanding they could not achieve in our twenty-first-century classroom—as well as a learning experience they will never forget.

This is why I teach.

I chose to introduce this book with a description of my students' visit to a one-room schoolhouse because I know the experience was transformational for them. I can require them to read about life in the past (as I often do), but history becomes far more relevant when they have the opportunity to relive it.

Similarly, I can try to explain electricity to them, or even have them diagram various types of circuits, but they will never achieve meaningful understanding until I give them wires, batteries, and lightbulbs and tell them to create light. When they conduct that experiment, they are no longer just studying science—they are scientists. Further, when they scream with excitement, "Dr. Smith! Come see! We got it to light!" I can hope that their enthusiasm will continue to lead them down a path of lifelong scientific learning.

If parents' comments are any indication, they too value most deeply these types of academic experiences. Although I want my students to master the competencies assessed by our state's mandated achievement tests—and they generally perform quite well on those measures—I have never had a parent thank me for raising a child's test scores. Instead parents express appreciation that their children have become avid readers and writers and have become enthusiastic about mathematics, history, and science. They talk about their children becoming "lost in books" at home and starting to regard reading as a pleasurable daily activity.

Like me, they are excited when students ask, as Brian and Joey recently did, "Can we read three chapters today instead of two?" Or when children beg, "Can we take the book home and finish it tonight?" Parents comment positively about their children's engagement in science projects and history simulations—but never about our classroom preparations for the standardized tests that dominate America's public discourse about education.

These parents are my allies in the classroom. We work together to enhance the learning experiences of their children, and we share many common beliefs about the characteristics of a quality education. Nonetheless, I know that my position as a teacher makes me privy to insights about our public schools that are not always evident to even the most well-informed parents and citizens.

I wrote *Restoring Honor to Public Schools: A Teacher's Vision for American Education* with these readers in mind. I hope that it clarifies for them the unanticipated effects of politics and educational policymaking on our nation's schools and provides them with the knowledge they need to advocate aggressively for positive change.

Because I was once a teacher educator and have a continuing interest in programs of teacher preparation, I also wanted to give attention in this volume to the needs and interests of educational scholars and their students. *Restoring Honor to Public Schools* contains firsthand perspectives that should provide useful insights to university professors and informative reading for education students who are studying public school climate and policy.

In addition, I hope that this book gives voice to the concerns of teachers and administrators, reflects their professional realities, and provides a vision of policymaking consistent with their expectations. We have known for some time that schools are most effective when they enlist the united support of parents, citizens, and educational scholars and practitioners, so I have tried to produce a volume that is useful to each of these groups.

I have been fortunate during my career to have taught in the elementary, middle, and high school grades, and to have served as an assistant principal, district administrator, elementary principal, teacher educator, and K–12 laboratory school director. By drawing upon the perspectives gained in these varied educational roles, I hope that I have been able to clarify in this book the dilemmas and challenges of education in the twenty-first century and to provide readers with a better sense of how our schools might become all that we want them to be.

In writing *Restoring Honor to Public Schools*, I have taken an approach that is atypical of most analyses of educational policy. Rather than producing a summary of research about the status of public schools, I have tried to illuminate the complexities of our educational system primarily by sharing experiences and reflections from my thirty years in the field. All of the stories in this book are true, but pseudonyms are used for the names of students and educators, including those mentioned above.

At times I could not address relevant issues solely through the sharing of personal experiences or reflections. I have cited educational research sparingly and trust that the few studies mentioned in this book are as clear and understandable to noneducators as they are to teachers, administrators, and scholars. Throughout the writing of this volume, I have strived to make it accessible and thought provoking to all readers who care deeply about the status of our public schools and the future of our children. I hope I have succeeded.

THE GOOD, THE BAD, AND THE UGLY: THE REALITY, THE IMAGE, AND THE DISCREDITING OF AMERICA'S PUBLIC SCHOOLS

Chapter One

———————O———————

Learning to Honor Education: A Lesson from Akina

FROM 1992 THROUGH 1996 I taught in the elementary education department of a state university in the Midwest. Those four years in teacher education provided me with many experiences that I fondly recall. However, none was as memorable or as enlightening as my brief friendship with Akina, a Japanese foreign exchange student who spent just one semester in our country but forever altered my perspectives about educational policy.

Akina's career goal was to be an English teacher in her homeland of Japan, and the intent of her visit to America was to enhance her understanding of our language, culture, and educational practices. Consequently, she signed up for a class in which I taught methods of reading and writing instruction to elementary education majors. Rather than enrolling as a regular student, Akina audited the course so that she could attend classes without having to fulfill all course requirements or receive a grade.

When I learned that I would be teaching a Japanese exchange student, my initial reaction was to hope that she could share insights about her country's schools. At the time, American education was still under the glaring spotlight created some ten years earlier by the federal government's publication of *A Nation at Risk* (National Commission on Excellence in Education, 1983). According to this report, our educational system was failing miserably and was causing America to lose its competitive edge in the global marketplace. *A Nation at Risk*

3

initiated more than a decade of intense scrutiny of public schools, with politicians and journalists frequently calling attention to test scores contrasting American students with those from other nations.

Like many educators at the time, I was especially interested in learning about schools in Japan, the country with which we were most often compared. I listened intently to the musings of elected officials and members of the media, and I read a sampling of the scholarly literature contrasting American and Japanese education, always hoping to identify characteristics that made their system more effective than ours. Perhaps, I thought, this young visitor from Japan could finally give me some genuine insight into the success of her nation's schools.

In retrospect, I was naive to believe that a young Japanese woman who had just entered our culture would be ready to interact freely in an American university classroom. When the semester began, Akina sat in the back of the room near the door. She rarely raised her head to make even the most momentary eye contact, and I did not hear her talk at all during the first few weeks of class, even to other students. I once tried unsuccessfully to draw her into a discussion, but she responded with such painful reluctance that I did not call on her again.

Akina finally spoke to me the day I broached the subject of our course's on-site teaching practicum. As one of the requirements in this language arts methods class, students spent twenty hours teaching elementary children in a local public school. (This field experience was one of several in our program that preceded actual student teaching.) As I began talking about the logistics of the practicum, Akina immediately raised her head and listened intently to my explanation and the subsequent class discussion.

To my surprise, she approached me at the end of the period, told me that she did not have any means of transportation, and asked if she could ride with me to the field experience site so that she could observe American teachers providing reading and writing instruction. When I said that she could, the smile that stretched across Akina's face revealed her true interest in my course—clearly, she had been waiting since the beginning of the semester for the opportunity to visit an American public school.

Akina's excitement on the first day of the practicum was palpable. The shyness she had exhibited over the past few months evaporated once we began the short ride from the university campus to the elementary school, and our conversation was virtually nonstop as she peppered me with questions about American education and culture. Once in the school, Akina and I began visiting in each of the classrooms where my students were teaching. After the first few stops, she asked if she could remain in one of the second grade classrooms we had just observed, so I left her there for the remainder of the afternoon.

Akina was beaming when I met her at the end of the school day. This diffident young woman whose voice I had not heard for the first few months of class immediately burst into conversation about all that she had seen during her two hours in the school. As we emerged from the building in to the light of a brisk, sunny afternoon, we continued talking until we were perhaps fifty feet from the door. At that point, she suddenly paused, turned, and bowed toward the building. When Akina and I realized what she had done, she blushed, giggled nervously, and explained that bowing to the school was such a habit that she had done it instinctively.

In the weeks that followed, Akina endeared herself to my wife and daughter on a visit to our home, and she and I had many engaging conversations about literacy instruction on our trips to and from the practicum site. However, despite my earlier hopes that she would inform my understanding about the effectiveness of Japanese schools, I never thought to ask her for such an assessment. In retrospect, I can only say that my perspective about what I hoped to learn from Akina changed the moment I saw her bow toward that elementary school.

If the Japanese people perceived at the time that their schools were superior to ours (and I'm not sure that they did then, or do now), it was irrelevant to Akina. She certainly never expressed that belief, and she seized every opportunity to learn as much as she could about American education until the day she left our country. In fact, from the time of Akina's bow, the particular methods used in Japanese schools seemed far less important to me than they had before. I sensed that Akina had already taught me what I most needed to know about Japanese education.

When Akina bowed, she was demonstrating more than her reverence for that school and its teachers. Most important, she was honoring education itself. For many Americans, *A Nation at Risk* raised the question, "What can we do to improve our educational system and, specifically, what can we learn from nations such as Japan?" Sadly, in the twenty-five years since the publication of that document, we have completely missed the point. If we fall short of the Japanese in any regard, it is that we do not share their cultural understanding that education is a sacred trust and should be honored.

At the time of my friendship with Akina, I was like so many educators who struggled to make sense of our nation's discourse about the "crisis" in American education. On the one hand, I doubted that our performance was nearly as abysmal as suggested by the hyperbolic *A Nation at Risk* or the political and media rhetoric that followed its publication. On the other hand, I knew that our public schools had their share of problems and that we could do much better.

Although I questioned whether there was much to be learned from *A Nation at Risk*, I too joined the intellectual search for solutions to "fix" our educational system. When Akina bowed, she jarred my thinking about what matters most in the educational change process and how we need to alter the course of reform we have followed for the last twenty or thirty years.

Akina accepted American education uncritically and celebrated every learning experience she encountered. If she perceived flaws in our schools—or Japan's, for that matter—those problems did not obscure for her all the rich opportunities that education offered. Further, it would never have occurred to Akina that educators here or in Japan are anything other than caring and competent professionals who work diligently and selflessly to improve their students' lives.

Unfortunately, our collective national disposition toward education contrasts sharply with Akina's. Figuratively speaking, too many Americans, particularly politicians and journalists, have stood outside our schools and peppered them with stones—only to disparage our educational system further when they find it is pocked and scarred.

At times these critics have questioned the motives, competence, and work ethic of our nation's teachers. Over the years they have made so many misleading claims about educational quality that it is now difficult for citizens to engage in thoughtful public discourse about how to improve America's schools, or even to identify clearly the real issues that trouble them. Based on a fraudulent portrayal of public school quality, elected officials have enacted legislative solutions that often missed the mark and were not educationally sound—usually without the advice of educators, the people who best understand children, curriculum, and the organization of schools.

In brief, our nation's politicians, pundits, and journalists have dishonored American education, and in the process they have compromised our children's future. Although these public figures may not have been aware of the damage they were causing, the effects of their behavior have been just as real and substantial as if they were intended.

In the years since I taught Akina, her bow has formed a framework for my thinking about how we can improve American education, and I recounted her story here for that reason. Her bow has become a metaphor for me—a single cultural act that reminds me that America's schools will never become everything we want them to be, or everything that our children deserve, until our society begins to treat education as a sacred trust deserving of our honor and commitment.

Akina's deferential and respectful behavior was clearly a reflection of her cultural heritage, and I certainly do not expect Americans to adopt the unique Japanese custom of bowing at the schoolhouse door. Nor do I want our citizens to refrain from expressing concerns about public education. It is imperative that Americans engage in critical—but thoughtful—discussions about our schools. However, we should no longer allow educational change in our country to be driven by misleading claims of school quality that satisfy the ambitions of a few while ignoring the needs of our young people, the desires of their parents, and the insights of our most talented educators.

If America is to have any hope of achieving the level of educational excellence that our children deserve, we as a people must begin to honor education. Conversely, if we permit elected officials to continue to approach school change as they have in recent years, public education will inevitably decline—perhaps irreversibly—and our children will suffer the consequences of our failure to act.

As indicated in the introduction, the purpose of this book is to provide readers with an understanding of the real effects of educational policy and to empower them to enact positive change in our schools. As a first step, parents and other citizens must have accurate information about the performance of our educational system. As suggested in the next chapter, a broad and objective examination of American education gives us many reasons to be optimistic about the potential of our public schools.

Chapter Two

═════════════○═════════════

The Good News about America's Schools

AS AN AVID CONSUMER OF PRINT AND TELEVISION NEWS, I often wonder how most American citizens make sense of the political statements, media reports, and commentary that dominate our nation's public discourse about education. Typically, the images of schools conveyed by these messages are so overwhelmingly negative and distant from my reality as an educator that they leave me scratching my head.

In this chapter, I call attention to just four indications of the strength of American education. By no means am I attempting to provide a comprehensive assessment of our public schools or to suggest that they are beyond reproach. Instead, my purpose is simply to raise questions about the increasingly popular assumption that our educational system is failing miserably. I hope that this chapter provides readers with a more even-handed and realistic portrayal of school quality than they encounter in most public discourse and therefore gives them greater optimism about the future of American education.

In any appraisal of public schools, we should begin by asking how well they have served society over time. When we assess their performance from that perspective, it is clear that public education has benefited our country enormously. By many measures, America has never been healthier or stronger than it is today. We are far and away the world's most preeminent nation, not only in economic

9

wealth and military power, but also in cultural output and techno-logical innovation.

In fact, we could argue that no group of people has ever achieved the creative productivity of present-day Americans. Surely our schools deserve some credit for our society's success in gener-ating so many of the world's inventions, medical cures, and other advances. Moreover, American citizens today enjoy a better quality of life and a greater level of personal freedom than any people in history—freedom that could not be sustained over time without an educated populace capable of participating actively in a democratic society.

There is little wonder that so many people from diverse cultures around the world continue to emulate our lifestyle and flock to our shores. They hope to benefit from all of our country's advantages, including the opportunity for their children to attend schools that they perceive to be among the best anywhere.

In spite of these achievements, public discourse about Ameri-can education has had a very negative tone for most of the last half century. After the launching of Sputnik in the late 1950s, pundits asserted that America's students were inferior to the Soviet Union's and predicted dire consequences for our Cold War competitive sta-tus. However, the Soviet Union has since crumbled, and America now stands alone as the world's only superpower.

During the social upheaval of the 1960s and 1970s, many Americans worried that public schools were failing to provide our youth with the basics, as well as the discipline and commitment to sustain our country's greatness. As the students of that era now ap-proach retirement, America continues to thrive and surpass every other nation's productivity.

Throughout the 1980s and early 1990s, elected officials and journalists suggested that we were losing our global economic edge, particularly to the Japanese, because we were supposedly lagging far behind them in educational performance. Since that time, how-ever, Japan's economy has experienced periods of stagnancy while America's has continued to prosper overall, in part because recent graduates from our nation's public schools have led the world's technological revolution.

Obviously, the collapse of the Soviet Union, the successes of the baby boomers, and the comparative economic health of Japan and the United States are complex issues that invite multiple explanations. Nonetheless, the fact remains that America is a dynamic, thriving nation, and our schools deserve at least some credit for the skills, creativity, and work ethic that have characterized our people and made our country the world's only current superpower.

In fact, when we consider the international status of the United States today, it seems illogical to conclude that our educational system has been inadequate. When we hear warnings of a crisis in American education, we should remember that politicians, pundits, and journalists have been making the same ominous predictions for the last fifty years, and America has continued to maintain its preeminence. I'd like to suggest that these doomsayers have always been correct in establishing a link between America's public school performance and the health of our nation. They've just always been wrong about the existence of an educational crisis.

A second reason for optimism about our public schools—and perhaps the most important one—is that our teachers have never been better. Improvements in teacher preparation have been especially impressive over the years. Through the early part of the twentieth century, prospective teachers in America attended normal schools where they received two years of training. Although a bachelor's degree is now a minimum requirement for teaching, half of the public school teachers in the United States have advanced degrees, more than double the percentage of those who had attained that level of education in 1961 (O'Neil, 2003, p. 27).

One reason that so many teachers now have higher degrees is that certification standards have become increasingly rigorous over the years. Many programs of teacher preparation have moved to a master's degree as their basic route to certification. Others have increased the number of required courses so substantially that it is becoming more and more unusual for a teacher candidate to finish in four years.

In addition to studies in general teaching methods, today's colleges of education give greater attention than ever to techniques for improving student behavior and teaching children with different learning styles. In fact, these institutions intensified their efforts to "leave no child behind" long before politicians at the national level proclaimed their interest in that cause.

Indeed, the realm of teacher preparation has steadily expanded as educators have addressed issues (such as school safety, special education, and instruction for non-English speakers) that were not even considered just a few decades ago. Although some politicians and journalists continue to suggest otherwise, teacher education has never been more demanding or more attuned to the changing needs of American society.

In recent decades, advancements in our knowledge about how young people learn have greatly enhanced the quality of instruction that teacher candidates receive. Unfortunately, the insights provided by educational research rarely grab the attention of the public with the dramatic impact of breakthroughs in fields such as medicine. In contrast to the biological and physical sciences, education is a complex behavioral science, and educational researchers must contend with unpredictable variables, including the willful and sometimes unexpected behavior of young learners. (As any parent will attest, children have minds of their own and often respond in surprising ways.)

Therefore, educational research—more than research in perhaps any other science—must be applied to changing contexts, with the result that there are few understandings about education that might be called absolute scientific truths. Nonetheless, the work of educational researchers, especially those in the United States, continues steadily and surely to open doors to our understanding about teaching and learning. Today we know far more than ever before about effective instructional practices in all academic subjects and methods for teaching children with unique learning and behavioral needs.

I would also suggest that America's public school educators have never been more committed to their work. In the thirty years that I have been in the profession, I have observed that teachers now spend substantially longer hours working after school than they once did.

When I was a laboratory school director from 1996 through 2000, a high-ranking administrator at the university where our school was located once asked me why teachers in our building worked such long hours. He said that he had taught in his first year after college but had not spent nearly as much time on the job as the teachers in our school. I explained that the paperwork demands of teaching had increased dramatically over the years, that teachers now work with more special needs students (and are more determined than ever to serve them effectively), and that teachers today spend more time preparing creative instructional approaches than in the past.

It might surprise most Americans to hear a former engineer and corporate vice president say that he now works harder as a high school math teacher than he did when he was in the business world, but Arnold Gundersen (2004) has done exactly that. As he explained, "Eight years of teaching have taught me that teachers face significantly more challenges, play many more roles, and are paid considerably less than their corporate counterparts" (p. 64).

In most of today's schools, teachers work collaboratively far more than they once did, with a resulting improvement in instructional quality. Obviously, teachers in one-room schoolhouses worked in isolation. Even as schools consolidated and growing towns and cities constructed large school buildings, teachers remained physically separated in their individual classrooms. Today an expectation of good schools is that teachers work together. They talk about dilemmas they encounter, ask colleagues how to resolve those issues, and share best practices.

In my return to the classroom, I have been very fortunate to enjoy a strong collaborative relationship with three outstanding fourth grade teachers. Although we share many similar beliefs, we have unique strengths, and each of us has grown professionally through our collegial interactions. Most important, when we work and plan together, all of our children benefit from our collective experience and instructional knowledge. Such collaboration is a positive dimension of today's schools that was not present in the past and another reason why we can say that teachers are better today than they ever have been.

Before going any further, I should acknowledge that our profession has its problems. Of the approximately four million teachers in our nation's public schools, some are undoubtedly incompetent, some are less committed to their students and to instructional excellence than they should be, and some are clearly unethical.

However, neither research findings nor my personal experiences support the suggestion that our educational system is overrun with bad teachers and that they alone are responsible for every real and perceived public school shortcoming. The percentage of teachers who should not be in the classroom is probably no greater than the percentages of people in other fields who are unfit for their jobs. In the end, although there is much that we can and should do to strengthen the profession (as explained in chapter 13), the quality of the American teaching force has never been better than it is today.

A third reason to be optimistic about American education is that test data indicate improvements in the academic achievement of our youth. That statement may seem surprising—even outrageous—to some readers, given our media's penchant for emphasizing the negative performance of America's schoolchildren. I am reminded of a report on the *CBS Evening News* several years ago when a positive test score was presented as a negative. In announcing that year's just-released Scholastic Aptitude Test (SAT) scores, the substitute anchor (whose name I do not remember) stated with obvious disgust in his facial expression and tone of voice that there was an improvement over the previous year of "only one point."

I was stunned. Over time I had witnessed misrepresentations of test data in the media, and I had known of journalists ignoring positive educational achievements while highlighting mediocre performances. However, I had never seen a test score gain, even one that was not significant, reported so negatively. Even though the improvement was not substantial, it was an improvement, but this journalist gave the impression that it represented school failure.

Those types of misrepresentations aside, anyone who objectively analyzes test data will find that our children have generally achieved quite well in recent decades and that most scores have held steady or improved over time. As promised in the introduction, I will not burden readers with extensive statistical findings to support that claim. In the following paragraphs, we'll just take a quick look at our students' performance in recent international comparisons and the SAT.

In an effort to bring perspective to the discussion of America's academic standing in the world, educational scholars Boe and Shin (2005) conducted an analysis of all major international assessments of industrialized nations between 1991 and 2001. Their concern was that critics of public schools often highlight a score in one academic area at one grade level on one test and then suggest that America's schools are struggling from top to bottom.

Boe and Shin combined data from six international assessments in all grade levels tested (fourth, eighth, ninth, and tenth) in each of the four subjects measured: mathematics, civics, reading, and science. In their analysis, America was first among all the world's industrialized nations in civics. In reading, the subject that many citizens would argue is the most important, only 13 percent of the industrialized nations scored above the United States, while 44 percent were statistically equivalent, and 44 percent were below. In science, 25 percent scored above the United States, 44 percent were equivalent, and 31 percent were below. Mathematics was the one area in which more industrialized nations scored above the United States than below. In that academic area, 44 percent scored above the United States, 37 percent were equivalent, and 19 percent were below. When Boe and Shin combined all subjects and grades to produce a single score for each country, only 19 percent of the nations scored above the United States, while 41 percent were equivalent, and 38 percent were below.

Like most Americans, I would like to see our students rank number one in the world in all subject areas. Nonetheless, as Boe and Shin noted, when we look broadly, rather than selectively, at all major international studies, the academic performance of our schools has not been poor in comparison to other industrialized nations. Instead, our students' achievement on these measures has been at least solid overall, and it has been comparatively excellent in some areas.

Our students' SAT performance over time has also been generally encouraging. Before examining SAT data, however, we should first acknowledge that the SAT was not designed to measure the overall effectiveness of our public schools, but rather to predict the success of students in college and university studies. It is also important to note that the SAT has traditionally assessed only math and verbal aptitude and gave no attention to other high school subjects or competencies until a writing test was added in 2006.

Like every instrument, the SAT has its limitations. However, it is a measure of students preparing to exit the public schools, and it receives perhaps the most media attention of any test, so it is worth examining.

Total SAT scores, and math scores in particular, have climbed slowly but steadily during the last few decades. Average math scores improved from 501 in 1987 to 520 in 2005, before dropping two points when the test was revamped in 2006. In fact, the 2005 math score was the best performance in math since 1967, and we cannot make valid comparisons to scores prior to 1967 because of changes in the way the College Board calculates scores. Even so, we can say that the 2005 math performance on the SAT was the best in thirty-eight years.

SAT verbal scores have remained more or less constant over the last twenty years. In fact, the average verbal score was 504 in 2002, the same as it was in 1981. Verbal scores increased to 508 in 2004 and remained there in 2005 before dropping to 503 in 2006 when the test was revised. Critics of public education may argue that SAT scores have not improved substantially over the last few decades, but the data do suggest that our students have more than held their own in recent years.

Especially impressive is the fact that SAT scores have remained steady or improved, even as increasing numbers of students from lower class rankings have taken the test. Since 1976 the College Board has gathered information on the class rankings of the students taking the SAT. As Berliner and Biddle reported in *The Manufactured Crisis* (1995, pp. 18, 19), a greater percentage of students from the bottom 60 percent of their high school classes have taken the test since 1976.

In other words, many students who once would not have expected to attend college—and therefore, would not have taken the SAT—are taking it today. With more lower-performing students taking the test, it would be reasonable to expect a drop in scores, but they have held steady or improved.

We should also take it as a positive sign that greater numbers of low-income and minority students are taking the SAT and that their scores are improving. Educational scholar Gerald Bracey (2003a) compared 1981 and 2002 scores on the math and verbal tests for different racial and ethnic groups (white, black, Asian, Mexican, Puerto Rican, and American Indian) and found that every group improved on both tests over that twenty-year period. In brief, when we objectively examine the SAT, we get a very positive picture of public school quality in America.

A fourth reason for optimism about our educational system is that most parents of children in public schools—the citizens who have the most direct experience with American education—express satisfaction with their schools. To illustrate this point, I would suggest that we first consider parents' reactions when faced with the possibility of substantial change to their children's schools. In most cases, what we see is a disposition toward school reform that is similar to the attitude many Americans had about winning Olympic medals during the Cold War.

Readers who remember that era will recall that every four years Americans would suddenly become very concerned about the Soviet Union winning more medals than the United States. However, when we considered that the Soviet Union screened its athletes at an early age into individual sports and then put them through a lifetime of rigorous, focused training in the singular pursuit of gold medals, we recoiled from that approach. In effect, we said, "If that's what it takes, they can have it. We'd rather have happy, well-rounded kids." Most of us then forgot about gold medals until the next Olympics rolled around four years later.

Similarly, we have at times engaged in national hand wringing when a prominent "expert" (usually not an educator) has suggested that our schools are falling behind those of another nation, such as Japan. However, when we consider that Japanese children typically attend school for eight hours each day, followed by three or four hours in after-school "crammies" to prepare for college exams, we say, "No thanks. That's not what we want for our children."

The desire of parents to keep the schools they have is presently being borne out by the response of American citizens to voucher programs. Some politicians continue to tell the public how desirable vouchers will be, but voters have consistently rejected that approach (Pons, 2002). Again, if we pay less attention to the political discourse about public education and more attention to the actual behavior of parents with school-age children, we'd have to conclude that most Americans don't want to change their schools significantly. To me, that's a solid indication that parents are generally satisfied with their children's education.

Survey data also indicate that most parents approve of their children's schools. Each year the educational organization Phi Delta Kappa conducts a poll in collaboration with the Gallup Organization on the public's attitudes toward the public schools. Since 1985 researchers have asked survey participants to give grades of A, B, C, D, or F to (1) the nation's schools, (2) the schools in the respondent's community, and (3) the school attended by that person's oldest child. Obviously, only parents of children in the public schools can answer the third question, whereas any citizen can answer the first two.

The parents who have given a grade of A or B to their children's schools have ranged from a low of 62 percent in 1998 to a high of 73 percent in 1991.[1] In my view, these ratings are exceptional. Imagine, for example, a political candidate with a favorable rating of 62 percent. You would predict a landslide victory for anyone held in such high regard by the public. When Lowell C. Rose and Alec M. Gallup reported the 2003 poll results in *Phi Delta Kappan*, they characterized the 68 percent A or B appraisal by parents that year as "a truly remarkable rating for any institution" (p. 44).

The percentage of respondents in the Phi Delta Kappa/Gallup poll giving an A or B to the schools in their community has been consistently lower. When we examine the survey over the last twenty years, the participants giving a score of A or B to schools in their community was at a low of 40 percent in 1988 and again in 1992, and it hit a high of 51 percent in 2001. Keep in mind that the

---

[1] Data from the Phi Delta Kappa/Gallup Poll appear each year in the September issue of *Phi Delta Kappan*. Readers can locate citations in the references by looking for the author Stanley M. Elam for the years 1991, 1992, and 1994–1996; Alec M. Gallup for 1986 and 1988; and Lowell C. Rose for 1997–2007.

Table 2.1.   Percentages of Respondents Giving a Grade of A or B to
Public Schools

Year	Nation's Schools	Community's Schools	Oldest Child's School
1994	22	44	70
1995	20	41	65
1996	21	43	66
1997	22	46	64
1998	18	46	62
1999	24	49	66
2000	20	47	70
2001	23	51	68
2002	24	47	71
2003	26	48	68
2004	26	47	70
2005	24	48	69
2006	21	49	64
2007	16	45	67

pool of respondents to this question included parents, as well as citizens who did not have children in a public school. Of course, parents were not only assessing the schools attended by their children,
but also other schools in the community—schools that they probably did not know as well.

That same group of participants—that is, parents of public
school children and other citizens—has given grades to the nation's
schools that have been substantially lower than the grades given in
the other two categories. In 2007, only 16 percent of respondents
gave an A or B to the nation's schools, and the highest rating was 28
percent in 1986.

A summary of these three categories of survey data for 1994
through 2007 is provided in table 2.1. As noted above, the differences between the figures in the three columns are dramatic. In
fact, the rating in the second column (the community's schools) is
approximately twice as large on average as the one in the first column (the nation's schools). Similarly, each rating in the third column (the oldest child's school) is roughly three times as high as
those in the first column.

In my view, these differences are startling—and revealing. Why, for example, would only 20 percent of the survey participants in 2000 say that the nation's schools deserved a rating of A or B, while a whopping 70 percent of America's parents gave an A or B to the schools they knew personally?

In this chapter I have expressed my heartfelt conviction that America has a sound, if not excellent, educational system. I base that belief partly on my thirty years of experience and observations in public schools in four different states. In addition, the data presented here on student achievement and parent opinions provide compelling statistical evidence that American education has performed at least reasonably well over the last few decades. However, the survey results in the table above also raise a perplexing and important question. Why do American parents give very high ratings to the schools they know, while the same parents and citizens without children in public schools give very low ratings to the schools they do not know?

Chapter Three

──────────○──────────

How Politicians and Journalists Shape Public Perceptions of Schools

MY FOURTH GRADE STUDENTS AND I were engaged in our usual morning routine on a Friday in late September 2003. As I slipped into the rocking chair at the front of the classroom, the children were settling into their desks in anticipation of the morning announcements. All of them seemed to have the necessary materials for the day's academic work and were quietly attentive when the principal spoke over the intercom immediately after the 8:30 bell—all, that is, except for Steven, who was just arriving and scurrying to the cubby area to put away his backpack. Mr. Williams concluded his terse morning comments, as he always does, by asking teachers to begin the daily moment of silence.

When we stood for the Pledge of Allegiance a short time later, Steven rushed out of the cubby area, his flattened right palm reaching for his chest even as he planted his feet and looked up at the classroom flag. Like all of the children, he was solemn and respectful during the recitation of the pledge. As I do so often, I glanced at their faces, noticed how intently they riveted their eyes on the flag, and wondered for the 10,000th time how any citizen who really knew these children could question the patriotism of today's youth.

During my planning period later that day, I quickly cleared away the minutiae that had accumulated on my desk so that I could spend time gathering materials for our upcoming unit on the American Revolution. As much as I enjoy all of American history, including the colonial period that I was currently teaching, the Revolution

21

is the era that holds the most fascination for me. I see it as a watershed event in the history of the world, and I remain in awe of the courageous men and women who enacted it.

My only dilemma in planning this unit each year is deciding how to teach it effectively in the limited time we have. To engage in any historical topic in depth is a challenge in fourth grade, given the requirement that we cover everything from early Native American cultures up to the Civil War. Nonetheless, I believe it is imperative that our children complete the study of the American Revolution knowing the brave sacrifices of our forefathers and the hardships they suffered in the pursuit of freedom.

As I leafed through materials from the previous year's unit, I could overhear Julie, the fifth grade teacher next door, through the narrow passageway that joins our classrooms. Coincidentally, she was teaching American history at that moment, a subject that in fifth grade begins with the Civil War and ends with contemporary America. Julie's forceful voice carries easily into my classroom when it is empty, so I find it difficult not to eavesdrop on her lessons. She is passionate about American history and civics, and she works hard to prepare her children for the day when they will be able to participate actively in public affairs. Last year I especially enjoyed hearing some of my former students debate political issues as they prepared for mock elections in Julie's classroom.

As always, my planning period sped by too quickly, but I was able to make substantial progress in preparing to teach about the American Revolution before picking up my children from physical education and resuming the day's instruction. With any luck, I thought, I'll be able to finish planning this unit with a few hours' work over the weekend.

The following morning the front page of the local newspaper featured an article about a speech made the previous night by U.S. Senator Lamar Alexander at a regional historic site—in fact, a location known especially for its significance in the Revolutionary War. As I read the article, I imagined the context. It struck me as interesting that our junior senator from Tennessee was giving a political speech in the same place where a statesman from an earlier era might have campaigned by standing on a stump with interested citizens gathered nearby.

I tried to visualize Senator Alexander warming up the crowd in his efforts to bring the assembled citizens to his point of view. I could almost hear his voice rising and falling in a rhythmic cadence as he stated the central point of his address: that it was time to "put the teaching of history and civics back in schools so children will know what it means to be an American" (Houk, 2003).

This was not the first time I had read a newspaper article about Senator Alexander—a former Tennessee governor and secretary of education under President George H. W. Bush—stating that history and civics are no longer taught in America's schools. The previous April he had used almost the same words as he called on educators in our state to put "American history and Tennessee history back in its rightful place in our schools" (Watson, 2003).

Senator Alexander's repeated public statements about the absence of history and civics instruction in our nation's schools were an apparent attempt to promote a bill titled the American History and Civics Education Act of 2003. The purpose of the bill was to provide funding for summer academies for teachers and students so that they could improve their knowledge of history and civics. In his comments to the Senate in introducing the bill, Senator Alexander noted that the two national issues that were most important to him were "the education of our children" and the historic principles that unite Americans (Alexander, 2003).

Since I was currently teaching my students about colonial America and excitedly anticipating our unit on the American Revolution, I was very disturbed to hear Senator Alexander assert once again that our schools no longer teach history and civics. I wondered if he had any data to support such a claim. (None of the reports I read about his speeches included any.) Had he spent substantial amounts of time in schools and personally observed that history and civics are no longer a part of our curriculum? (None of the articles suggested that either.) Senator Alexander was certainly ignoring the international comparisons that show America's students leading the world in civics achievement (as noted in chapter 2).

As I considered all of the classrooms in the schools in which I had worked as a teacher and administrator and the many I had visited as a teacher educator, I could not think of a school where history and civics are not taught. I knew that it was outrageous to suggest that these subjects are not taught in Tennessee. Like presumably every other state, we have a very explicit and detailed curriculum, and it includes a comprehensive list of concepts related to civics and the histories of America and Tennessee.

Since Mr. Alexander had once been the U.S. secretary of education and had stated recently that our children's education and the promotion of our nation's historic principles were his primary concerns as a senator, I thought he should probably know about mandates in his own state requiring the teaching of history and civics. That information is certainly not hard to obtain. With a quick visit to the Tennessee Department of Education website, he could easily find a copy of our required curriculum.

And what did Senator Alexander mean when he suggested that our children do not know what it means to be an American? Like all of my colleagues, I certainly try to imbue the values that are such a critical part of our nation's heritage and democratic way of life. In fact, that is one of the goals I try to achieve each year in teaching my students about the American Revolution. Surely, if Senator Alexander visited our classroom one time and witnessed my children reverently reciting the Pledge of Allegiance or attentively engaged in the study of state and national history, he would realize that I want them to know what it means to be an American.

Worst of all, what influence would Senator Alexander's comments have on the people who heard his speeches? In particular, I wondered about older citizens and others without school-age children. Since many of them lack firsthand experience with today's schools, there would be no reason for them not to believe this distinguished statesman and "education expert" who was saying that our schools no longer teach history and civics. What image of teachers would his remarks create in the minds of these listeners? Would those who have little direct contact with public schools conclude that today's educators are unpatriotic or delinquent in preparing young people for American citizenship?

Clearly Senator Alexander was presenting to these citizens a very negative, misleading, and unsubstantiated portrayal of teachers and schools. In the speech near my home, he made his assertions at a historic landmark on an occasion commemorating the courage, sacrifice, and commitment of early American patriots. In the context of that event, the picture he painted of today's educators must have provided a startling contrast to the memory of the brave and unselfish Revolutionary War heroes who were being celebrated that day.

At the end of chapter 2, I called attention to the striking disparity between parents' positive appraisals of the schools their children attend (the schools they know) and the public's negative appraisals of our nation's schools (the schools they do not know). As Berliner and Biddle (1995) asserted in *The Manufactured Crisis*, the primary reason for that dramatic difference is the unrelenting and unjust criticism of education by politicians and journalists over the last few decades.

Unwarranted attacks by these two groups have given most Americans the faulty perception that our public schools are floundering—even as parents report that the schools they know are quite good. Only by considering the cumulative weight of years of unsubstantiated political and media criticism can we understand, for example, how only 20 percent of the respondents in the 2000 Phi Delta Kappa/Gallup poll gave our nation's schools a rating of A or B, while 70 percent of the parents gave an A or B to their children's schools—the schools that they know best (Rose & Gallup, 2000).

Statements like Senator Alexander's are not merely criticisms that may upset educators like me. In a democratic society, citizens should express their concerns about institutions such as education, and elected officials and journalists should actively engage the public in thoughtful discourse about school improvement.

However, there is simply no place in such discussions for comments that are not supported by data and are not motivated by a sincere desire to improve our schools. As explained in the following chapters, when politicians, pundits, and members of the media misrepresent educational problems and use them to gain personal advantage or to achieve goals other than positive school change, their behavior too often leads to educational policy that is unnecessary or badly conceived.

From a historical perspective, the unwarranted criticism of public schools by politicians and journalists seemed to accelerate in the 1960s and 1970s. At that time, the baby boomers were coming of age as the first American generation that viewed a college education as a birthright. In particular, larger numbers of rural and minority students were aspiring to be the first in their families to obtain a college degree.

At the same time, America's involvement in the Vietnam War influenced many young men to enroll in college to avoid the threat of the draft. Consequently, there was a sudden and dramatic increase in the number of students taking the SAT who were from the lower rankings of their high school classes or who came from more humble backgrounds than previous pools of test takers. The result was a predictable and widely publicized decline in SAT verbal scores. (As explained in chapter 2, that decline has largely been reversed by score improvements in the years since.)

Readers who were of age during the 1960s and 1970s also remember that period as a time of social upheaval and loss of trust in public institutions. As I think back to my early years of teaching in the 1970s, citizens often complained that public schools were abandoning their focus on the basics. I rarely heard or saw any evidence of such a curricular shift, but many people believed that it was happening.

In retrospect, the perception that education was changing for the worse was certainly logical. With all of the social strife we experienced during that era, it probably made sense to assume that schools were in upheaval too. The well-publicized drop in SAT scores supported that assumption and substantiated many citizens' fears that school quality was declining.

During the 1980s, the publication of *A Nation at Risk* surely exacerbated public concerns about our educational system. This official statement of a commission established by the Reagan administration to recommend changes to education opened with the words, "Our Nation is at risk. Our once unchallenged preeminence in commerce, industry, science, and technological innovation is being overtaken by competitors throughout the world" (National Commission on Excellence in Education, 1983, p. 5).

A Nation at Risk was short on data and useful recommendations but long on rhetoric about the alleged mediocrity of our schools. Its primary intent was to establish a relationship between the alleged decline of our public schools and America's slip from dominance in the worldwide economy. According to this publication, Japan and other nations were moving ahead of us, and the failure of our educational system was the reason why. (Curiously, when we experienced an economic boom in the middle and late 1990s, politicians, journalists, and corporate leaders did not assert the same causal relationship and suggest that improvements in our schools were saving American business.)

It is noteworthy that A Nation at Risk was published in 1983, one year before a national election. President Reagan established a political strategy that year that Republican and Democratic candidates for the presidency, congress, governorships, and state legislatures have mimicked for the past two decades. Simply stated, part of the campaign script for running for virtually any elected office became, "Our schools are failing miserably, and I'm going to fix them." The widespread use of that political strategy has clearly influenced many Americans' beliefs about the quality of our nation's schools.

In fact, criticisms of schools have assumed so much momentum in public discourse over the last twenty or thirty years that they have taken on a life of their own. Recall from the previous chapter the news anchor who implied that a small improvement in SAT scores represented failure. Also consider how often we hear campaigning politicians state that they have the answers for our nation's failing schools without providing any evidence that American education is, in fact, failing.

Members of the television media—who should provide objective analyses of facts—sometimes open news reports with comments that assume viewers' agreement with the assertion that our schools are struggling. For example, in the midst of the 2004 Democratic National Convention, Lou Dobbs of CNN began his coverage of that event with a statement about the party's plan to "fix America's broken schools." Although he did not provide any data to support his unsubstantiated opinion that American education is failing, Dobbs confidently concluded at the end of his commentary that most citizens would agree that our nation's schools are floundering.

Americans are continually exposed to so many political and media misrepresentations of educational performance that it would be impossible to convey the breadth of that problem adequately in this chapter. The examples that follow simply illustrate some of the types of fraudulent appraisals of public school quality that dominate our nation's discourse about education.

Although I include a number of misleading statements by politicians and journalists from my own region, I am not attempting to portray a local or regional concern. I believe these examples characterize a dilemma that is national in scope, and I challenge readers to think about similar misrepresentations in their own areas of the country.

Political campaign rhetoric has been especially damaging to the image of public education, simply because each election-day promise to fix education reinforces the perception of school failure. When Tennessee's Democratic candidate for governor in 2002 reminded voters that he once initiated a back-to-basics curriculum in Nashville, he employed the popular political strategy of suggesting that schools are failing to teach basics skills.

When his Republican opponent said that he was going to pay teachers and principals who do a good job (another very popular political strategy), he clearly implied that many educators were performing badly. Of course, I never heard him say how he would determine who was doing a good job and how much money they would receive. Nor did he mention how much bureaucracy and expense such a plan would create, especially in the context of his promises to maintain minimal and low-cost government. The only certain effect of these two campaign statements was that they sent subtle but powerful messages to voters about the alleged (but unsubstantiated) shortcomings of our schools and teachers.

Similarly, when two Tennessee legislators proposed a bill to "allow" children to say the Pledge of Allegiance in public schools (Watson, 2002), they clearly suggested that students in our state were somehow being denied that opportunity. Since there obviously is not a prohibition in Tennessee against the recitation of the Pledge of Allegiance in public schools, we can only infer that the state's educators would try to keep children from saying the pledge unless they were compelled by law to do otherwise.

It is hard to imagine what these two politicians were trying to accomplish, unless perhaps they wanted to distract the public's attention away from their role in the legislative impasse over the state's budget that was then threatening the jobs of thousands of teachers. Whatever their intentions, they engaged in the kind of political behavior that causes the public to question the integrity of educators and the quality of our schools. It is no wonder that many citizens without school-age children have come to believe that America's schools have lost their moral and patriotic groundings.

Sometimes members of the media disparage public education because they simply do not understand educational data. When I read a local newspaper editorial indicating that the percentage of Tennessee high school students scoring proficient on a science test required for graduation had dropped from 39 percent in 2002 to 36 percent in 2003, I immediately knew something was wrong. Surely, I thought, the percentage of students passing a test required for graduation had to be higher than 36 percent.

A quick check of the state website revealed that student scores were reported in three categories: not simply the percentages of students below proficient or proficient, as implied by the editorial, but also those scoring advanced. By not reporting the percentage of students scoring advanced, the author completely misrepresented the actual data.

Indeed, the 3 percent decline in students scoring proficient (from 39 percent in 2002 to 36 percent in 2003) was because the number scoring advanced had increased from 56 percent to 59 percent. In other words, the scores had actually improved. That is, the same percentage of students had passing grades (either proficient or advanced) in both years, but an additional 3 percent scored advanced in 2003.

By not reporting advanced scores, the author of this editorial not only misinterpreted an improvement as a decline, but also gave readers the impression that only 36 percent of Tennessee high school students had passed the science test that year, instead of the actual 95 percent. The scores on the math and English tests were reported in the same manner, indicating that fewer than half of the students in the state were competent in these essential academic subjects.

On realizing the newspaper's errors, I immediately wrote them a letter pointing out the mistakes. However, it is unlikely that the published letter to the editor received nearly as much attention as the initial editorial, which was titled "Report Card Shows Where State Falls Short" (2003). The damage had already been done.

On a national level, one of the most revealing and disturbing media misrepresentations of education occurred in April 2006 and concerned the reporting of test information for the No Child Left Behind Act (NCLB). As is explained further in chapter 7, this education law requires schools to report test results each year and to "disaggregate" the scores for eight subgroups (white, Hispanic, African-American, Native American, Asian/Pacific Islander, economically disadvantaged, students with disabilities, and limited English proficient).

That is, schools must state how many students in each of these eight subpopulations met state standards. Since many schools do not have significant numbers of students in certain groups, the law allows such schools to omit the reporting of scores for these small subgroups. Further, each state has been permitted (with federal approval) to decide how large the groups must be before reporting is mandatory.

In other words, if a school has fewer children in a subpopulation than the state cutoff number, it does not report the percentage of students passing or failing in that group. Of course, the scores of all students are included in the report of the school's total population.

The primary reason for this provision is that drawing conclusions about a school's performance based on extremely small numbers of children would not be statistically sound. For example, if there are only two Hispanic children in a school, their scores—whether passing or failing—would not be a true indication of the school's success in teaching Hispanic children any more than randomly telephoning two American citizens would constitute a valid political poll.

I would suggest that there is another very compelling reason for not reporting such small groups of students. If there were only a few students in a particular subpopulation and all of them passed or failed, then the entire community would know how these children performed academically. To violate their confidentiality in that way would be ethically unacceptable, if not illegal.

But such considerations apparently will not deter some members of our nation's media. When the Associated Press (AP) broke the story about public schools not reporting some subpopulation scores in April 2006—more than four years after NCLB was signed into law—journalists could not resist the opportunity to lambaste educators.

For example, the editor's note introducing an AP article on April 17 said, "States are exploiting a legal loophole that is giving a false picture of academic progress" ("'No Child' Loophole," 2006). In the opening sentence of the article, the author then asserted, "States are helping public schools escape potential penalties by *skirting* (my emphasis) the No Child Left Behind law's requirement that students of all races must show annual academic progress" (my emphasis).

Later in the same article, the AP writer commented on "the breadth of schools' deliberate undercounting." In addition to repeating the term "loophole" (including in the title), the author also included a reference to schools "gaming" the system. Other journalists picked up on the theme of this article. For example, a *New York Times* editorial referred to the AP report by saying "school districts were deliberately failing to break out scores for nearly two million minority children" ("Congress Adds Issues," 2006).

As suggested above, this news episode is both revealing and disturbing. First, the NCLB provision regarding the reporting of subpopulation test scores has been in the law since it was passed in early 2002—more than four years before America's journalists apparently became aware of it. If this allowance truly undermines the purposes of NCLB, our nation's media should have recognized that problem and written about it much sooner.

Second, when journalists did learn about a stipulation in the law that virtually every public school administrator and teacher in America had known about for four years, these reporters and commentators presented their finding as if they had uncovered a sordid plot by disingenuous educators everywhere. Instead of just saying that the need to guarantee statistical soundness had resulted in a dilemma that lawmakers had not anticipated, the media suggested that America's educators were avoiding accountability.

In truth, school administrators and state education departments were just doing what NCLB mandated. For that, the media painted them as devious and irresponsible and essentially gave a free pass to the elected officials who enacted the flawed legislative requirements these educators were simply following.

The use of selective data by politicians and the media has also been damaging to the image of public education. In *Bail Me Out!* Gerald Bracey (2000) explained that one of the key indicators for the claim in *A Nation at Risk* that America's schools were in crisis was a slight decline in science scores for 17-year-olds. As Bracey noted, this statistic came from the National Assessment of Educational Progress (NAEP), also known as the "Nation's Report Card."

The authors of *A Nation at Risk* did not mention that the nation's 9-year-olds and 13-year-olds were also tested at the same time as the 17-year-olds, and that all three groups were assessed in science, math, and reading. Eight of these nine NAEP scores had steady or positive trends, while one—science performance for 17-year-olds—showed a very small decline, but it was the only NAEP score mentioned in *A Nation at Risk* (Bracey, 2000, pp. 24, 25).

There are many examples of the selective use of data by the media to disparage schools, but I'll share just one more that I think is especially revealing. A few years ago, my local newspaper published an editorial asserting that only 26 percent of Tennessee's eighth graders were proficient readers. To emphasize the seriousness of this alleged literacy problem, the author called it a "shameful secret."

Of course, the source of the data was also a secret, since the editorial only stated that the information came from "a recent study." The author added that a "crisis" could be averted if only schools would make some "key changes." Although the editorial did not describe these changes or the "definitive steps" educators should take to improve reading achievement, it closed by saying that citizens of Tennessee should be "angry" if schools do not enact such initiatives ("State's Shameful Secret," 2005).

When I read this editorial, I checked the website for the Tennessee Department of Education to try to locate the score of 26 percent. The only figure I could find relating to eighth grade reading was from our state's "Report Card." It indicated that 86 percent of kindergarten through eighth grade students scored proficient or advanced on the most recent reading and language assessments for the state.

I'll acknowledge that this statistic does not separate the grade levels and give a separate score for eighth grade. However, I doubt that there is a discrepancy in performance of 60 percent between eighth graders and students in the previous seven grades and kindergarten. You also have to wonder why the author wanted to use the figure of 26 percent from "a recent study," when data reported by the Tennessee Department of Education represent the only assessments for which the state's teachers and administrators are held directly accountable.

I suspected that the score of 26 percent proficient was from an NAEP assessment, so I checked the website for that test and verified my suspicion. Unfortunately, most readers of the editorial would not know that NAEP scores are always substantially lower than scores on essentially every other known assessment and that educational statisticians have questioned the credibility of its standards for years.

Nor would most readers be aware of the enormous discrepancy between the unreferenced "statistic" given by the editorial writer and the valid data provided by the state. Instead, they would be left with the faulty impression that most Tennessee middle school children cannot read at a proficient level.

As seen in this example, the omission of accurate references is a problem that is just as significant as the selective reporting of data by journalists. In this instance I was able to locate the source of the score provided in the editorial—but only because I am a career educator with an interest in educational statistics.

Even so, I sometimes encounter media statements about unnamed studies that I cannot identify or locate. Until I know the source of an educational statistic, I am not going to take that figure very seriously. Knowing how journalists and elected officials often misunderstand or misrepresent educational statistics, I would like to be able to confirm that the figures they present are valid and that their conclusions are justified. I do not doubt that these folks have some kind of data. However, I will always be skeptical about their interpretations if I cannot read the original study and judge for myself.

Unfortunately, most consumers of print and television news and commentary are more likely to believe—as I might in reading about findings in fields other than my own—that a test or a study that is not named is absolutely the final word on that topic. When no other findings are mentioned, the implication is that there are no others, or that additional tests or studies would probably yield the same results. As explained in chapter 9, that is often not true.

There are compelling reasons why Woodward and Bernstein could not reveal the true identity of Deep Throat, but providing the name of an educational study or researcher does not compromise anyone or anything. If journalists are sincerely interested in giving the public accurate information about educational assessments, all they have to say is that their statistics come from the NAEP, the SAT, or whatever test is being referenced.

If they are referring to educational studies, they can simply state where the findings were published or mention the names of the researchers. When members of the media do not give that information, they leave me wondering if providing the truth is really their goal, or if they are more interested in presenting an ideological position that cannot be supported with sound data.

Maybe the problem is just sloppy journalism. Whatever the reason for their lack of references, each unsubstantiated report of a "crisis" in our educational system chips away at citizens' perceptions of public school quality and adds to the impression that only drastic (and probably unproven) measures will stop education's alleged decline.

Our media have also shortchanged education by simply not reporting positive news about America's schools. The parents of students I teach are intelligent, well educated, and very involved in their children's schooling. However, I have yet to meet a parent who has heard of the Sandia Report—a study that seems to be known only by educators (and not very many of them). The saga of the Sandia Report is a story that every parent, educator, and interested citizen should know, because it reveals much about the influence of politics and media on our children's education.

In 1990, at the request of the secretary of energy, Sandia National Laboratories conducted a comprehensive analysis of educational data in order to prepare a report on the status of America's public schools. By that time President George H. W. Bush had already stated his intention to become the "education president" on the basis of assertions that our schools were failing and should be overhauled. As Berliner and Biddle (1995) suggested in *The Manufactured Crisis*, Bush's efforts to gain reelection would certainly benefit if Sandia Laboratories could produce evidence to support the president's claims (pp. 166, 167).

The Sandia researchers examined dropout statistics, test scores, international comparisons, educational funding, and numerous other measures. When possible, they compared data over time. As Mary McClellan (1994) reported, the Sandia researchers stated, "To our surprise, on nearly every measure, we found steady or slightly improving trends" (p. 2).

Unfortunately for America's educators and public school children, the Sandia Report was suppressed until after the Bush administration left office, apparently because it did not serve the political ambitions of the president. Even after its delayed release, it received very little attention from the media—so little, in fact, that few Americans outside of the educational community have ever heard of the report. Apparently, positive findings about education do not win elections or sell the news.

Misrepresentations and omissions of information have not only eroded Americans' faith in the nation's schools, but have also poisoned public discourse about educational issues. In an article in *neatoday* (Flannery, Holcomb, & Jehlen, 2004), an Iowa math teacher who has been a lifelong Republican expressed dismay after participating in a poll from the national Republican Congressional Committee and reading the question, "Why is public education failing?"

This educator's concern was that the survey did not ask respondents for their appraisal of American education and then state, for example, "If you believe schools are succeeding, proceed to the next question. If you believe schools are failing, then skip the next question." Instead, the authors of the poll clearly asserted—without any opportunity for respondents to express a different opinion—that schools are failing. Case closed. End of discussion.

As this Iowa teacher explained, he was not only disturbed by the unchallenged assumption of the Republican Party that America's schools are floundering, but also by the fact that one of the reasons listed in the poll for public education's alleged failure was "really poor teachers." In addition, he said he had become increasingly frustrated by his inability to make proposals about educational issues at party caucus meetings in his area. Apparently, other citizens there were so convinced that schools are in crisis that the informed opinions he tried to inject as a veteran educator were not given any credence. As this example demonstrates, when most people have accepted the false premise that education is hopelessly failing, the thoughtful exchange of ideas about school improvement is not possible.

Unfortunately, the political and media repetition of the theme that schools are failing has been so constant and pervasive that it has become an accepted "truth" in our culture. Even so, it was not until February 23, 2004, that our nation witnessed an event that I believe was the most disturbing example yet of the effects of more than two decades of dishonoring American education.

On that date, while addressing America's governors at the White House, Secretary of Education Rod Paige referred to the National Education Association (NEA) as "a terrorist organization" (Toppo, 2004). In the aftermath of this assertion, several governors expressed dismay, although the majority did not respond publicly—at least, not compellingly enough to attract media attention.

For his part, Secretary Paige later said that his statement was "an inappropriate choice of words." He also explained that he was frustrated by the NEA's opposition to certain provisions of NCLB, the centerpiece of the Bush administration's education policy. However, he did not offer a direct apology to the NEA.

As a member of the NEA, I share that organization's objections to NCLB. I also understand that political rhetoric in our nation's capital has become increasingly vitriolic and divisive in recent years. However, it is worth noting that more than half of America's public school teachers (approximately three million) form the union that Secretary Paige called a "terrorist organization." In effect, he labeled the majority of our nation's teachers and many of its administrators as terrorists. Further, he issued this appalling characterization less than three years after September 11, 2001—at a time when America was fully engaged in a war on terrorism.

No matter how virulent politics in Washington may have become, a cabinet member calling over three million of America's public servants "terrorists" is not within the bounds of acceptable political banter, and certainly not when our government is fighting a war against terrorism. As I considered Secretary Paige's statement in the days after he made it, I was certain that he would soon be fired—or at least publicly reprimanded—and that the White House would deliver an apology to the nation's public school teachers.

I read my local newspaper the morning following Paige's comment and diligently watched network and cable news every opportunity I had during the next twenty-four hours. To my surprise, I was able to locate only one report, a brief article on page 8 of my local newspaper. *NBC Nightly News*, the network program I view each evening, made no mention of Paige's comments or any reaction to it. One of the cable networks had a short statement scrolling across the bottom of its screen with other news briefs as its anchor reported on stories of presumably greater importance. However, in the hours I watched that cable network and others present the same stories repeatedly, I heard nothing about Secretary Paige's speech.

Late that night, as I reflected on Secretary Paige's comment and the lack of response to it, I recalled Akina's bow. As I did, I concluded that it was inconceivable that a government leader in Japan could characterize that nation's teachers as terrorists and not elicit a fierce public reaction. Surely, I thought, if a high-ranking Japanese official—even in a moment of duress—somehow made a statement like Paige's, the response of journalists, citizens, and politicians would be immediate and overwhelming.

I could not imagine the people of Japan allowing an assault on one of their most revered institutions to occur without a strong backlash. A country that honors education simply would not allow such an unwarranted attack on its teachers. In contrast, Rod Paige's statement received no comment from the White House and little coverage from the nation's media. Both entities seemed to give their implicit approval, and the American public—perhaps because it heard so little about the incident—hardly blinked.

In the following days, my colleagues and I had numerous conversations about Secretary Paige's statement and the astonishing lack of reaction to it. Julie, the teacher next door, commented one morning that it had been harder for her to come to work and teach with her usual enthusiasm since Paige's speech. When she did, I was relieved to know that someone else was experiencing the same emotions that I was feeling.

Like most educators, I see my work as a calling, and I regard myself as a dedicated public servant. As someone who tries to contribute positively to his community and nation, I found it demoralizing to be called an enemy of the state by such a high-ranking government official. Just as disturbing was to know that America's elected leaders were—by their silence—complicit in Secretary Paige's disturbing characterization.

When we hear politicians, media members, and other "experts" contrasting American schools negatively with those in other nations, we should ask ourselves if an event like this could occur in those cultures. We might also wonder what the reaction would have been if the U.S. surgeon general had called the American Medical Association a terrorist organization, or if a high-ranking law enforcement official had characterized our nation's police in that way.

My guess is that such statements would draw a firestorm of reaction. Certainly, there would have been a vigorous response if a White House official had used an ethnic or racial slur in a public address. Is the application of the term "terrorist" to a group representing the majority of America's teachers less offensive than an ethnic slur?

The fact that such a disturbing condemnation of our nation's most prominent teacher organization took place virtually unnoticed should disturb any American citizen who values public education. If we sincerely want American education to be the best that it can be and to occupy a position of international preeminence, shouldn't we show greater respect for the people who serve that institution?

Secretary Paige's comment and the lack of reaction to it also suggest how much our nation's discourse about education has changed in recent decades. Imagine, for example, a high-ranking government official in the 1940s denouncing teachers as Nazis without a response from politicians, the media, and overwhelming numbers of citizens. If a cabinet member during the Cold War era had characterized America's teachers as communists, surely America would have reacted differently than it did in 2004 to Secretary Paige's characterization of public school teachers as terrorists.

In recent years politicians and journalists have publicly bemoaned the status of American education, usually asserting without sound evidence that we have slipped from a once loftier standing. Sadly, these "experts" fail to see the irony in their statements. They do not recognize that the most meaningful change in American education over the last few decades has been their own propensity to dishonor public schools and the professionals who serve them.

When all is said and done, America's schools have not failed. Instead, the elected officials and members of the media who have consistently misrepresented the quality of our schools have failed our children. Whether they realize it or not, the consequences of misleading American citizens about public school performance are real and substantial.

Chapter Four

---○---

The Consequences of Misrepresenting Public School Quality

SUZIE WAS UNUSUALLY SHY AND HAD FEW FRIENDS, but she was a pleasant child and a hardworking and compliant student. Her teacher from the previous year had warned me about Suzie's mother, saying that she was hard to please and quick to anger. I filed that admonition away, as I typically do with such advice, believing that I could win over Mrs. Butler with sound teaching and an extra measure of diplomacy.

For most of the first half of the year, that approach worked, and I stayed in her good graces, although maintaining harmony between us required that I be especially cautious and conciliatory. Of course, the mother was a secondary concern. My first priority was Suzie, who came to school each day with a smile and a willingness to do whatever was necessary to please her teacher and succeed academically.

I cannot recall the issue that finally ignited Mrs. Butler, but I remember thinking that it was petty and that she had reacted unreasonably. I also recall that the problem did not seem to concern Suzie initially—only after she had gone home from school that day and had a chance to talk with her mother.

By the next morning, I fully understood what my colleague had meant when she warned me about Mrs. Butler. In one day I went from being the reasonably competent professional to whom she reluctantly entrusted her daughter's education to yet another in the long line of Suzie's teachers who were unfit for the classroom.

41

The bigger problem, however, was that Suzie immediately adopted her mother's disdain for me and my teaching. The little girl who once brought a pleasing disposition to every task and had gone far beyond my expectations on most assignments was suddenly sullen and angry. She seemed to view every classroom event through the cynical lens of her mother, and academic work was now a burden that she shouldered dutifully but begrudgingly.

As hard as I tried to regain Suzie's trust, she maintained that approach until the end of the school year. It would be impossible to measure how much her learning was compromised that year, but it was clear that she would have benefited far more had she been able to sustain the positive attitude she had at the beginning of the year.

By no means would I suggest that Suzie and her mother were typical of American students and parents (if, in fact, anyone is typical). Both had an extreme reaction to the mistake Mrs. Butler thought I committed, and neither one of them was ever able to forgive me. Nonetheless, their story does demonstrate what can happen when a child loses faith in a teacher.

Classroom success depends largely on the willingness of students to follow their teacher's lead, and their achievement is clearly compromised when they are unwilling to follow. Just as it is impossible to know how much less Suzie learned in my classroom than she might have, we will never be able to determine exactly how much public school performance in America has been diminished by the incessant political and media denigration of education.

However, I would like to suggest that we consider for a moment the population of students in American public schools as analogous to Suzie and wonder whether constant verbal assaults on education are really a good idea. In my view, it just doesn't seem likely that students will achieve as much academically if they're continually hearing that their schools stink.

Although it is difficult to support that suggestion with data, there are other consequences of misrepresenting public school quality that are more easily established. In the remainder of this chapter, I briefly consider five that I think are especially important.

One effect of the constant disparaging of public schools is that Americans are less likely to support educational funding if they believe schools are failing. For many years, a popular political strategy has been to suggest that we are committing more and more money to education, but quality is declining. Any citizen hearing that assessment would be justifiably concerned. Although there are many factors that influence educational funding, the widespread belief that our schools do not provide a good return on our investment is probably one reason why funding sometimes suffers.

When politicians allege that schools are failing in spite of receiving generous resources, they suggest that there is no relationship between money spent on education and the resulting quality. Thus, they relieve themselves of the responsibility to commit necessary funding to education and do not have to make difficult and politically unpopular decisions about how to obtain money for schools. In the end, asserting unfairly that teachers and schools are failing is a winning strategy for politicians but a losing strategy for our children.

In recent years, some politicians have campaigned on the promise of delivering "world-class schools." Those who elaborate on this slogan typically express concern that America is not number one in international comparisons and that the key to achieving that status is increased accountability for teachers.

The premise behind a call for greater accountability is that teachers are not working hard enough or do not possess the teaching competence or knowledge to help students attain high standards. Politicians who invoke such rhetoric know that they do not have to ask taxpayers to make a financial commitment, and they can appeal to citizens who want them to get tough with public servants who are allegedly not doing their jobs.

As an educator, my version of world-class schools is quite different from the view proposed by most politicians. For starters, I would like all students to have greatly expanded access to the latest computer technology. I believe every public school student in America should have access to a laptop computer throughout the day. I would also like to prepare our young people for the rapidly changing global society by introducing regular foreign language instruction in all elementary and middle schools.

In addition, I'd like all high school students to be able to take larger numbers of advanced math and science courses. In international test comparisons, our high school students have fared least well in math, and to a lesser degree in science, partly because they often compete against students from other nations who have already taken calculus and two years of physics.

You see, I too want all of our children to attend world-class schools. My answers may not be the right ones, but they are grounded in educational experience and study. Unfortunately, mine are also a lot more expensive than the popular political proposal to simply increase accountability and regulations.

It is a lot easier to say that the solution to all educational dilemmas is to get tough with students, teachers, and administrators than to examine issues thoughtfully and propose workable solutions, especially when they require a commitment of funding. Unfortunately, when politicians, pundits, and journalists create a fraudulent image of public school failure, they obscure the real issues and make inexpensive get-tough measures seem like effective strategies.

A second consequence of misrepresenting educational quality is that it justifies the exclusion of educators from educational policymaking. If we assume that America's public school teachers and administrators are not performing as well as past generations or their contemporary counterparts in other nations, then why should we trust them to give sound advice about how to improve education?

In Tennessee, our state education organization lobbied for a law that went into effect in January 2004 requiring that at least one representative of the twelve-member State Board of Education be a teacher. Previously there was no requirement that the board include a single educator. Now it must include one. Imagine that. One out of the twelve members of an education board must be a teacher.

Then imagine a board governing medical practice that included only a single doctor or hospital administrator, or a group to recommend economic policy that included only one businessperson. It is hard to conceive of a medical group not being dominated by medical practitioners or a business group not being dominated by businesspeople. In contrast, it is not uncommon for commissions to be established to recommend educational policy that do not include a single educator.

The widely publicized National Reading Panel is a good example of a powerful policymaking group that had minimal educator representation. Even though the work of this group focused on reading in the elementary grades and is already influencing literacy policy nationwide, it included only one teacher—not an elementary school teacher who might have informed the commission's central purpose, but a middle school teacher at that.

No group of professionals is more underrepresented in decision making about their own area of expertise than educators. The exclusion extends not only to teachers, but to administrators and educational scholars as well. As a result, the people who are shaping public school policy in America have little or no knowledge about educational research or practice.

The current secretary of education, Margaret Spellings, is a good example. She has a bachelor's degree in political science and has never taught or worked in a school. As the highest ranking official of an agency that oversees millions of dollars in educational research grants, it seems unlikely that she can offer useful guidance for the dissemination of those funds. Nor can she provide the president and the rest of the cabinet with informed opinions about educational policy, and it is doubtful that she will ever be able to garner the respect of the millions of teachers, administrators, and scholars she is supposed to lead.

Sadly, most of our secretaries of education have shared Margaret Spellings's lack of experience and degrees in education. The Republican and Democratic presidents who have selected noneducators for that key cabinet position have sent a very clear and disturbing message that knowledge of education is not valued at the highest levels of our government.

A third negative consequence of misrepresenting public school quality is that it diminishes the professional image of teaching, thus making it a less attractive career choice. We need to be especially concerned about this effect as the baby boomer teachers approach retirement and the grandchildren of that generation enter school. Both trends will only exacerbate the problem of teacher attrition with which our educational system has struggled for decades. More than one third of the teachers who enter the profession leave within three years, and almost one half within the first five years (Kaufman, 2005).

Obviously, the difficulty of attracting and retaining good teachers is not new. However, in light of current population patterns, teacher shortages may become even more severe in the near future, especially if the relentless political and media denigration of America's teachers and schools continues as it has over the last two decades.

Consider for a moment that the generation from which we draw today's new teachers was born in the early 1980s. They are our first group of young people to have lived their full lives in the era of overwhelming negative public discourse about education that accelerated with *A Nation at Risk*. We have to wonder what the cumulative weight of that verbal onslaught has been on their perceptions of teaching as a profession. Even if they do not articulate it, I suspect that they understand intuitively from the cultural messages they have heard all of their lives that teaching is not honored in our society.

In fact, our country's dishonoring of education may already have had an effect on our teacher population. A survey by the National Education Association revealed that only 21 percent of our nation's teachers are men, the lowest number in 40 years. Similarly, the proportion of African-American teachers declined from 8 percent in 1991 to 6 percent in 2001 ("Teacher Demographics," 2004).

I would suggest that we view the decrease in both of these teacher populations as the canary in the coal mine. That is, if we as a society truly care about the "children left behind," we should be deeply concerned about the decline in male and African-American teachers. African-American children need to experience teachers with cultural sensitivity to their lives, and children of all races and ethnicities need to see African-American teachers in their classrooms.

In addition, children of every background, particularly those who do not have fathers in their homes, would benefit from having more males as teachers. In the end, teaching should be neither a female nor a male profession, and it should have appropriate numbers of men and women from every race and ethnicity. However, we will probably not achieve that result until we begin to honor education and educators in our nation's public discourse.

A fourth consequence of the misconception that schools are failing is that many Americans tend to look backward, rather than forward, when they consider school improvement. When Americans seek medical treatment, most of us want our doctors to use the most contemporary equipment and techniques. When we purchase automobiles or audiovisual equipment, the majority of us want the newest innovations. Isn't it ironic that Americans—who seem to value the latest technological wonders—so often demand a return to the past in educational practice?

Consider for a moment the typical American classroom of 1900 and compare it to today's classrooms. Then imagine seeing a doctor in 1900 and think about how much the delivery of medical services has changed over the last century. Although there certainly have been substantial changes in education, they are clearly less dramatic than changes in many other fields. In my view, that is partly because so many Americans cling to the belief that our schools were once better and have been steadily declining ever since.

I often encountered that attitude when I was an administrator. During my first three years in the K–12 laboratory school where I was the director, we enhanced the curriculum in a number of areas. We increased the size of the foreign language faculty and the number of advanced foreign language courses, reduced high school English class sizes and added electives (which students could take in addition to the required four years of English), increased the number of advanced high school math courses and teachers, added foreign language for elementary and middle school students, and increased the number of advanced placement courses for college credit—all while maintaining the same student population.

In brief, each change we initiated was part of an effort to enhance the academic rigor of the school's curriculum. However, even after all of these positive changes, when we reconfigured our advanced high school science courses to reflect current national science guidelines, we immediately heard the charge that we were dumbing down the curriculum.

Although that criticism ignored our history of only making changes that increased academic rigor, it was a heartfelt concern of some parents. In my view, it grew out of the popular perception that schools were once better and that any move away from traditional practice is clearly a change for the worse. Unfortunately, the promotion of that belief limits the ability of educators to use the most current teaching strategies and precludes thoughtful consideration of ways to prepare our children for the future. It is simply impossible for schools to meet the needs of tomorrow while continually looking backward.

A fifth consequence of unfairly disparaging public school performance is that it enables elected officials to enact educational reforms that are based on false assumptions. In any problem-solving process, the first step is to clearly identify the problem. Unfortunately, the misrepresentation of educational quality in America has obscured our schools' thorniest dilemmas and fixed the attention of legislators and the public on a fraudulent premise—that teachers are either not working hard enough or lack the knowledge or competence to perform adequately. In brief, we have been trying to address problems that do not exist and ignoring those that should demand our attention.

We might compare this dilemma to what happens when a medical examination of a genuinely sick person yields a misdiagnosis. Mistakenly believing that the patient has an ailment that is completely unrelated to the real problem, the doctor prescribes the wrong remedy. At best, the application of the incorrect therapy defers the time when the doctor will take appropriate measures to help the patient recover from the actual malady. At worst, the undetected illness becomes more severe, and the patient also suffers from the faulty cure.

In recent decades, our educational system has been much like the patient who has been misdiagnosed and mistreated. The difference is that most patients eventually receive the appropriate treatment (or they sue on the basis of medical malpractice). In contrast, the image makers who have contrived a fraudulent view of failing schools continue to shape our citizens' negative perceptions of public education and to prescribe false remedies. In brief, the misdiagnosed patient usually learns the truth in time, but our schoolchildren continue to be victimized by distortions of the truth.

Over the last twenty years, false assertions about the quality of our schools and their teachers have spawned state and federal laws designed to increase accountability. Much like a medical misdiagnosis, these laws have usually failed to address real problems, have hampered the efforts of educators to utilize best practices, and thus have kept our schools from becoming as effective as they might have been. Moreover, because they are invariably based on an assumption that teachers are not doing their best, or will not perform up to expectations without incentives or the threat of punishment, they have dishonored America's teachers.

This fifth consequence of creating a fraudulent image of public school failure is important to understand and requires much closer examination. In the following three chapters, I draw upon personal experiences to provide an understanding of the real effects of accountability legislation on American classrooms. In chapter 5, I demonstrate how these laws have actually compromised academic achievement and have resulted in illusions of quality.

ILLUSIONS, MISGUIDED NOTIONS, AND QUESTIONABLE INTENTIONS: HOW EDUCATIONAL POLICYMAKING HAS GONE WRONG

Chapter Five

―――――――――○―――――――――

High-Stakes
Accountability Measures
and Illusions of Quality

I BEGAN TEACHING IN 1974 AND SPENT THE NEXT FIFTEEN YEARS in my home state of South Carolina, usually working in facilities that were outdated and in need of repair. One of these schools was constructed in the 1930s and had not been renovated or painted in the years since. The others were built in the mid to late 1950s to accommodate the explosion in the student population that came with the baby boomers' entrance into school.

In the Lowcountry, where I grew up and started my educational career, most of these newer buildings were one-story structures with open corridors and flat roofs that eventually leaked. Many schools in our area lacked air conditioning, and students and teachers endured stultifying heat and humidity during the months of August, September, April, and May.

In fact, in most South Carolina communities in the 1970s, the buildings in which public school children were educated had seen little or no significant maintenance since their construction decades earlier. When I managed to finesse the meager resources to paint the exterior trim, offices, and main hall of the school where I was a principal in the 1980s, it was the first coat of new paint that any portion of that drab building had received in the thirty years since it had been erected. Despite my best efforts, I was not able to obtain funding to paint the rest of the school during my three years as principal.

The conditions of these facilities reflected the minimal commitment to public education of the communities that built them. In fairness, I should note that there was little industry in South Carolina at the time, so the tax base in most locations was limited. Historically, however, neither the state government nor the small towns of the Lowcountry had made education a budgetary priority.

In addition, white support for public education had dwindled in many areas with the federally mandated racial integration of public schools in the 1960s and 1970s, especially in communities with large African-American populations. Private schools with names like Jefferson Davis and John C. Calhoun sprang up in most Lowcountry towns and quickly filled with white students.

In some cases, the recently integrated public schools became almost entirely African- American with the exodus of white children to the hastily erected "academies." The departure of so many white students meant that much of the local political power abandoned the interests of public education in numerous communities.

In spite of these conditions, black and white public school educators in South Carolina remained committed to a vision of successfully integrated schools. There were substantial racial tensions in some schools in the late 1960s and early 1970s, and maintaining an effective learning environment posed challenges that few teachers and administrators had previously experienced. Nonetheless, they persisted, and their dedication ensured a more promising future for the young people they taught.

Full racial integration of South Carolina's public schools was in its fifth year when I began teaching, so I cannot claim to be part of the generation of educators who worked under such difficult circumstances during the previous four years. However, I was close enough to many of them and that era to have some perspective on how meaningful their contribution was. Public schools played a more important role than any other institution in altering the racial climate of most Southern communities. Although there are still many shortcomings in the region's achievement of racial harmony, they should not overshadow the significant accomplishments of the educators who worked in the early years of public school integration to bridge the cultural gap between black and white students.

I started my educational career with a one-year stint as a high school English teacher. Over the next few years I taught middle school social studies and reading before settling into a position as a sixth grade self-contained teacher (teaching all academic subjects) in a small rural community.

There were approximately even numbers of black and white students in this district, and both groups took great pride in their school system—which was one of the smallest in South Carolina. Although there were subtle racial tensions in the schools and community, black and white parents provided solid emotional support for public school educators, and the town's two schools—one kindergarten through seventh grade and the other eighth through twelfth—enjoyed a strong academic reputation.

Because of the size of the system, some employees had to wear many hats, and I enjoyed numerous opportunities that simply would not have come my way in a larger school district. During my first five years in that system, I was a full-time teacher and coach in two sports. For the last two years, I was the assistant principal for the elementary school and a district administrator responsible for special education and programs mandated by South Carolina's landmark Education Improvement Act (EIA) of 1984.

The enactment of the EIA was a watershed moment for schools in South Carolina. Governor Richard Riley (later the secretary of education under President Clinton) forged the political support for the law's passage, including the adoption of a one-cent sales tax to pay for its numerous provisions.

In the years between the federally mandated racial integration of the state's schools and the implementation of the EIA in 1984, public education in South Carolina had evolved substantially. Overt racial tensions seemed to have quieted in most schools, and many formerly divided communities where white citizens had once tried to resist integration now purposefully went about the business of educating black and white children together. The time was right in 1984 for galvanizing the state's supporters of public education and moving its schools to a new level, and the EIA was heralded as the mechanism for accomplishing that aim.

Part of the funding generated by the increased sales tax went to school building renovations and maintenance. The intent was that every district would receive money for this purpose each year. In the system where I worked at the time of the law's passage, EIA funding enabled us to make some minor but necessary building improvements that had been deferred for many years.

Most provisions of the EIA, however, related directly to academic achievement, including requirements eliminating any interruptions to learning. I remember telling stunned teachers in a graduate class in the Midwest a decade later that I simply refused to speak over the intercom during the instructional part of the day while I was a South Carolina principal. In contrast to their schools, where office personnel often interrupted instruction to make announcements, the EIA forbade such disruptions to academic learning, and compliance with that directive was absolute in most systems.

The EIA focused educators' efforts squarely on student achievement as measured by the state's basic skills tests. We had begun giving these tests in reading, math, and writing several years earlier. However, the EIA mandated substantial consequences for success or failure. School systems that did not make adequate yearly progress would be identified as "impaired" and receive direct intervention from the State Department of Education. Individual schools that made exceptional improvement would receive special recognition and additional funding—essentially cash prizes for the school to use at the discretion of the faculty.

Within a few years of the act's implementation, the Teacher Incentive Program began, and teachers could receive annual cash awards of $3,000 for meeting certain criteria. Winners had to show that their students had achieved substantial academic growth, and teachers almost invariably chose basic skills tests to document such improvement. In 1989 the Principal Incentive Program went into effect. Principals had to demonstrate proficiency in a variety of administrative competencies but could not qualify for a cash award unless the school had at least adequate progress on test scores.

Some EIA funding was earmarked for special education, but a more substantial amount was for assisting nonhandicapped students who failed any of the state's basic skills tests. Administrators could choose from a number of instructional options, including tutoring and smaller classes, but it was mandatory that they provide service to these students in an approved manner.

Without question, the EIA was a comprehensive program that made achievement on basic skills tests the singular focus of the state's educational system. Excuses and apologies for low achievement by poor and minority students—what President George W. Bush has more recently called "the soft bigotry of low expectations"—would not be tolerated.

Administrators and political leaders in South Carolina pointed with pride to an article published in the *Wall Street Journal* praising the EIA and predicting positive changes in our schools. Not only were we on the threshold of a new day educationally, but people in other parts of the country were commending us for our foresight and tough, businesslike approach to school reform. Like many educators in South Carolina, I felt a great sense of pride that my home state was being recognized nationally as a leader in educational accountability.

Although some South Carolina educators surely had concerns about the effectiveness of this comprehensive reform initiative, I think most supported it and felt a strong sense of efficacy—a belief that the act would give us the resources and backing to make a profound difference in our students' lives. Our schools had come a long way since the early 1970s, and we were ready to take another significant step forward.

When implementation of the EIA began, any doubts about the toughness of the act's provisions surely disappeared. The first four school systems to receive the dreaded impaired status were all poor, rural, and predominantly African-American. As promised, the State Department of Education sent teams of consultants to work in each of these districts.

Although I do not know all the details of these interventions, the word quickly spread to administrators in my area that being in an impaired system was absolutely the last thing they would want in their professional lives. Educators in those districts were engaged in extensive work above and beyond their regular responsibilities, and rumors abounded of harried administrators with elevated blood pressure. If the intent of the penalties imposed by the EIA was to get educators' full attention, it was clearly having that effect in the region where I worked during the early years of the law's implementation.

From the passage of the EIA in 1984 until I left South Carolina to attend graduate school in 1989, I can also verify that the two districts in which I was an administrator focused their instructional resources and efforts almost entirely on the improvement of test scores. My impression was that the same was true in virtually every other system in the state.

The analysis of previous years' test data became the primary topic of discussion at faculty meetings and grade level meetings. Principals were required by law to provide summaries of test score information to all school parents each year, and administrators' reputations rode on their schools' published test scores. District administrative meetings were also dominated by discussions of test score improvement and strategies for achieving that aim.

Principals conveyed to their teachers the sense of urgency associated with positive test performance, and the quality of teachers' relationships with their principals depended primarily on how well their students performed on test days. Educators knew exactly what skills were tested, and teachers learned to look over children's shoulders to memorize as many items as possible so that they could teach them to their students in future years. Almost two decades after leaving South Carolina, I can still recite the six reading subskills assessed in the elementary grades during the 1980s.

Administrators received voluminous test score reports analyzing data from varying perspectives. Some indicated how many children in each grade level mastered each subskill. Principals could determine from another report exactly how students performed on particular types of questions. For example, this summary stated the percentage of fifth grade children who correctly added fractions with unlike denominators.

Teachers received copies of these reports so they would know how to focus their instruction. If a skill wasn't tested, it usually wasn't taught. If a skill was tested, it was taught and taught and taught—until presumably everyone mastered it.

As test dates approached in the spring, most schools engaged in intensive review and practice in test-taking skills, such as answering questions in a multiple-choice format and correctly bubbling circles. Many schools held pep rallies to stress to students the importance of the tests and gave them free pencils with engraved slogans in hopes of inspiring higher levels of test performance.

The EIA was implemented in South Carolina more than twenty years ago. Although I have been away from the state for the last nineteen years, I remain in close contact with family, friends, and educators there and know that raising test scores is still the major focus of the educational system.

There have certainly been improvements in South Carolina's schools, particularly in the quality of facilities. Further, the state has actively involved legislators and business leaders in working with educators and parents to improve public education, and it has begun some innovative programs, such as the South Carolina Reading Initiative and the Master Teacher Program. However, these initiatives are not related to the high-stakes accountability measures of the EIA.

I should also mention that South Carolina modified its testing program under the 1998 Education Accountability Act. This law called for a new and supposedly more rigorous set of tests than those used before and gave the state the power to remove administrators and seize control of districts that do not improve test scores over time.

Obviously, the determination to improve test scores in South Carolina has not abated, and the measures used to achieve that aim are as hard nosed as ever. However, after two decades of focused effort on the improvement of test scores, the state has not experienced the dramatic and sustained academic growth that advocates of the EIA predicted.

For example, South Carolina's SAT scores have shown moderate improvement over the last twenty years but have not closed the gap with the rest of the country. In fact, the state's 2004 average total score of 986 ranked fiftieth among the states and exceeded only the District of Columbia's. Further, despite some improvements since 2003, South Carolina's schools are struggling more than those of most other states to meet the federal requirements of No Child Left Behind (NCLB).

In the end, the legislature's tough, business-inspired, common-sense accountability measures simply did not catapult the state's educational program to the forefront nationally and did not enable South Carolina to overcome completely its earlier legacy of minimal commitment to the education of all children. When policymakers enacted the EIA in 1984, it was hailed as the answer to all of the state's educational problems. Sadly, however, South Carolina is still looking for answers.

I was born in South Carolina, lived much of my life there, and love the state and its people. I get no pleasure from reporting its educational struggles (or anyone else's). Nor do I want to appear to be second guessing the intentions or wisdom of Richard Riley. I have always thought that his commitment to public schools was genuine, and he was clearly successful in making education a priority in South Carolina. Moreover, I would be less than honest if I did not confess that I believed in 1984 that the commonsense provisions of the EIA would substantially improve our students' achievement.

I have two reasons for recounting the early years of the EIA. The first is that I experienced the act as an administrator and can share personal perspectives about its implementation. The second reason is that South Carolina's experience with the EIA provides many insights about school reforms that are driven by high-stakes testing—that is, the use of standardized tests for which there are substantial consequences for success or failure.

Since leaving South Carolina I have lived and worked in three other states in the South and Midwest, and I have witnessed or experienced most of the practices described above in each of those states. In fact, many of the high-stakes testing provisions of South Carolina's EIA have become commonplace across the nation over the last twenty years, and the federal NCLB Act essentially guarantees that all states adopt such strategies—if they haven't already.

South Carolina's experience with high-stakes testing makes it an especially useful case study for other reasons. As suggested at the beginning of this chapter, the context for school improvement in South Carolina was extremely positive in 1984. There appeared at last to be a collective recognition by the state's citizens that educational reform would move the state forward, and most politicians, educators, and parents seemed to endorse the provisions of the EIA.

Further, there was a comprehensive focus on test score improvement at every level of the educational system, and the law's package of incentives and punishments certainly had teeth. No one could say there was a lack of willingness or determination to raise test scores in South Carolina in the years following the passage of the EIA. Policymakers who continue to assert that schools can dramatically improve student performance simply by establishing high standards and enforcing them through tough-minded measures are ignoring the history of laws such as the EIA.

In the following pages I highlight a few of the dilemmas of high-stakes testing and accountability that I experienced in South Carolina and have since observed elsewhere. Hopefully this discussion will help readers, especially parents and other noneducators, to understand the unexpected consequences of the commonsense provisions of the EIA and other reforms like it.

I have learned in the years since the passage of the EIA that a total focus on test score improvement results in three illusions of school quality. One is what I call the *illusion of reform success*—a perception that high-stakes testing measures are improving education, when in fact they are not.

In the first few years of EIA implementation, many South Carolina schools were able to show impressive test score gains, especially in the early grades. The reason is that most schools were for the first time becoming very diligent about teaching exactly what was tested. Teachers were not working harder, and they were not necessarily teaching better. They were simply doing a better job of teaching to the test.

Of course, when gains were announced, teachers and administrators were congratulated, and lawmakers were able to proclaim that the EIA was working. The successes of the first years became seductive, leading educators to attempt to align instruction even more closely to the tests.

The problem came later. Once you have closely matched your curriculum to a test, it is hard to improve that alignment significantly.

It's much like giving a tune-up to a car that needs it badly. When you first tune the car, its performance improves substantially. However, that doesn't mean that you will get the same amount of improvement if you give it another tune-up every day.

Educators face the same dilemma in high-stakes testing situations. After the first year or two of matching what is taught to what is tested, scores flatten out, and people look for someone to blame (in most cases, teachers). We usually fail to see that our basic strategy is flawed because we can point to early successes and say that it worked then. Unfortunately, our trust in the efficacy of that faulty approach discourages the consideration of other alternatives for improving instruction. Most schools fall into the trap of simply trying harder to make the same strategy of curriculum alignment work again and again.

I have also learned from over two decades of observing the testing game that a singular focus on basic skills improvement can result in an *illusion of academic excellence*. After several years of EIA implementation in South Carolina, some state-level administrators began to herald the achievement of excellence. The basis for that claim was that very high percentages of students, especially in grades one through three, had passed the state's basic skills tests in math and reading.

However, the standardized tests in South Carolina at that time were not capable of identifying excellence. They were tests of minimum basic skills. Every child in the state could have passed the tests, and we would not necessarily have achieved academic excellence.

Imagine, for example, giving a test of basic physical fitness in which a student passes by doing five sit-ups and then running one lap around a basketball court. If everyone in the class demonstrated that minimum level of fitness, we would have 100 percent passing the test, but we could not necessarily say that anyone was in excellent shape. Some might have been, but we would not know it from that assessment.

In truth, all we could establish from such a measure would be the universal achievement of mediocrity. Unfortunately, when supporters of high-stakes testing assert that 95 percent or more of a group of students has reached an academic standard, most observers are inclined to perceive that attainment as an indication of excellence, no matter how low the standard for demonstrating proficiency might have been.

Most citizens do not realize that a very disturbing change occurs when schools focus all of their efforts on the achievement of test score standards. The problem with a curriculum driven by tests of basic skills is that we assume teachers will help all of their students attain that minimum level and then immediately move on to higher levels of learning.

Unfortunately, when intense pressure is associated with ratcheting up test scores as high as possible, instruction usually does not move beyond what is tested. High-achieving students lose out because they are not challenged academically. Low-achieving students—especially if they are grouped by ability—lose out because they are rarely exposed to anything beyond the tested curriculum. Teachers are expected to keep plugging away to master tested skills, even if it means students never experience any other kind of learning.

The pressures of high-stakes testing invariably cause teachers to place such restrictions on our children's education. If we are only teaching what is tested, we are limiting instruction to skills that can be assessed in a multiple-choice format and can be answered quickly. For ease of scoring, test items often require students simply to regurgitate information, and questions can be very trivial.

For example, standardized tests are more likely to ask students which amendment to the Constitution guarantees the right to bear arms than to ask them to explain the meaning of this right or why it was important to the founding fathers. These tests do not require students to engage in the kind of critical thinking that is the foundation of democratic citizenship or advanced scholarship. Nor do these assessments measure creativity, sophisticated problem solving, or any of a range of higher thinking processes valued by educators, parents, and even the politicians, journalists, and business leaders who usually advocate accountability legislation.

At best, standardized tests measure a thin slice of academic learning, and that thin slice becomes our children's only curriculum when test score improvement takes precedence over all other educational priorities. Clearly, we cannot legitimately claim to have achieved academic excellence under such circumstances.

However, as America's schools complete the early years of implementation of NCLB, we are hearing giddy assessments from the architects of that law that are eerily similar to the reports that came out of South Carolina in the 1980s. For example, at the 2004 National Republican Convention, both President Bush and Secretary of Education Rod Paige proclaimed that America's elementary schools had been transformed.

As a teacher in one of those elementary schools, I would suggest that we are just seeing the effects of increased efforts by teachers to teach to the test under the threat of the stinging sanctions of NCLB (which are discussed in greater detail in chapter 7). The history of laws like the EIA should tell us that the only transformation caused by NCLB has been the narrowing of our children's curriculum to the skills that can be tested in a multiple-choice format.

The third illusion of accountability reforms does not occur until well after the first two. As noted earlier in this chapter, test scores flattened out after the first few years of EIA implementation in South Carolina. In fact, the same pattern is invariably repeated as a result of all high-stakes initiatives. At that point we experience the *illusion of educational failure*.

Once teachers have carefully aligned their instruction to a test, it is extremely difficult to make continuous gains. That is, no matter how hard students and teachers work, they will eventually reach a performance plateau. Unfortunately (especially for the educators involved), improvement over the previous year is the acknowledged standard of success in many high-stakes testing situations. Because the advocates of accountability laws have often convinced citizens that schools were floundering badly before the enactment of reform legislation, anything less than substantial and steady improvement is often seen as a sign of failure.

Further, because there were usually impressive test score gains in the early years of the reform effort, school observers now wonder why educators cannot demonstrate continuous progress. Most teachers and administrators who have played the testing game for any length of time know how difficult it is to maintain constant test score improvement. Even when you have implemented a positive schoolwide instructional strategy and actually enhanced the learning experiences of children, their scores are not necessarily going to jump each and every year.

Assuming that schools are failing when their performance eventually reaches a plateau is analogous to saying that a college football team with a nine-win season did not do well because it did not exceed its nine wins of the previous year. In truth, both records were solid. When a child is at the 98th percentile in a subject one year and climbs to the 99th percentile the next, we cannot say the student failed to make acceptable growth. The 99th percentile is the highest score possible.

Unfortunately, test score gains are often the primary focus of reports provided to the public. In Tennessee, where I presently reside and teach, one of the most highly publicized analyses of test scores on our annual State Report Card uses letter grades to indicate growth from one year to the next. As it happens, I work in a very high-performing school. If we have exceptional reading scores one year and reproduce the same outstanding scores the next year, we get a grade of C, the letter grade for not substantially increasing or decreasing scores. Consequently, the local media and many of our parents may conclude that our test performance has been mediocre, when actually it has been consistently excellent.

The same dilemma tends to occur on the state and national level within a few years after any school accountability reform. No matter how diligently and efficiently teachers and administrators work to improve student performance, scores will eventually hit a plateau, thus creating an illusion of mediocrity or failure. Politicians and the media—who understand little about test statistics and less about what actually occurs in classrooms—will proclaim it a crisis.

Within a few years the same elected officials may impose on children and educators even more stringent requirements and pressures. This cycle of illusions of quality—the illusions of reform success and academic excellence, followed ultimately by the illusion of educational failure—has clearly profited politicians but negatively affected educators and students.

Other dilemmas accompany high-stakes accountability acts like the EIA. Citizens in South Carolina have been justifiably concerned about their state's average SAT scores for several decades, and many of them expected those scores to climb when the stringent accountability measures of the EIA took effect. In fact, SAT scores remained relatively flat over time, even as scores on the state's basic skills tests improved.

It might seem illogical that scores on a high school reading test could rise while SAT verbal scores of the same population remained about the same. Actually, the reason is fairly straightforward. We can say that a test measures reading, for example, but that does not mean it measures everything about reading, or that every test of reading or verbal skills assesses the same competencies.

As an avid college basketball fan, I recall that there were several universities that were less successful than they had previously been when the three-point shot first went into effect. In the past, these teams had been very adept at getting the ball inside to a big player or working efficiently for a short jump shot. That was considered good basketball before the rules of the game changed. In the new era of basketball, a long jump shot that formerly would have been considered a bad shot was now an effective strategy. Consequently, some of the formerly dominant teams that did not quickly recruit or develop three-point shooters struggled until they adjusted to the new rules.

Similarly, I think that South Carolina's struggle to improve SAT performance could be related to the state's narrow focus on basic skills. If classroom teaching is closely aligned to the state's basic skills tests, many students will not perform well on the SAT if it does not test the same kinds of skills as the state's test.

As is explained further in chapter 9, an analogous situation may occur when students in America are compared to students from other countries on international assessments. If there is a mismatch in the types of competencies measured by state-mandated tests and international assessments, our students will be at a distinct disadvantage on international comparisons because the instruction they receive is so narrowly focused on their states' tested curricula.

When elected officials talk about high-stakes tests, they generally equate performance on these measures with rigorous academic expectations. Typically they also suggest that teachers who question the wisdom of high-stakes legislation do not want to be held accountable. The history of South Carolina's EIA and other states' accountability reforms should raise doubts about these simplistic assertions.

Teachers question the use of high-stakes testing for two important reasons. One, they have learned through personal experience that these assessments provide false impressions about school performance. Two, they know that high-stakes accountability measures invariably compromise our children's education. Under the pressure to produce higher test scores and little else, educators are forced to narrow the curriculum to only those skills that are tested.

The result is curricular mediocrity, not excellence. Politicians can proclaim that their tough measures have led to educational excellence when test scores show temporary improvements, but teachers know that students in high-stakes testing environments learn less, not more.

Educators also recognize that high standards and the threat of punishment are not adequate remedies for all of the difficulties faced by low-performing schools in low-income areas. At the beginning of this chapter I commented on the status of public education in South Carolina before the 1984 implementation of the EIA. I thought it was important to describe the context for the law's passage, not only to affirm that this initiative arrived at a time when most South Carolina citizens were ready for change, but also to suggest that the problems facing many of the state's schools required more than standards, penalties, and incentives.

Clearly, the accountability provisions of the EIA did not address issues related to the state's considerable poverty and its legacy of segregation and educational neglect. One of the important lessons of the EIA—in fact, the lesson we most egregiously neglected in the passage of NCLB—is that we need to provide more than tough rhetoric and penalties to our neediest schools if we genuinely want all children to achieve academic excellence.

Chapter Six

———————○———————

A Tale of Two Teachers: The Passionate Professional and the Dispirited Functionary

AS A HIGH SCHOOL SENIOR, I was predisposed to dislike English literature. Although I know he meant well, my father often related to me his belief that fiction was a waste of time, especially for males. He had found English literature particularly distasteful and warned me at an early age about authors like Shakespeare and Coleridge. To demonstrate the impracticability of their writings, he frequently and disdainfully quoted the passage, "Water, water, everywhere, nor any drop to drink."

Of course, my father wanted me to be a successful student. He encouraged and supported me in all school endeavors, and he certainly expected me to do well in senior English. He just thought he should give me fair warning that I probably wouldn't like it.

My father could never have anticipated Mrs. Elkins. Her energy and passion for her subject captivated me from the first moment I sat in her English class. She often talked about the expectations of college professors and how she wanted to prepare us for the rigors of undergraduate coursework. When she did, it was with such earnest conviction that I was confident I would succeed at that level if I simply followed her lead.

When she spoke of life beyond our provincial little town, I knew for the first time that I wanted to experience worlds I had never before considered, and I was certain that her sophistication and mastery of language would grant me passage—if only I could gain a small measure of all she possessed in those realms. For the first time in my life, words truly mattered. When they rolled off her tongue, I wanted to understand them all—to grasp their nuances and combine them in ways that produced clarity and beauty, just as she seemed to do so effortlessly.

It wasn't long before I embraced the writings of those English masters about whom my father had warned me so many times. When Mrs. Elkins introduced us to their works, she strode gracefully across the front of the classroom, holding a book in front of her and melodiously delivering their words. Every reading was a celebration. The enthusiasm in her demeanor revealed her love of the ideas and music that poured from those literary classics, and she invited us to ponder their messages and revere them just as she did.

When we searched beneath the surface of those passages for deeper meaning, we felt a sense of scholarship that was new and exhilarating. Mrs. Elkins listened intently to our ideas and genuinely engaged us as intellectual equals. We shared our interpretations with each other and her, and I suddenly imagined being part of the stimulating academic discourse of the university classes that awaited me one year in the future.

Every week I labored to produce an essay that was due on Friday. And each weekend she took home the tortured prose my classmates and I wrote by hand, along with pages of vocabulary exercises—all of that from five sections of twenty-five to thirty students each—and graded and returned every paper on Monday. As a teacher today, I marvel at the sheer magnitude of that Herculean task. Even as teenagers, my classmates and I knew what a powerful sense of caring she conveyed with that act of selfless commitment to our learning.

Of course, we always knew that she cared. We saw that daily in the warmth of her demeanor, the respect she communicated to each of us as students and people, and the joy she exuded in teaching English. In return, we gave her our best academic efforts simply because we knew that she gave so much to us.

I know that I am much more today than I would have been without the good fortune of having been Mrs. Elkins's student. She is one of the primary reasons I am a teacher, and if I possess any competence as a writer, it began with her. She taught me to be open to every perspective and possibility and yet to consider each one critically. She instilled in me a love of learning and of reading from a variety of genres, and she launched a desire for understanding that time has not diminished. Perhaps most important, she changed my view of the world, invited me to take it all in, and enriched my life daily by challenging me to experience it fully and deeply.

In contrast to Mrs. Elkins, Mr. Jackson is a teacher I do not know personally. I learned about him through colleagues and conducted an interview with him about his classroom teaching experiences.

When Mr. Jackson completed his education degree in 1999, he aspired to make a difference in young people's lives. During the first four years of his career, he taught in a middle school that provided him with a clearly defined set of instructional goals but with the academic freedom to decide how to achieve them.

Mr. Jackson brought energy and enthusiasm to the classroom every day, and he worked diligently to engage his students' interest in learning. A former colleague described him as genuinely caring toward his students and passionate about teaching. In those beginning years, Mr. Jackson believed he was making a difference and was realizing his dream of becoming an exemplary teacher.

When his wife accepted a professional transfer to a large city in a bordering state, Mr. Jackson obtained a position there as a fifth grade teacher. In contrast to his first teaching assignment, students in his new school were required by state mandate to pass an end-of-year test to advance to the next grade. Faced with these high-stakes pressures, his school adopted a program that focused almost entirely on instruction in test-taking strategies. It provided a day-by-day, hour-by-hour script for elementary teachers to follow in all academic subjects.

For the first time in his career, Mr. Jackson was not able to exercise his professional judgment in the classroom or to assume responsibility for instructional decisions affecting his students. He was no longer able to draw upon his knowledge and instincts or to utilize his creative energies. Every hour of every day, he provided his students with prepackaged activities designed to prepare them for end-of-year tests.

In each subject, the emphasis was on how to read and answer passages written in the format of the state tests. His supervisor explicitly directed him to focus more on test strategies than on academic content, even in mathematics, the subject that Mr. Jackson once taught with the most passion and creativity. Day after day, he struggled with the ethical dilemma of being required to teach in ways that contradicted his beliefs about best educational practices.

The restrictions imposed on Mr. Jackson stripped him of the passion he once had for teaching. His students responded to his diminished enthusiasm and their impoverished curriculum with apathy and disinterest. Boredom dominated their days, and there were significant behavior problems in his classroom. When Mr. Jackson diverged from the school's required curriculum and relied on his own professional knowledge and instincts, students responded with the excitement and interest he had known from previous teaching experiences.

However, he did not feel comfortable straying from his new employer's mandates very often, even though he knew that "the kids were burned out from the tedium of constant test preparation." They had been engaged in the same kinds of activities for several years, and Mr. Jackson struggled on a daily basis to sustain their interest in learning. In contrast to the less regimented environment in which he had once taught, he noted that he had never seen so many children who disliked learning and simply hated to read.

Sadly, Mr. Jackson came close to leaving the profession. "I didn't know if I was a good teacher anymore," he said. "I didn't think I made a difference in any kid's life." After one year in that restrictive environment, Mr. Jackson was able to find a position in a school that gave its faculty a little more academic freedom. In fact, he was one of numerous teachers who left his former school at the end of that year. When I asked him what he would do if all schools were like the one from which he resigned, Mr. Jackson said that he would simply have to quit teaching.

Obviously, I wanted to provide a striking contrast between the depictions of Mrs. Elkins's and Mr. Jackson's classrooms. I also hoped that the description of Mrs. Elkins would stir readers' memories of teachers who changed their lives as much as she did mine.

To be fair, I should acknowledge that I wrote about Mrs. Elkins as a student who experienced her teaching, and I cannot provide the same perspective of Mr. Jackson. I can only report what he and his former colleagues said about his teaching and his children's response to the tightly prescribed curriculum in his school. I should also admit that I recall Mrs. Elkins's classroom nostalgically, and we should be careful not to view past educational experiences through the lens of nostalgia.

However, my emotions and personal perspectives notwithstanding, I am certain that I can attribute substantive results to Mrs. Elkins's teaching. I know that she inspired in me a love of literature and of learning in general. I also know that I was far better prepared for freshman English at the undergraduate level than most students in those classes, and I've heard high school friends say that they had the same experience at the colleges and universities they attended. Most important, however, I drew upon my memories of Mrs. Elkins because I did not think that I could adequately convey the magic of a classroom where the teacher and students were so passionate about learning without personalizing the experience.

I hope that my description of Mrs. Elkins caused readers to think back to the teachers who influenced them the most and the qualities that distinguished those teachers. I assumed that most people would recall teachers who were knowledgeable, enthusiastic, creative, and inspiring. I also assumed that readers would attribute to those teachers a sense of caring and concern for students that extended far beyond their academic performance.

Obviously, I expected readers to react quite differently to the portrayal of Mr. Jackson's teaching. Nonetheless, it is important to reiterate that Mr. Jackson sincerely wanted to inspire his students and make a difference in their lives—perhaps just as much as Mrs. Elkins did. Unfortunately, the mandate to use a prescribed curriculum designed solely to improve test scores deprived him of the opportunity to teach in the ways that he knew he should.

In contrast to Mr. Jackson, Mrs. Elkins taught in the years before high-stakes testing and accountability measures replaced teachers' academic freedom with restrictive mandates. She was able to make instructional decisions based on her knowledge of English

and her personal views about how to teach that subject most effectively. If Mrs. Elkins taught today, I am certain that she would continue to serve dutifully, but I suspect that some of the passion, creativity, and energy that enabled her to inspire so many young people
and forever change their lives would be compromised.

If there was anything better about schools in the "good ole
days," it was that teachers were allowed to draw upon their professional knowledge and follow their conscience in making instructional decisions. Parents who recall teachers like Mrs. Elkins
should not automatically assume that their children's teachers possess the professional autonomy that earlier generations of teachers
enjoyed.

Increasingly, teachers everywhere are being denied that opportunity, and the result is that students often experience instruction
that is inferior to what their teachers are capable of delivering. Ironically, at a time when teachers are better prepared than ever before
in both academic content and instructional methods, they are more
constrained than ever in their ability to use that professional knowledge in the classroom.

If we genuinely want our schools to be the best that they can
be, we should wonder whether it really makes sense to deprive educators of the opportunity to be passionate about what they do. It
seems unlikely that any teacher will possess the passion of Mrs.
Elkins when told exactly what to teach and when and how to teach
it. In schools like Mr. Jackson's, we are stifling teachers' creativity
and enthusiasm, and we are reducing learning to repetitive, tedious,
and intellectually stultifying activities for both them and their students. As most of us will probably agree, if there is little joy in a
teacher's experience of the classroom, there probably won't be
much excitement for students either.

Almost all public school teachers in contemporary America
have experienced Mr. Jackson's frustration to some degree. Beginning in the years following the publication of A Nation at Risk and
continuing to the present time, state educational mandates have
become more and more restrictive. As they have, teachers have increasingly lost the academic freedom that Mrs. Elkins and her generation enjoyed.

Linda McNeil (2000), who has extensively studied public school accountability in Texas, reported that the "margins" of the classroom where teachers have always been able to "really teach" have been steadily shrinking (p. 730). That is, in the beginning years of accountability legislation, teachers could comply with the restrictive mandates these laws imposed on their teaching but still manage to provide at least some of the kinds of meaningful learning experiences that interest and engage students. These educators' academic freedom had certainly shrunk, but they retained a portion of their instructional autonomy (in the margins) and could still find the passion in their work that has always driven professionals like Mrs. Elkins.

Unfortunately, because of the pressures of state and federal mandates, many systems now require their teachers to use distilled and prescribed curricula that closely match the format of multiple-choice tests. When that occurs, the real losers are our children. Not only is the passion and excitement for learning disappearing in too many classrooms, but teachers are also losing the professional discretion to adapt their teaching to student differences.

The measure of any teacher's professional autonomy depends on the expectations of the state educational system, the local school district, and the principal. Typically, the degree to which the state emphasizes high-stakes testing will determine the school system's focus and, subsequently, the principal's emphasis.

I feel fortunate that my home state of Tennessee is not quite as test driven as some states, that my school district is not yet entirely consumed with test score improvement, and that my principal is more respectful of his teachers' professional autonomy than many administrators. Still, I have noticed that external intrusions on my instructional decision making increase year by year and have accelerated rapidly during the beginning years of No Child Left Behind (NCLB).

That encroachment on my classroom teaching takes varied forms. In an effort to improve math test scores, my school district instituted a system of assessments that each math teacher must conduct, grade, and analyze by certain dates throughout the year. For example, one of the fourth grade tests checks for students' mastery of a variety of geometry concepts. Like all of my colleagues, I am required to indicate on a summary report the percentage of students in my class who master each of the various concepts tested. Teachers submit these reports to their principals, who then forward them to a district supervisor.

The message is very clear, isn't it? If teachers want to be perceived by their administrators as successful math instructors, they had better teach exactly the concepts tested for that period. I especially resent being directed to teach certain concepts in the order and amount of time that someone else has determined. On occasion, I have thought that my students would have greater success following a different order than the sequence mandated by the district.

There are also times when my students are struggling with a particular math concept and I feel compelled to move forward because there were other math objectives to master before the due date for the assessment. Each time that happens, I face the ethical dilemma of wondering if it is best for my students to develop a better understanding of the difficult concept or to forge ahead to new material.

This dilemma reveals one of the many ways in which test-driven curricula are counterproductive to their intended purpose of increasing learning. I think most educators would agree that it is more desirable to develop a thorough understanding of a manageable number of concepts than to have a shallow understanding of a larger number of concepts.

When I was a beginning administrator in South Carolina, my superintendent frequently reminded me that wide coverage, not depth of understanding, would result in better systemwide test scores. Indeed, that philosophy is evident in the thinking of accountability advocates and the content of our standardized tests. When supporters of high-stakes testing talk about higher expectations, they usually mean that the tests cover more material, not that they assess more intellectually rigorous levels of understanding. Thus, a major problem with test-driven curricula is that they tend to be a mile wide and an inch deep. When the curriculum becomes so shallow, there is little opportunity for students to dive in and become deeply engaged in learning.

As a teacher, I struggle with these concerns throughout the year. I want my students to perform well on any assessment they encounter. Therefore, it is impossible to ignore our standardized tests, even though I question their validity. For example, I wonder if I should sacrifice a hands-on approach to science in order to cover (quickly read and discuss) more science content. Is it really in my students' best interests to abandon the scientific method and cut back significantly on the number of experiments and reports we do? Although our curriculum would be less interesting and rigorous, we could probably improve our test scores that way.

Similarly, should we decrease the amount of research, the number of classroom reenactments, and other engaging social studies activities in order to learn more historical facts? Is it really more important for students to memorize which amendment guarantees freedom of religion, or should we want students to be able to explain the meaning of that right and why it was so important to our founding fathers? Still, if we just learn the facts, we'll probably have greater gains on our social studies scores.

I also wonder if I should compromise the amount of time my children spend writing. I probably teach writing more passionately than any other subject, and each year my students enhance their skills in writing personal narratives, reports of various kinds, poetry, book reviews, and biographies of classmates. They learn how to write effective beginnings and endings, to develop their ideas fully and clearly, and to use figurative language and appropriate word choice. They also learn how to combine sentences and use a variety of sentence types in order to improve the flow of their writing.

And, of course, they learn correct usage and the mechanics of writing: spelling, punctuation, and capitalization. In truth, those last few writing skills are about the only ones assessed on our state's standardized test for language. If all I cared about were test scores, I'd skip everything else and just drill the children on those few tested skills. The Tennessee writing test comes in fifth grade: I could just let the fifth grade teachers worry about writing.

Similarly, I wonder if I should change the way I teach reading. Should the children quit reading novels, biographies, and nonfiction books and focus instead on skill sheets with short reading passages and multiple-choice questions? After all, if performance on standardized tests is all that matters, there's little point in challenging students to read compelling literature. They certainly won't be asked to read and interpret a book on the day of the reading test.

Perhaps I should quit reading to my students. In the past, I have read to them orally each day for fifteen minutes or so, and we usually manage to complete five or six novels together during the school year. I typically choose books that most of them would not choose on their own: fiction that challenges their thinking and offers opportunities for us to discuss literary devices that may not be present in the literature they select for recreational reading. Their parents and I believe that "teacher read aloud" increases their appetite for books and pushes them to choose more mature and sophisticated literature. But if we used that fifteen minutes for cramming some more facts, our test scores would probably improve.

As you can see, my primary concern about teaching to the test is that I feel compelled to make instructional decisions that reduce the rigor and excitement of my children's curriculum. As stated at the end of the last chapter, high-stakes accountability measures almost invariably result in less learning for students, not more. No matter how long and convincingly elected officials repeat their mantra that they are improving our schools by imposing the commonsense strategy of increased testing and accountability, their reforms result in illusions of quality. Children learn less, and their enthusiasm for learning suffers.

In fact, a complete focus on teaching basic skills for standardized tests can result in instruction that is dysfunctional. In my first year as an elementary school principal in South Carolina, I walked into one of the fourth grade classrooms one day and found the teacher completely exasperated with her students. She had been attempting to teach them how to identify the main idea of a reading passage: that is, what the passage was basically about. Because the concept was one of our state's six reading subskills, it was a major focus of instruction from the first grade on.

The children told this fourth grade teacher that their first and second grade teachers had taught them that the main idea would always be stated in the first sentence of a paragraph. As it happened, the teachers in those grades had noticed that pattern on the state reading tests. If first and second grade children simply selected the answer choice that was the same as the first sentence in the reading passage, they would be assured of getting a passing score on the main idea subskill.

However, by fourth grade the reading passages were more difficult, and very often the main idea was not stated in the first sentence. In other words, students at that level had to comprehend the author's message. They had to be able to read. In effect, the teachers in the lower grades had been teaching children a test-taking skill instead of teaching them to read for understanding.

If you believe, as I do, that it is more important to read effectively than to pass reading tests, you have to be disturbed by that situation. Because of pressures to score high on the tests at even the earliest grade levels, we were teaching children a dysfunctional reading strategy at perhaps the most important stage of their reading development.

I have wondered in the years since if that problem at least partly explained why children in South Carolina seemed to do well on reading tests in the early grades and then perform less successfully as they got older. As this example suggests, the overzealous pursuit of improved test scores can lead to instructional practices that provide a short-term fix but result in diminished learning over the long haul.

In fact, the primary reason that America's students have often scored higher in the early grades than in the middle and high school grades on state, national, and international assessments may be even more straightforward. As noted earlier, Mr. Jackson believed that his students were burned out by fifth grade because they had experienced the same tedious and boring curriculum for several years. Even in schools where teachers' autonomy is not so severely limited, test pressures still tend to result in practices that diminish teachers' and students' excitement about learning.

Thus, high-stakes accountability measures may be having the same cumulative effect on our middle and high school students as they did on Mr. Jackson's students. As most parents of teenagers will attest, young people at that age have a lot on their minds, and contemporary American culture certainly provides them with many compelling distractions. If we continue to impose on our students learning activities that are designed solely to raise test scores, we should not be surprised that our young people lose interest in learning and achieve less academically as they move through the grades.

High-stakes pressures can have other unexpected results for children's learning. When we communicate to teachers that test score improvement is paramount to all other concerns, we clearly indicate that subjects not tested are not very important. In South Carolina, where writing was not tested until the sixth grade, there were teachers in the K–5 school where I was principal who were understandably resistant to committing class time to writing.

In fact, most states do not test students in writing in the primary grades and, consequently, many teachers de-emphasize that essential competency in order to spend more time drilling students on other skills. Ironically, most literacy experts agree that writing instruction reinforces children's reading skills. If we reduce the amount of time spent on writing to improve scores on multiple-choice reading tests, ultimately we are shooting ourselves in both feet. Not only are we shortchanging children's competence as writers, but we are also unwittingly compromising their reading achievement.

It is important to reiterate that problems related to an overemphasis on testing are not unique to South Carolina or Tennessee, the two states I mention most often in this book. In her studies of classrooms in Texas, Linda McNeil (2000) found that high school students were not actually reading the passages on their state's tests or practice activities but were simply matching key words from answer choices with key words in the text. Their teachers had purposefully taught them this strategy, committing instructional time to a test-taking technique that might have been spent instead on teaching sound reading strategies.

McNeil (2000) also observed students in many Texas schools spending large amounts of class time practicing how to correctly "bubble," or fill in, the circular answer spaces used on standardized tests, as well as learning to recognize "distracter" answers. Young children were taught the "pep rally cheer, 'Three in a row? No, No, No!'" The point of this activity was to remind them that test makers would probably not design three consecutive multiple-choice questions with the same letter for the answer (p. 730). Clearly, mastery of test-taking strategies was trumping any concern for meaningful learning in these Texas classrooms.

Many readers may perceive that instructional practices in their states and communities are quite different from those that I have described here. However, it is important to note that NCLB—the act that is changing teaching and learning in schools across the country—was based on the so-called Texas Miracle.

Since the passage of NCLB, children in America's public schools have been spending more time reviewing for and taking mandated tests than ever before. Each year my fourth graders spend almost a full week on Tennessee's standardized tests. In addition, my system recently purchased a program designed to give students practice on test items and to assess their proficiency on these items. We administer these tests three times during the year, committing about half a day to each session. Of course, teachers also engage in varying amounts of review as the time for statewide testing approaches, with particular emphasis on answering multiple-choice questions and bubbling answers.

The irony in this situation is that high-stakes accountability has resulted in a significant reduction in the amount of time spent on actual teaching and learning in our public schools. If we add the time required for the administration of standardized tests to the time spent on review and practice test-taking strategies, we can conservatively estimate that students in American schools commit up to 10 percent of their academic year taking state-mandated tests or preparing for them.

In some locations, such as Mr. Jackson's former school, the investment of time in these activities is even more substantial. Even at a commitment of 8 percent each year to testing and test preparation, students lose approximately a full year of instruction by the time they graduate from high school. If state legislatures across America announced that budget concerns were forcing them to eliminate the twelfth grade, there would be a great public outcry. Shouldn't we be just as concerned that many of our children spend a full year of their academic lives preparing for and taking standardized tests instead of learning new material and concepts?

I believe we should be equally concerned that the exclusive focus on test score improvement is slowly eroding education's ethical foundation. One afternoon a principal and a group of teachers in my area were discussing an instructional approach in a grade-level meeting. The teachers noted that this particular strategy had prevented them from spending sufficient time with learning disabled students and thus had a negative effect on those children's achievement.

The principal suddenly interrupted one teacher and stated emphatically, "I don't care about those kids!" He then explained that when test scores for their school were disaggregated (separated to show the performance of different groups such as special education, African-American, white, and non-English speakers), the learning disabled children had made the test score gains required by NCLB the previous year.

However, the nonhandicapped students had not improved their scores as much as the principal had hoped, so he was suggesting that the teachers give preference to them—and less attention to the learning disabled students—in making instructional decisions. When I reflect on that situation, I cannot help but wonder how the parents of the learning disabled students would react if they were aware of that comment.

It is also worth noting that the principal's response would probably have been the same if the school's more intellectually gifted students were performing well on statewide tests and the teachers had expressed concern about an approach shortchanging them. The high-achieving students would then become "those kids"—students who were to be given a lower instructional priority so that test score gains could be achieved with another group. The point is, too many educators have become so driven to improve test scores that they no longer think about what is best for the welfare of all children.

Another principal was simply being candid when she declared, "We're not about the 'whole child' anymore!" That is, test scores are all that matter in the present culture of schools. Other concerns about students are irrelevant.

It is tragic that test score improvement has become so ascendant that it has distracted otherwise caring and committed educators from the noble purposes that first attracted them to the profession. As NCLB has increased the pressure to improve test scores, administrators in some systems are explicitly directing teachers to focus their instructional efforts most intensely on the students in the middle and to give less attention to other children.

That is, these administrators are telling teachers not to worry about the most capable students, because they will probably pass state-mandated tests anyway, and not to be too concerned about the lowest performing children, because they have little hope of passing no matter what their teachers do. The idea is that schools will get more bang for their buck if teachers give greater attention to students who are on the bubble. Getting those children to achieve scores of proficient will boost their schools' totals and help them to avoid being labeled as failing schools.

In fact, at a workshop for beginning teachers in my area, one of the trainers—who is also an elementary principal—displayed a student writing sample that was severely flawed. The presenter then told the audience that she would not recommend spending much time instructing that student in writing because he would probably never pass the state writing test anyway.

I have even heard of local elementary principals considering putting their weakest teachers in third grade—the lowest grade in which Tennessee schools must conduct statewide testing—so that the presumably lower scores produced at that grade level would be easier to improve upon the next year, and perhaps in the years to come. Thus, the school would be able to demonstrate that it was making impressive year-to-year gains.[1] I do not know if principals have actually begun to employ that strategy, but it is disturbing that it is even being suggested. We should never make educational decisions on the basis of criteria so removed from a consideration of what is best for our children.

---

[1] Each school's "Report Card" in Tennessee provides letter grades indicating how much improvement has occurred in each subject and grade level that is part of the state's testing program.

Traditionally, teachers and administrators have prided themselves on making decisions in response to the question, "How would I want my own child to be treated in this situation?" As the pressure increases to produce better test scores—instead of helping young people grow intellectually, emotionally, and socially in ways that we would endorse for our own children—public education is losing its ethical grounding.

I worry especially about the effects of the testing culture on beginning teachers. Nontenured teachers seem to express far more concern about their test scores than tenured faculty. In fact, it is not unusual to hear younger teachers talk about their fears of being fired if their scores are not high enough.

As our statewide tests approached a few years ago, I was talking with one of my nontenured colleagues, a very promising and talented educator, about cramming material at the last minute because we knew it could be on the tests. When I commented that I was not going to engage in that practice, she replied that her status as a nontenured teacher compelled her to do so. She then added ruefully, "I know it's wrong, but I'm afraid I'm being judged on test scores."

My greatest concern about beginning teachers is not simply that they are temporarily compromising their ethical concerns for our children until after they are tenured. I worry even more that they are entering the culture of teaching at a time when standardized tests are so important that these teachers will perceive that education's only purpose is to improve test scores.

For the most part, teachers of my generation will continually struggle to protect the margins of the classroom that Linda McNeil described. Like Mrs. Elkins, these educators entered the profession at a time when they were allowed to teach from the heart, and they will always find a way to engage in teaching that matters. They know how personally and professionally rewarding real teaching can be, and how powerful and transformational it can be for their students. They know that only a rich and meaningful curriculum can change young people's lives, and they know that compromising our children's curriculum in the interests of improved test scores is no less unethical than showing up at school unprepared to teach.

Unfortunately, that generation of teachers is rapidly moving toward retirement and is being replaced by beginning teachers who will never have the experience of teaching from the heart. To them, teaching simply means playing the test score game that Mr. Jackson was compelled to play. Those who are troubled ethically by that expectation will eventually quit the profession, as Mr. Jackson almost did, leaving our children in the hands of those who are willing to collect a paycheck for simply enacting the mandates imposed on them by lawmakers far removed from the realities of public school classrooms.

I have to believe that most Americans do not realize that these disturbing changes are occurring in their children's classrooms. The parents of the students I teach are committed to their children's academic growth, including their performance on standardized tests. However, I have never had parents suggest that they would like for me to care less about their children. No parent has ever said to me or any other teacher I know, "I'd like for you to quit treating my daughter like a human being and start regarding her as a statistic."

However, in today's high-stakes climate, we have provided educators with incentives to do exactly that. When we adopt policies that diminish—and perhaps even extinguish—the ethical motivations for teaching and serving children, we tread on very dangerous ground. Before we allow the erosion of ethics in our schools to progress too far, perhaps we should ask whether Americans really want our educational system to adopt a do-whatever-it-takes attitude toward test score improvement.

I believe America's parents would answer that question with a resounding no if they understood fully the impact of high-stakes testing on their children's education. The parents of the students I teach share my desire that their children perform well on any and every assessment. However, as I indicated in the introduction, I have never had a parent thank me for raising a child's test scores. Instead they express interest in a range of student competencies that are not tested and are therefore rapidly becoming low educational priorities.

Ironically, it is the media—the same journalists who have helped to promote high-stakes accountability—who consistently affirm our

society's interest in an educational system that does more than simply produce high test scores. When newspapers and television news shows are not suggesting that our schools are in crisis because of unsatisfactory test performance, they are often reporting about creative and academically engaging school projects.

In recent years I have seen stories in my area about unusual student publications, election debates, drama productions, fundraising for tsunami relief, a project to study and restore an old cemetery, and students learning math and economics by playing the stock market. Clearly, we Americans celebrate and want these kinds of interesting and intellectually challenging school activities for our children. Apparently members of the media recognize that fact and present such stories in an effort to be fair: to spotlight positive events in our schools that offset the negative news of our alleged achievement test failures.

Sadly, however, these journalists do not see the striking contradiction between the two extremes that dominate their coverage of education. They do not realize that students receive fewer and fewer opportunities to engage in projects like those mentioned above when schools focus entirely on raising test scores. In fact, if the momentum continues toward curricula that emphasize test score improvement to the exclusion of all other educational goals, such projects may all but disappear.

In the introduction, I described my students' field trip to a restored one-room schoolhouse. It is always far and away the highlight of our academic year, not only because of the children's excitement and joy of discovery that day, but also because their participation in this extraordinary experience increases their interest in the study of history and teaches them more about life in the nineteenth century than I ever could in a typical day's instruction.

Recently I spoke with the director of this program and learned that not a single class participated in this program last year until Tennessee's standardized tests were over in late April—and then the one-room schoolhouse was booked almost every day. In other words, even the teachers who most value this powerful and transformational learning experience deferred it until almost the end of the year because they did not believe that they could take one in-

structional day away from their preparations for statewide testing. (And, yes, I was one of the teachers who scheduled the trip for a date after the tests were over.)

Even worse, only one class from the county school system in which the museum is located took part in this historical reenactment, and other nearby systems had minimal participation. The program director said it was her understanding that schools in these districts were eliminating almost all field trips so that they could concentrate their instructional efforts solely on test score improvement. The opportunity to spend a day engaged in a living history experience had become unnecessary fluff.

At the end of chapter 2, I examined the extraordinary disparity between Americans' positive perceptions of the schools they know and their negative perceptions of the schools they do not know. I have to wonder—when parents who approve of education in their own children's schools hear politicians promise to fix American education with stringent accountability measures, do these parents imagine that such initiatives are for other schools—the failing schools somewhere else that they keep hearing about—and, therefore, not for their own children's schools?

I think we should be very clear. If mandates like the ones that throttled the enthusiasm, passion, and professional decision making of Mr. Jackson have not already become a part of classrooms in every community, don't be too sure that they won't in the very near future. No Child Left Behind has already fundamentally changed the educational experiences of students in schools across America and promises to alter teaching and learning even more profoundly as time goes on.

Chapter Seven

─────────────────○─────────────────

The No Child Left Behind Act: Illusion and Reality

THE NO CHILD LEFT BEHIND (NCLB) ACT, which was signed into law in January 2002, is the most far-reaching piece of educational legislation in our nation's history. It has substantially altered public school policy in every state, and its impact on teaching and learning—as well as the very status of public education in America—will probably be more profound with each passing year. To begin our examination of this landmark federal act, please imagine turning to the sports page of your local newspaper one morning and reading the following article.

COLUMBUS HIGH GIRLS CONTINUE TO STRUGGLE

Columbus—The woes of the Columbus High School girls' basketball squad continued Friday night in its game versus conference rival Lewis and Clark. Afterward, Coach Suzie Johnson could not hide her frustration with the persistent failure of this year's team.

"It seems as if there's a different problem every night," she lamented. "Sure, we outscored them 56 to 38. Heck, we've outscored 16 of our 18 opponents this season, but what does that mean when you don't make the national standard for rebounds in one game and the standard for assists the next?"

Coach Johnson's frustrations are understandable. In the contest against Lewis and Clark, the team met federal standards for rebounds, blocked shots, steals, and turnovers. They also posted exceptional percentages for free throws, three-point attempts, and overall shooting from the floor. However, the girls fell one short of the standard of ten assists per game that the National High School Athletic Board has designated as this year's measure of adequate progress.

Johnson lamented, "This has been another very difficult season. As coaches, we've tried to do the right things, but nothing seems to be good enough. It's disheartening to all of us—the players, the coaches, and the fans. It hurts to look up at the scoreboard and see that we had more points than our opponent and met seven national standards, but failed to achieve just one.

"I don't know how the girls keep coming to practice. In fact, two of our most promising young athletes quit just last week. On top of everything else, attendance at our games has been steadily dropping. And don't tell me that we can take consolation that everyone else is failing to reach these standards! The board has given us the standards for success, and we've got to find a way to achieve them. If we don't soon, I'm afraid our players are just going to give up. Every day they have to face family and friends who can't accept the team's continuing failure. That's the really hard part. I hurt for the kids."

If the measures for basketball success depicted in this article seem puzzling, consider the accountability provisions of NCLB. As explained in the following paragraphs, the requirements of this federal act impose a burden on public schools that can be as daunting and demoralizing as the plight of the fictitious team from Columbus High. Much like the basketball standards that required the girls to attain statistical targets in every dimension of the game before they could claim success, public schools must now meet multiple testing criteria every year in order to avoid harsh penalties and a public perception of failure.

NCLB mandated the annual testing of students in grades 3 through 8 in mathematics and reading and the testing of high school students in these subjects at least once during grades ten through twelve.[1] Beginning in 2007–2008, states were also required to test students in science at least once in grades three through five, once in grades six through nine, and once in grades ten through twelve. The law allows each state to select its own tests, thus permitting states to use assessment measures they already had in place.

Many states had been conducting all of these tests and others for years. However, NCLB went a step beyond any previous accountability legislation and mandated that every student be at least proficient on its state's mathematics, reading, and science tests by the 2013–2014 school year. States were required to establish at least three levels of student achievement on their tests: basic (unacceptable), proficient (acceptable), and advanced. To demonstrate progress toward the noble goal of 100 percent proficiency in 2013–2014, every state also had to devise a plan showing increasing percentages of students scoring proficient on the tests each year. These annual targets showing steady incremental gains are called adequate yearly progress (AYP) goals.

A second provision that distinguishes NCLB from other accountability measures is the requirement that schools achieve these annual AYP standards not only for their overall populations, but also in each of eight student subgroups: white, Hispanic, African-American, Native American, Asian/Pacific Islander, economically disadvantaged, students with disabilities, and limited English proficient.

Further, at least 95 percent of the students in each category must be tested—meaning that no more than 5 percent of any subgroup can be absent on testing dates. Schools that do not meet their overall AYP goals, as well as the goals in each of the eight subgroups, receive the designation "in need of improvement." The consequences for not meeting AYP goals become increasingly stringent when schools do not achieve them in consecutive years. (An explanation of these penalties begins on page 101.)

---

[1] Although the law required states to begin this testing no later than 2005–2006, many (if not most) systems had begun to comply with the testing requirements of NCLB within one year of the law's January 2002 passage.

Much like the fictitious Columbus High School girls' basketball team, a school could be successful in meeting its overall test achievement goals but could fail because any one group, including students with disabilities (mentally handicapped students), did not reach the state AYP standard on one academic test. Similarly, a school might meet its targets for the total student population and for every subgroup except children who speak limited English, and that school would be regarded as failing.

In other words, since schools must ultimately meet their goals for the overall population and each of eight subpopulations on three different tests, a school could fail by not achieving any one of twenty-seven different criteria.[2] Further, because 95 percent of the students in each subgroup must be present for testing, the absence of too many students in one particular group during testing would cause the school to fail. (In some states, two or three student absences in one group would result in failure.)

With this attendance provision, the number of standards that must be achieved annually by some schools is potentially fifty-four—since each school must meet the attendance and academic standards on each of three tests in each of nine population groups. A school could meet fifty-three of fifty-four criteria and would still be identified as a failing school and suffer the consequences of that shortcoming.

The reputed purpose of these requirements is that schools will be accountable for closing the long-standing achievement gap between middle-class white students and poor or minority students—thus, the politically inspired name No Child Left Behind. The idea is that schools will no longer shortchange children through what President George W. Bush and members of his administration have repeatedly called "the soft bigotry of low expectations."

My first experience with NCLB was in April 2003 when my principal asked me to administer state-mandated tests to two third grade students in the subgroup known as limited English proficient. Felipe and Maria both came from Spanish-speaking homes.

---

[2] As explained in chapter 3 and below on page 95, schools with few or no students in a subgroup do not have to publish that group's test scores or meet the achievement standards for that student category.

Felipe was in the first grade when his family came to America and he began attending public schools. His spoken English was quite fluent, but his reading was somewhat below grade level, as one would expect for a child who spent his first few years in school just learning to understand and speak English. That is, it is difficult to read a language before achieving some proficiency speaking it—a fact we often forget when we discuss the education of children who come to school not knowing English.

Maria had arrived in America just a few months earlier. Her family had previously lived in a remote Central American village that did not have a school, so she could not read even in her native language. Further, she understood virtually no spoken English. In the two days I tested her and Felipe, it was clear that she understood hardly anything I said.

Before the testing, Maria's teacher tried to communicate to her that she should use her pencil to darken bubbles next to any words on the tests that she might recognize from the few English sight words she had learned in her one month of schooling. In truth, I'm not sure that Maria was capable of employing even that basic strategy. Throughout the testing, she closely observed Felipe and simply imitated his actions.

To begin each of our testing sessions, I read verbatim the script provided to all third grade test administrators. Anyone who has ever taken a standardized test probably recalls directions like these: "During this reading test, you are to answer only the questions in this part of the test booklet. When you come to the word STOP, you may not turn the page. You may go back and check your work on this test, but you cannot work on any other test."[3]

Knowing that I would be in violation of statewide testing policy if I did not read the text exactly as it was written in bold print in the administrator's manual, I dutifully carried out the absurd travesty of slowly and deliberately reading each word of test directions to a child who could hardly comprehend anything I said. Thankfully, Felipe

[3] I am reciting these directions from memory and probably do not have the words exactly right. There are strict prohibitions in Tennessee against copying test materials.

understood the directions, but Maria clearly did not have a clue what I was asking her to do.

When I told the children to begin the first test, Maria did not respond, so I turned the page of her booklet to the beginning of the test. She then watched Felipe and tried to copy his answers, so I communicated to her as well as I could that she had to work on her own. I guess she thought we were engaged in a cooperative activity and that it was acceptable for her to seek help from Felipe.

When Maria learned that she could not depend on Felipe, she simply went down each page randomly filling in answer bubbles and pausing intermittently to pretend to be pondering the choices. She often glanced at Felipe to see what he was doing and occasionally at me to determine if she was doing anything else that was impermissible.

I tried not to be too obvious but watched her carefully, suspecting that she would not know where the test ended. Sure enough, she finished marking all the answers on the first test and tried to proceed to the next page before I stopped her. (Heaven forbid she should move forward and blindly guess the answers to another test before being directed to do so.)

We followed this procedure for most of two afternoons until the testing was completed. After randomly darkening bubbles throughout each test, Maria would usually put her head down and close her eyes. When she did, I wondered what she must have been thinking about American education and how she must have felt devalued by the process to which I was subjecting her.

My fourth grade colleagues teased me for several days because I felt compelled the second day of testing to bring snacks for Felipe and Maria. Knowing that I could not communicate to Maria my regret that we were putting her through such a foolish and demeaning exercise, I hoped that giving her a treat would somehow let me off the hook.

In the end, it was the dishonesty in the process that troubled me the most. By administering standardized tests to Maria, I was complicit in the lie, acting as if she should be able to perform the academic tasks in the test booklet and that this whole futile exercise served a useful educational purpose.

Worse, we forced Maria to be part of the dishonesty, and she responded in the only way that a child could in that situation. To save face and endure what must have been a perplexing and uncomfortable situation, she pretended that she understood what to do and how to answer the test questions. As happens so often in the enactment of educational accountability measures at the classroom level, the teacher and child simply played the game they were compelled by law to play.

The reason for testing Felipe and Maria separately from their classmates was to provide them with additional time so that they might be more successful on the tests. That allowance may have helped Felipe, but it was useless to Maria. Giving her extra time made as much sense as shouting words slowly and distinctly in the face of a foreign visitor who does not understand English. Anyone who has ever witnessed that situation knows how foolish an exercise it is. If a person doesn't know the language, hearing the words spoken loudly and clearly isn't going to help. Nor was more time on the tests going to help Maria read a language she couldn't speak or understand.

Of course, the purpose of testing children like Maria is to demonstrate our determination under NCLB to hold every student accountable for learning basic skills. No longer will teachers be allowed to exercise the "soft bigotry of low expectations" by modifying the standards for children who cannot speak English. With NCLB, we're going to hold all students' feet to the fire by mandating that they perform at a proficient level and penalizing their schools if they do not.

In fairness, I should remind readers that there is a provision in NCLB that waives the requirement for schools to meet AYP targets in subgroups with small populations (as explained in chapter 3). For example, a school with only four African-American children would not have to meet the AYP standard for that group, because the performance of such a small sample would not be a valid measure of the school's effectiveness in teaching African-American children.

With federal approval, each state is allowed to decide what number of students to use as its cutoff (for example, forty-five in Tennessee and thirty in Florida). Therefore, some schools do not have to publish the results of certain subpopulations and do not receive penalties for failing to make the AYP standards for those student categories.

However, many schools, especially large schools with diverse populations, have to meet the standards for most or all of the eight subgroups. Besides, the fact that Maria's scores did not have to be reported on my school's Report Card does not alter the fact that she had to endure a demeaning and futile exercise when she should have been in her classroom increasing her knowledge of English and academic content.

I should also note that the regulations regarding the testing of limited English proficient children—also called English Language Learners (ELL)—have changed somewhat since the passage of NCLB. For example, states may now allow ELL students to take statewide tests in their own language for three years. Of course, since Maria had never been to school and could not read in any language, this provision would not have helped her.

Further, Tennessee only offers its tests in English, probably because of cost considerations. I do not know how many states provide tests in languages other than English, but I think we can be confident that none have a full complement of assessments in Sanskrit, Russian, Swahili, Vietnamese, Chinese, Japanese, Korean, Spanish, and all of the other myriad languages spoken by the more than five million ELL students enrolled in America's public schools.

Since the passage of NCLB, there has been one other important change regarding the testing of ELL students. In the absence of tests in their own language, these children can now demonstrate progress in reading using specially designed alternative measures of assessment. However, they must still take tests in all other required subjects in English even if they just arrived in America, and they must take the reading test in English after being enrolled in our schools for three years.

In Tennessee, and presumably most other states, math and science tests have few, if any, questions that do not require some reading. Therefore, in states that only have assessments in English, passing the math and science tests will be a daunting task for even those ELL students who are very accomplished in these subjects but are not yet proficient English readers.

For this reason, it is questionable whether schools with substantial ELL populations will ever be able to meet their AYP targets, particularly in future years when the expectation for success approaches 100 percent. Years ago I conducted a study in a school located in an ethnic neighborhood that was the cultural destination for recent immigrants from one of the Caribbean nations. On a typical day, multiple families with children spending their first hours in America enrolled in this school. Portable classrooms were installed on a regular basis as the school population exploded and, at one point, only about half of the students came from English-speaking households.

This elementary school had a competent and dedicated staff, including many educators who spoke the language of the new students. Nonetheless, it is hard to imagine that school and others like it meeting the AYP standards of NCLB and avoiding the inevitable label of "failing schools."

Similarly, schools with more than minimal numbers of students with disabilities face a daunting challenge under NCLB. Although the law will allow 1 percent of a school's student population—those whose IQ is below 70—to take an alternative form of statewide testing, it is hard to imagine that most schools will be able to attain AYP standards for disabled students consistently, especially as requirements in future years approach the ultimate goal of 100 percent proficiency. Even with the most effective regular and special education teachers, it is simply unreasonable to expect all children with learning disabilities or mild mental retardation to pass most standardized tests.

There are politicians and journalists who suggest that teachers in opposition to NCLB standards for mentally handicapped students are coddling and underestimating these children. Of course, it is unlikely that any of these critics have ever taught a child with severe learning disabilities. To understand special education and its effects, we might compare it to a ramp that gives physically handicapped people access to a building.

A person without the use of both legs can enter the building using the ramp and a wheelchair and can then move around with some degree of effectiveness, assuming there are no obstacles inside. However, the ramp does not guarantee that people in wheelchairs will be able to race into the building and negotiate twists and turns, crowded hallways, changes in elevation, and every closed door with the same ease as a person with no physical limitations.

In much the same way, special education enables mentally handicapped children to access learning opportunities and grow academically as much as possible, but it does not ensure that all of them will keep up with their more intellectually gifted classmates. In other words, special education does not altogether compensate for every disabled student's academic difficulties. It does not fix mentally handicapped children.

By definition, mentally handicapped means that grade-level performance may not be expected, certainly not for every child within that category. That's not a low expectation or excuse making. It is simply one of the realities teachers face every day. Educators strive to help every student succeed, and sometimes handicapped children achieve far beyond expectations. However, we shouldn't expect grade-level performance from all mentally handicapped children any more than we should expect people with wheelchairs to cover 100 meters as fast as able-bodied and accomplished track athletes.

With excellent instruction and considerable support, some children with disabilities may achieve NCLB targets, but not all of them will. To demand that they attain those standards annually under the threat of punishment for their schools dishonors those students, their parents, and their teachers and administrators. We should not put any group of children and adults in the position of receiving the designation "failing school" because a small percentage of mentally handicapped students do not pass a standardized test at a given moment in time.

The belief that schoolchildren of varying backgrounds and abilities will benefit across the board from a law that sets the bar at an arbitrary standard and says "Just get there" is based on very simplistic assumptions about high expectations for student learning. One way to understand the complexity of that educational concept is to examine its implementation in different classrooms.

As a principal, I once worked with two second grade teachers who provided an interesting contrast in their beliefs about high expectations for children. I call them Angela and Regina and hope that their stories clarify the difference between genuine high expectations and arbitrarily imposed standards.

Angela was African-American and had grown up in a rural community near our school. Each year she established with her children the strong personal connections that make exemplary teaching possible. She was sensitive to the individual perspectives of all of her students, whatever their race, circumstances, or abilities.

Like all good teachers, Angela knew when to offer encouragement or understanding, when to nudge a child academically, and when to provide a stern reprimand. On the rare occasions when she found it necessary, her expressions of disapproval were professional and respectful. Her acceptance and nurturance of every child communicated a reassuring sense of approval to each of them and an unspoken expectation that they should treat each other with the same thoughtfulness that she modeled in her behavior toward students.

Consequently, Angela's classroom was a safe, orderly, and productive learning environment—the kind of place you'd want to be if you were a young child. In that positive context, Angela pushed her students as far as each of them could go and made no apologies for varying her expectations for individual students based on real differences in ability and past achievement.

Regina was white and also grew up in a community near our school. However, she did not possess the cultural sensitivity to all of the children from our rural area that Angela displayed, and Regina's classroom demeanor clearly revealed her belief that it was not important for her to connect personally with the students she taught. From the most gifted to the least capable student, Regina expressed the same performance expectations. I cannot recall ever seeing her offer encouragement or comfort to a struggling student, and she frequently and publicly expressed her disapproval for poor behavior or academic performance.

Regina's classroom was not a happy place for young children. The climate was tense, and conflicts between students seemed to occur more often than in other classrooms. Nonetheless, Regina regarded herself as a strong teacher. Whenever I questioned her instructional practices (as I often did), she proudly characterized herself as tough, demanding, and uncompromising.

She also reminded me that I advocated high expectations for all students, and that was exactly what she thought she was expressing. She clearly indicated to students what they needed to achieve and, in her view, that constituted high academic expectations. In truth, however, I don't believe Regina sincerely expected her struggling students to succeed. Her job was to set the bar, deliver uniform instruction to everyone in the classroom, and winnow the wheat from the chaff.

When school began each year, I assigned Angela and Regina classes of children who were comparable academically. Nonetheless, by the end of each year, Angela's students had outperformed Regina's on a variety of measures, including standardized tests. The differences were especially dramatic in comparisons of children who began the year as low achievers, particularly low-income African-Americans.

Angela's cultural sensitivity and ability to connect personally with all of her children paid substantial dividends. Most important, she understood how to show students at the bottom of the academic ladder how to reach the next rung, and then another, and so on, until those children went as far up the ladder as possible. All of her lowest achieving students may not have attained grade-level proficiency by the end of the year, but they made impressive progress, often demonstrating more than one year's academic growth.

In contrast, Regina took students at the bottom of the ladder and simply pointed to the distant top rung. Some of them apparently concluded they would never make it and quit trying. By demanding that every child function at an arbitrary standard that did not necessarily reflect where they were academically or where they needed to go next, Regina doomed many low-achieving students to a year of frustration and academic inertia.

Angela had genuine high expectations for students, and her understanding of that fundamental teaching disposition was one of the primary reasons why she was so successful. In contrast, Regina's notion of high expectations was analogous to the requirements of NCLB. The target of 100 percent proficiency is a noble aim that every educator should work tirelessly to attain, and most already do. However, like Regina, NCLB has established standards that are unrealistic for some students, and then it simply demands that they somehow achieve those milestones.

Given the failure of the Bush administration and Congress to fund NCLB adequately, we can only assume that these elected officials believe that greater effort by teachers and students is all that is needed to meet the law's ambitious targets. As I hope the story of Maria and the earlier discussion of special education demonstrate, sometimes effort alone will not enable every child to reach grade-level academic proficiency.

However, the one certainty is that there will be serious consequences for schools that do not attain all standards of NCLB. The law requires every state and school district to provide detailed reports of test results to the public each year, and school systems must clearly identify schools that fail to meet all of their AYP targets. As the most recent reauthorization of the Elementary and Secondary Education Act (first passed in 1965), NCLB encompasses Title I, the federal government's program for disadvantaged students.

Therefore, the law also includes penalties for those schools that receive money through this legislation and do not meet AYP standards. These funds are allocated to about two thirds of American public schools and 95 percent of the nation's school systems, so most schools are affected directly by the sanctions of NCLB (Popham, 2004). The bulleted points that follow provide brief summaries of the consequences for failure to reach AYP targets from the first year through the fifth.

- Schools that do not attain all performance objectives for the first time receive the designation "in need of improvement."
- When a school fails to meet all standards for two consecutive years, the district must provide technical support to help it improve, and its students may transfer to other schools within the same system, with the costs of transportation provided by the system.
- In schools that do not reach their target goals three years in a row, technical support and school choice continue. In addition, students must receive supplemental educational services from the

school or may use their share of the school's Title I funding to obtain tutoring from outside groups.

- Schools that fail four years in a row must continue all of the services required in the third year. They must also implement an improvement plan that may require the development of a new curriculum or the replacement of school personnel.
- In the fifth consecutive year of failure to achieve standards, governance changes will go into effect. These may include state takeover, conversion to charter school status, or the assumption of control by a private management company.

Even schools that do not receive federal funding for disadvantaged students are feeling the effects of NCLB, and most are giving as much attention to the law's requirements as those that are vulnerable to the penalties outlined above. Perhaps the surest consequence of a school's inability to reach all of its AYP targets in any year is that the public will perceive it as a failing school. In newspaper articles about schools not achieving all NCLB standards, some form of the word *fail* often appears in the title and almost invariably throughout the text (just as I have used it often in this chapter).

One day when I was driving home from school, I heard what appeared to be a public service announcement stating the options available under NCLB for children who attend a "failing school." I was surprised by the explicit use of that label and listened unsuccessfully to the same station for days hoping to hear a repetition of the announcement in order to clarify its origin.

I have wondered ever since if perhaps it was pulled from the airwaves because of the too-obvious use of the term "failing school." Although I believe that the authors of NCLB wanted America's schools to have to wear that label publicly, perhaps the officials who removed the announcement realized that it too clearly betrayed one of the law's real purposes.

James Popham, an educational scholar who has studied and written about standardized testing for several decades, obviously has no doubts that the designation "failing" will be applied to any school that does not meet all standards of NCLB. Popham (2004) has written a book titled *America's "Failing" Schools* in which he attempts to explain to our nation's parents and teachers how even our best schools run the risk of not meeting every NCLB standard and then being labeled as failing schools.

It is hard to know if educators' fears of being seen as failures are as great as their trepidation at the thought of the chaos, expense, and difficulty that will certainly befall schools that do not meet NCLB standards for two or more years. The image of students transferring in and out of schools, the mandate to provide tutoring to students without adequate funding, and the requirement to make staffing or governance changes are enough to intimidate any well-meaning and hardworking administrator. Even so, it is perhaps just as troubling to most teachers and principals to accept the notion that the schools to which they commit their professional lives might be publicly labeled as failing. After all, that suggests that they have failed.

Whatever the cause of their trepidation, public school educators are clearly marching lockstep down the path of test score improvement described in the two previous chapters. In my own school and the outstanding system to which it belongs, the emphasis on standardized tests to the exclusion of all other educational goals has increased substantially in each of the last few years. Discussions about statewide testing, the implications of not performing well, and strategies for improving scores (not children's lives) dominate faculty and grade-level meetings.

It's hard to imagine that the same pattern is not being repeated in virtually every school across America. Each year, school systems in Tennessee (and across the nation) adopt new textbooks in particular subjects, perhaps social studies one year and science the next. The most substantial change I have noticed in textbooks in recent years has been the increasing emphasis on test score improvement. Textbook publishers have clearly gone to greater lengths to provide materials and strategies for raising test scores with each new version of their products. In fact, the determining factor in local textbook selection is often the amount of test preparation activity provided by the various companies.

Tennessee schools adopted new mathematics textbooks in 2005. In a meeting to explain features of the books our system had purchased, a representative from the publisher proudly explained the multiple ways in which her company's product leads to improved test scores. In this textbook series, which is now being used in thousands of systems across the country, every lesson has a brief accompanying activity designed to help children perform on standardized tests and a more substantial multiple choice assessment at the end of each chapter. Teachers who assign these exercises will commit instructional time to test score improvement instead of teaching new mathematical concepts or increasing students' depth of understanding of skills and content already learned.

Moreover, teachers in Tennessee are now evaluated according to whether or not they assess daily student progress using the types of multiple choice questions found on standardized tests. On the revised evaluation instrument that our state published in 2004, teachers who want to receive the highest rating for their ability to measure student achievement must use "assessment items written in formats similar to state assessment items." In other words, to be a good teacher in the era of NCLB, you must now use multiple choice questions rather than essay questions or other forms of assessment that might require higher level thinking and more rigorous standards of student performance.

Having experienced a similar climate during South Carolina's implementation of the Education Improvement Act (EIA) in the 1980s, I am seeing a repetition of patterns that characterized that era, and the reports I'm reading and hearing from across the country affirm those perceptions. In 2005 a presenter from New England who provides workshops nationwide on classroom computer use told teachers in my system, "I see innovation being crushed out of schools."

That reaction to NCLB is certainly very evident in my area. As reported in chapter 6, many schools in the region are already eliminating or sharply curtailing field trips to focus on test score improvement. Some have also substantially reduced instructional time in social studies to increase skill and drill activities in math and reading.[4] In fact, according to a 2006 survey by the Center on Education Policy, 71 percent of America's public school districts have

---

[4] Many educators have begun to refer to these activities as "drill and kill" because a steady diet of this type of instruction has the effect of killing student interest and enthusiasm for learning.

decreased the amount of time spent on history and other subjects in order to meet the math and reading test standards of NCLB (Campbell, 2007).

Typically, however, the effects on instruction are more subtle. Teachers who might have conducted a science experiment or had students complete a research project in years past now have children simply read from their textbooks and complete worksheets that resemble the multiple-choice, darken-the-bubble format of standardized tests. More and more schools are telling teachers to abandon the reading of chapter books in the classroom and to return to skill and drill activities to improve reading scores. In brief, the encroachment on instructional autonomy and creativity that crushed the spirit and innovative instincts of Mr. Jackson (in chapter 6) is rapidly accelerating in school systems across America.

Administrative creativity is also surely on the wane. We have known for some time that one of the key measures of a successful school is the instructional leadership of the principal. In the context of NCLB and the fear it has engendered in most school personnel, there simply isn't any room for innovative school leadership.

No longer are the most highly regarded administrators the ones who can stimulate reflection and discussion among parents and educators about all that their schools might accomplish. Nor are they the people who devise creative ideas for school improvement, or those who inspire and harness the energies of everyone in their buildings to address the unique challenges of their student populations and communities. The mission of educational administrators at all levels has been narrowed to a single focus—improved scores on the tests that measure achievement of NCLB targets.

One of the strengths of American education has always been the ability of enterprising teachers and administrators to generate unique responses to their schools' problems—solutions whose effectiveness can then be replicated in other contexts. It is important to remember that every accepted and proven educational strategy we use today began as an alternative approach that someone had the courage and insight to try. When we engender in educators a fear of straying from a single approved script, we all but eliminate the kind of innovation that might provide answers to education's most troubling dilemmas.

Our children are the ones who stand to lose the most from the misguided vision of public education embodied in NCLB. Like South Carolina's EIA, NCLB is based on the assumption that pressures to improve test scores will compel educators to work harder. But what if that premise is wrong?

Most of the teachers I know from personal experiences in four different states work very hard and use the best methods available to them. If these teachers are already working as diligently and effectively as possible to improve student achievement, then teaching to the test is the only rational response they can make to the pressure to ratchet up test scores higher and higher.

They have little choice but to narrow the curriculum to that thin slice of academic learning that is tested, and then skill and drill students ceaselessly on assessed concepts and proficiencies. Many teachers in schools with large numbers of disadvantaged students fear that any diversion from "drill and kill" will compromise their students' chances of passing the tests. Thus, the children that NCLB promises to save are truly left further and further behind.

As suggested in chapter 5, higher performing children also suffer because they experience a watered-down curriculum that does not challenge them. In the end, students of all ability and achievement levels lose in this high-stakes testing environment because they must endure instruction that does not interest or engage them and fails to address higher level thinking and creativity.

Nonetheless, under the pressures imposed by NCLB, there will be an early illusion of success, as demonstrated already by the pronouncements of President Bush and other NCLB supporters. As test scores have shown improvements, we have heard how our broken public schools have been fixed and how elementary schools across America have been transformed.

In truth, the only change that has occurred under NCLB is that teachers everywhere are now compelled to teach almost exclusively to their states' standardized tests. Scores may improve as educators fine tune the alignment of curricula and tests, but types of learning that are not tested—but are nonetheless important to our children's total academic development—will increasingly fall by the wayside. As suggested by the comparison of Mrs. Elkins and Mr. Jackson in chapter 6, teaching that truly matters will become a rarity.

We should also prepare ourselves for politicians promoting the illusion of academic excellence. As educators everywhere teach to the test under the fear of NCLB's sanctions, scores may make substantial improvements in some schools and systems. As they do, we will hear elected officials proclaim that their reforms have resulted in educational excellence.

However, as explained in chapter 5, what we will probably have in these locations is the universal achievement of mediocrity. There may be high percentages of students passing their states' standardized tests, but those high percentages do not indicate the achievement of excellence. Although there is variation in the quality and difficulty of the tests being used to establish compliance with NCLB, students do not have to demonstrate academic excellence to attain a score of proficient in most states.

That last statement may seem to contradict my earlier assertion that the standards of NCLB are too high. Let's be very clear. When teachers and administrators complain that NCLB sets impossible standards, they don't mean that the academic expectations are too rigorous for average and exceptional students. Most of those students will easily meet mandated targets.

However, it is unreasonable to demand that educators elevate all children—including those who are mentally handicapped or speak limited English—to grade-level proficiency or face punishment for not achieving that absurd standard. We don't demand that doctors cure every patient, including those who are near death when they first seek treatment, and we don't subject those physicians to penalties or public embarrassment for not meeting that outrageous expectation. We simply require that they use sound practices, perform according to professional and ethical standards, and do their best.

In time, educators and schools everywhere will experience the sting of the illusion of educational failure. In the early years of NCLB, elected officials will claim credit (as they already have) for the perceived success of NCLB and the alleged attainment of excellence.

However, as suggested in chapter 5, once educators have aligned their teaching as closely as they possibly can to their states' standardized tests, scores will level out.

No matter how hard and effectively teachers work toward the aim of test score improvement, they will inevitably hit plateaus. As they do, their schools will fail to meet the increasingly high AYP targets of NCLB, and the public will perceive that these schools are failing. At that point, educators, not politicians, will feel the displeasure of citizens demanding answers for the apparent widespread failure of our nation's public schools.

In fact, large numbers of schools across the country failed to meet the law's standards even in its beginning years. Approximately 26,000 of America's 91,400 public schools did not achieve their AYP goals for 2002–2003 (Goldberg, 2005), and 45 percent of California's schools—including 77 percent of its high schools—did not attain NCLB standards that year (Asimov, 2003).

However, it is important to note that many of these schools did not fail because of poor academic performance. Of the 723 California high schools that did not meet AYP standards in 2002–2003, the problem with 84 percent of them was that fewer than 95 percent of the students from each subpopulation group were present during testing. Several of the state's most exemplary high schools, including some in the prestigious Palo Alto district, failed because groups of high-performing juniors decided to skip testing in order to prepare for advanced placement (AP) exams. As an official in the system explained, high AP scores have direct personal benefits to outstanding college-bound students, but the state tests do not, so these young people opted to study for AP tests (Asimov, 2003).

In some cases, schools failing to meet NCLB standards posted excellent scores on other measures during the same academic year. Education author Thomas Newkirk (2004) noted that New Hampshire had the best reading and mathematics scores in the country on the 2002 National Assessment of Educational Progress (NAEP), but that almost one third of the state's schools failed to meet AYP standards in the same year.

Maine experienced the same problem, with one fourth of its schools failing to achieve AYP even as it scored in the top 10 percent nationwide on the NAEP. The urban Norfolk, Virginia, school district won the Broad Prize for Public Education, a prestigious national award given to systems that successfully raise the test scores of poor and minority students, but nonetheless failed to attain NCLB targets in the same year (Sharma, 2006).

In Florida, 827 of the 1,262 schools that received the coveted grade of A under their state's rating system failed to make required AYP standards. North Carolina and California were two other states where large numbers of schools identified as outstanding according to their own state criteria failed to achieve AYP ("Mixed Messages," 2005).

As suggested earlier, a school will most likely be perceived as failing no matter what the cause of its inability to meet AYP standards. As a high-ranking California education official noted in a television appearance, "A fail is a fail is a fail." An obviously troubled administrator from Savannah, Georgia, commented in a television news interview in July 2004 that parents in his system were concerned and confused about the label "in need of improvement" that was applied to their children's schools. In one instance, five absences within a subgroup led to a school's failure, and in another situation, special education students did not meet their AYP, even though they demonstrated exceptional academic growth from the previous year.

The number of schools failing to achieve NCLB standards will undoubtedly explode in the future, especially as we approach the year 2013–2014, when every student is expected to be academically proficient. According to Mark Goldberg (2005), the Connecticut Education Association projected that more than 90 percent of its elementary and middle schools will not meet the standards of NCLB in 2013–2014.

I believe that estimate is too conservative. No school can guarantee that virtually every student will be present on testing dates and that not one child will fail to be proficient on three academic tests. Some educators are predicting school failure rates at or near 100 percent in 2013–2014.

How can educators be held responsible—and, in effect, punished—because a small number of young people do not attend school on testing days? In fact, what happens when students are actually sick during the tests? In my first year of teaching fourth grade, I had six students absent on the day of the statewide writing test because we were in the midst of a flu epidemic. Since this test is administered on only one day, with no opportunity for makeups, the absences in my class alone would have put my school at risk of failure under the standards of NCLB.

We should all wonder what purpose is being served by labeling schools as failures because of too many student absences. Who will benefit from outstanding schools being assessed the penalties prescribed by NCLB because of such a trivial shortcoming? Moreover, how can anyone expect schools with large numbers of special education students or children who are just learning English to achieve 100 percent proficiency, especially when the federal government is cutting funding to the programs that serve those two groups? I am one of a large and steadily growing number of educators who have arrived at a troubling answer to these questions, an answer that is revealed in the following anecdote.

A professional couple who are close friends of my wife and me moved away from our area and returned to a small city where they had previously lived. When they visited our home a few months later, they expressed concerns about the school their older daughter would attend in their new community. As it happened, the performance reports required by NCLB had recently been released to the public, and the results were unsettling to our friends.

Having once resided in that city, they perceived that the area in which they bought a house had excellent schools. In fact, before purchasing their home, they studied achievement indicators for each of the city's public high schools, and the data they found confirmed that impression. They also talked with parents of young people enrolled at the high school their daughter would attend, and everyone consistently reported that it was an excellent school.

Now our friends were alarmed. As it happened, this high school that they had always regarded as outstanding had been identified as failing because it had not met one of its AYP standards. Our friends turned to my wife and me with numerous concerns. Is this not a good school? Have we been deceived by its reputation? If it's the best of the three high schools in the city, are none of them any good? Are we going to have to send our child to a private school to provide her with a quality education? As well as I can recall, their last question was, "What does all of this mean?"

I replied, "It means that No Child Left Behind is working." For more than two decades, politicians and journalists have chipped away at the American public's confidence in its educational system. Now we have a federal law that ultimately ensures a perception of failure for even our most exemplary public schools. If hardworking, patriotic American citizens like my two friends purchase a home in a particular neighborhood so they can send their children to the best public schools available, and even those schools are failing, how long will it be before they demand vouchers so that they can obtain a private school education for their children?

In my view, the real purpose of NCLB is to promote the privatization of public education. If that conclusion seems unjustified, please know that large numbers of America's public school administrators appear to have the same opinion. According to a September 2004 article in *Education Week*, almost half of our nation's public school principals and superintendents agreed that NCLB was "politically motivated or aimed at undermining public schools" (Rebora, 2004, p. 5).

When I asked my former superintendent her opinion of NCLB in an informal conversation in 2004, she asserted without hesitation that it was a scheme to bring about vouchers and the privatization of public schools. Like the thousands of other administrators who apparently share that perception, she never stated it publicly, perhaps believing that it would sound irresponsible for someone in her position to suggest that the elected officials who crafted this law could be so disingenuous—especially in light of their many public professions of concern for our youth.

Still, she had expressed a view that I formed when I first learned about the accountability measures of NCLB. As I listened to a presenter in early 2003 explain AYP standards and the penalties for failing to achieve them, I scribbled on my notepad, "Is this a way to promote vouchers?" By the end of the meeting, I was certain that it was, and everything I have learned since has only confirmed that perspective.

I am not a person who is quick to impute sinister motives to other people. Nor do I believe that every elected official who supported

NCLB saw it as a way to disparage American education so thoroughly that citizens would finally demand the privatization of our schools. The advocates of NCLB are from diverse backgrounds and political perspectives. I'm sure that most of them believe that the law is exactly what it purports to be: a tough-minded, commonsense solution to the long-standing problem of racial and social inequities in our students' academic performance.

Further, the imagery contained in the title No Child Left Behind is very powerful and compelling, and we should all support the aim it implies. However, I just wish that every political leader and journalist who supported NCLB had simply read the act (or talked to someone who had) and taken the time to discuss its implications with an educator who would understand its impact at the school and classroom level.

Surely, if they had done that, some of them would have wondered if it's really a good idea to label a school as a failure and penalize it because three students in one population subgroup were absent for a few days, or because a handful of handicapped students or children who don't understand English failed a single academic test written in that language. Most important, they might have questioned whether this law effectively serves the children left behind or, for that matter, any of our children.

The positive intentions of some NCLB advocates will not undo the real damage being caused by this law, and they do not obscure the fact that the authors of this landmark act surely must have understood its implications. It is hard to imagine why they would have written into the legislation so many ways for schools to fail unless they hoped to disparage public education and promote privatization. In addition, please consider the following:

- President George W. Bush sponsored and signed a law establishing the first federally funded voucher program in American history (affecting schools in the District of Columbia). Public discussions of vouchers and privatization as an educational reform strategy first surfaced during the administrations of President Reagan and President George H. W. Bush, the leaders whose philosophies and policies so clearly influenced the George W. Bush administration.

- President George W. Bush and members of his administration frequently called attention to the need to improve the academic performance of children of color and those living in poverty, and they touted NCLB as the answer to that problem. However, they severely underfunded the law from the first year of its passage. According to the National Education Association (NEA), funding for NCLB was shortchanged by $32 billion as early as 2003, with the result that 5 million (or 60 percent) of the nation's eligible disadvantaged children did not receive services that year. In fact, the federal mandates of NCLB were so seriously underfunded that the NEA filed a legal challenge that was supported by six states and the District of Columbia in 2006. If the Bush administration sincerely believed NCLB was the solution to America's educational problems, you would think that these leaders would have supported it with appropriate funding.
- Similarly, the Bush administration proposed or carried out the elimination or reduction of funding to the following programs at various times: the Even Start family literacy program for non-English-speaking immigrants, Head Start, teacher preparation initiatives, after-school programs, arts education, and the Eisenhower math and science initiatives, as well as social programs to improve rural and urban housing and juvenile crime prevention. Although federal educational funding for programs for handicapped students has never matched the promise in 1975 that it would amount to at least 40 percent of the total cost of special education, the Bush administration kept that funding at approximately 20 percent, even as it increased the pressure on handicapped children to perform as if they had no disabilities. These cuts and reductions just don't reflect the policies of an administration deeply concerned about the welfare of disadvantaged children.
- Privatization was one of the central political themes of the Bush administration, as evidenced by the president's efforts to privatize Social Security.
- The concept of vouchers has been especially appealing to some wealthy Americans and evangelical Christians. Not only were these two groups a solid part of President Bush's political base,

but they have also been strong supporters of private and religious schools. Because so many of them do not send their children to public schools now, vouchers would be for them a kind of educational rebate.

- Especially revealing is that President Bush's original proposal for NCLB called for vouchers to provide students with the funding to attend private schools. Congress did not include this provision, in part because voters in California and Michigan demonstrated the political liability of that strategy by soundly defeating voucher proposals in the 2000 election (Bracey, 2003c).

When we consider all of the evidence, it is hard not to conclude that NCLB is a backdoor approach to legitimizing vouchers. Supporters of privatization argue that this approach will provide citizens with choice and will improve academic performance by bringing free market pressures to our educational system. They say that public schools will perform more effectively in order to compete with private schools and that students using vouchers to attend private schools will be better served in those settings. However, there are four compelling reasons why we should reject these unproven assertions.

One, the existing research simply does not support the suggestion that voucher initiatives force public schools to improve or that students using vouchers to attend private schools perform better than their counterparts in public schools. In fact, the few available studies suggest just the opposite (Pons, 2002).

Two, voters have consistently and overwhelmingly opposed vouchers. Seven states have had referendums on vouchers since 1972, and every initiative has failed. Only the 1972 referendum in Maryland, with 45 percent in favor and 55 percent opposed, was even reasonably close. Since that time, no vote in favor of vouchers has been higher than 36 percent and, in the most recent referendums in 2000, only 30 percent of the citizens in Michigan and California voted for them. If public education is supposed to serve the public, we should acknowledge the public's adamant rejection of vouchers (Pons, 2002).

Three, the few voucher experiments that have been tried have not been cost effective and have often been plagued by mismanagement and scandal. For example, four of eighteen voucher schools in Milwaukee were closed in 1995–1996 because of mismanagement and fraud, and an audit of vouchers in Cleveland revealed almost $2 million in "questionable expenses," including charges from a taxi company for transporting students who were actually absent from school. In fact, almost two thirds of the students who received vouchers in Cleveland had never attended public schools: vouchers were essentially rebates for parents who had always sent their children to private schools (Pons, 2002).

Four, vouchers have not resulted in equality of opportunity, as advocates have argued they would. In Milwaukee some private schools have refused to accept students with vouchers, and others have excluded students on the basis of ability, gender, religion, and race (Pons, 2002).

It is also important to note that voucher programs have been ruled unconstitutional by the Florida Supreme Court and the Colorado Supreme Court. In spite of this fact and the problems just cited, conservative politicians continue to aggressively promote the view that this type of choice will improve education. As disastrous as voucher experiments have been, we have to wonder if Americans will one day weaken in their opposition to this ideology—and if members of the judicial branch will also change their perspectives—if they continue to hear the fraudulent claims of voucher advocates and persistent reports that our public schools are failing miserably.

In fact, a fairly substantial number of Americans have a vested interest in the privatization of our educational system and are likely to continue pushing for that change so long as there are elected officials who promise to pursue it. As noted above, the adoption of a voucher system would provide cash rebates to members of the religious right and many wealthy and middle-class Americans who already send their children to parochial or private schools.

If NCLB succeeds in privatizing public education, we will be dismantling an institution that has served our nation well and replacing it with a false promise. We can only imagine what American education will be like if vouchers are implemented across the country, but we can be certain that it will not serve the needs of the "children left behind." In addition to the concerns discussed above, it is important to remember that private schools typically do not provide services for mentally handicapped or ELL students, and they often do not have the resources for effectively teaching other kinds of struggling learners.

More to the point, if the parents of most school-age children in America were provided a voucher, the gap in quality between the education of the poor and that of children from more affluent families would probably be more dramatic than ever before. Low-income students would be able to access only those schools for which their vouchers would pay. Many would attend the kind of hastily organized for-profit schools that have performed so poorly in the voucher experiments cited earlier.

In contrast, middle-class and wealthy families would be able to supplement their vouchers and obtain better quality offerings. In areas where large numbers of parents choose to use their vouchers and send their children to private schools, the students who remain behind will attend schools decimated by the exodus of their classmates and the dismissal of educators who are no longer needed.

Of course, I am talking about a hypothetical situation. However, the setting I am describing is a part of the scenario that politicians advocating vouchers often present. They talk about a competitive educational marketplace where everyone has a choice, but they do not mention the ramifications I am discussing here. Let's be very clear. In addition to dismantling public education, school privatization would widen the academic gap between rich and poor and would increase the social and racial segregation of America's schools.

Even if NCLB does not result in widespread privatization, we know that it is already seriously compromising the quality of education in schools across America. In chapters 5 and 6, I described the negative and unanticipated impact of high-stakes accountability measures like South Carolina's EIA. Well, NCLB is the EIA on steroids. It is bad enough that we have dishonored American education by once again imposing on our schools a reform strategy that has an established history of failure. It is even more shameful that we are now enacting a law whose effects will be exponentially more harmful than any previous accountability legislation and that its damage will be felt most severely by the very children it purports to serve.

Chapter Eight

———————○———————

The Truth about the Children Left Behind

A FEW YEARS AGO, A KINDERGARTEN STUDENT in my area carried an unloaded automatic pistol to school. It wasn't until he was returning home on the bus that he showed the gun to other students and they informed the bus driver. When I read the newspaper account of this incident, two thoughts occurred to me. First, although this situation certainly was a problem for the school, I couldn't help but wonder: was it really a school problem?

Clearly, the school did not bear any responsibility for the carelessness of the parents who left a dangerous weapon where their five-year-old child could access it. In fact, short of installing metal detectors, what could educators have done to prevent this boy from bringing a pistol into his elementary school? Even if there were metal detectors at the doors of the building, they would not have kept him from taking the gun onto the bus (unless it had metal detectors too) and potentially endangering a large number of students on the way to school. My second thought regarding this incident was that it serves as a powerful reminder that our children quite literally bring everything with them to school.

Much of what students bring to school profoundly affects their academic achievement. To illustrate the differences between young people who arrive at school with all the ingredients for success and those who come with considerable disadvantages, I describe in the following paragraphs two unforgettable students from sharply contrasting backgrounds.

I taught Jennifer when she was in the fourth grade. Her parents purchased a home near our suburban school, and she walked the short distance to and from school from the time she enrolled in kindergarten until she left us at the end of fifth grade. Her father was a professor at a nearby university, and her mother stayed at home so she could give full attention to Jennifer's development.

Both parents were actively engaged in the life of the school, and her mother volunteered in a variety of roles during Jennifer's kindergarten through fifth grade years. Her parents attended virtually all school and class meetings, and both of them met with me for a lengthy conference during the first few weeks of school. In addition, her mother and I talked periodically throughout the year about Jennifer's academic and social development, as well as our views on school dilemmas and broader educational issues.

Even after Jennifer moved on to fifth grade, her mother and I had occasional discussions about her school experiences. In fact, her mother seemed to maintain with each of Jennifer's former teachers the relationships they established when Jennifer was in their classrooms, and we all continued to have an interest in her ongoing academic success.

When school was not in session, Jennifer and her family traveled extensively both in and out of the country and often visited museums and historical sites. At home she had access to a computer and a variety of desirable reading materials, and her parents attentively nurtured her intellectual growth and avid interest in books. Of course, there was never any question about her physical needs. Jennifer was a healthy, attractive, well-dressed girl who interacted positively with all of her classmates. Not surprisingly, she was an exceptional student. Jennifer had an intense intellectual curiosity, a strong work ethic, extraordinary general knowledge for a child her age, and superior skills in every academic subject.

Tommy entered my sixth grade classroom one winter day about twenty years ago. He had attended numerous schools from kindergarten through sixth grade, including, as well as I can recall, two others that academic year. His absences were frequent, and he was as dirty and unkempt as any child I have ever taught. His hair was invariably tousled and uncombed, and even on the rare occasions when his clothes were clean, they were torn, stained, and far too small. During warm weather, he wore plain white T-shirts that were so inadequate they left some of his midsection exposed.

When I learned of Tommy's personal circumstances after a few weeks of teaching him, I knew why his appearance was so bedraggled and why his family had been so transient. He, his three brothers, and their parents lived in an old, barely functioning, midsized automobile. I was never able to establish contact with his mother or father, and I do not know whether they had jobs during their short stay in our community or, for that matter, whether the family had enough to eat.

I do know that Tommy received free lunch and ate so ravenously whenever food was put in front of him that other children's snickers and stares were inevitable. In fact, although the students in my class were generally thoughtful and considerate of each other, Tommy's appearance and behavior limited his ability to form meaningful friendships at school. He tried hard to give the impression that he did not care, but it was obvious that he did.

Tommy was a very bright boy, and I have often wondered how successful he might have been in school if he had been able to stay in one place and his parents had been able to meet his basic physical needs more adequately. Like many children living in poverty, he was absent so often and changed schools so frequently that teachers rarely had the opportunity to connect with him, fully assess his academic competencies, and learn how to teach him effectively before he was on his way again. In addition, when he did come to school, he was usually exhausted after struggling to get sufficient rest in the car where he and his five other family members slept.

The first few times he put his head on his desk to sleep, I awakened him, but I soon realized that he was so sleep deprived that learning was close to impossible. Following a morning nap to compensate for the lack of rest the night before, Tommy was usually able to engage in classroom activities for the rest of the day. He began to experience a modicum of academic success as winter turned to spring, but then his family picked up and moved again.

I hope that the dramatic contrast between Jennifer's and Tommy's experiences outside of school illustrates the relationship between the conditions of young people's lives and academic achievement. While Jennifer had every opportunity for school success, Tommy had the odds stacked high against him. Jennifer came to school each day physically refreshed and excited about learning. On the other hand, Tommy came to school exhausted, hungry, and emotionally distraught over his family's unstable situation.

Jennifer's parents continually challenged her intellectually and supported her learning with activities that reinforced classroom experiences. In contrast, Tommy received little or no intellectual stimulation outside of school. During the summer Jennifer traveled widely and visited educational sites, read good books, and used the computer in her home. Tommy, however, spent those months immersed in his family's hardscrabble existence and divorced from any kind of academic learning.

One of the most daunting challenges in helping students like Tommy maintain grade-level proficiency is addressing the issue of summer loss. Richard Allington (2002), a noted scholar in children's literacy, has examined studies of this problem and concluded that low-income schools are often as effective as wealthier schools in helping young people improve their reading achievement during the academic year. However, over the summer, poor children regress in their reading proficiency by about three months, while more affluent children maintain or enhance their reading skills.

The reason for the difference between these two groups is really quite simple. Like Tommy, most children living in poverty do not have access to reading materials when they are out of school, while middle- and upper-class children like Jennifer usually do. We can fully appreciate the significance of this problem by considering that three or four years of summer loss add up to one full grade level of academic achievement.

Although teachers have expressed concern about this dilemma for many years—and researchers such as Allington have now confirmed it empirically—there doesn't seem to be any discussion of it by the elected officials who make policy for our schools. Until we can find a way to provide poor students with reading materials over the summer, it is obvious that they will always be at a distinct disadvantage to their more affluent classmates in attaining long-term school success. However, instead of acknowledging and addressing this problem, elected officials have usually chosen to blame the achievement gap entirely on educators and to devise educational reforms on the basis of that faulty assumption.

Before and after the passage of NCLB, President Bush and its other advocates consistently stated that poor children who underachieved academically were simply the victims of educators' "soft bigotry of low expectations." Research does not support that assertion, and teachers, administrators, and educational scholars know that it oversimplifies a complex dilemma.

Children like Tommy do not fail to achieve school success because of educator bigotry, either soft or hard. Most teachers and administrators work diligently to help all students succeed, and they commit even greater effort to helping young people who struggle academically. If educators are uniquely guilty of anything, it is not bigotry or low expectations, but rather their persistence in calling attention to the range of social problems that affect many children's school success.

Educators are more likely than any other group of adults to acknowledge young people's personal difficulties simply because they are the public servants who are closest to our youth. Teachers and administrators see far too well the effects of poverty, violence, substance abuse, and family instability on children's lives. Educators strive to help disadvantaged youth move beyond their personal circumstances, so naturally they express disappointment when social conditions pose obstacles for these children.

People choose to become teachers because they want to make a difference. They lament the struggles of some students because they know that problems they cannot control prevent them from making as much of a difference for every child as they would like.

When citizens hear statistics relating to the harsh conditions of some children's lives, they may lack the personal connections to disadvantaged youth that give meaning to such data, but teachers do not. In our thirty years as educators, my wife and I have worked with young people who were physically or sexually abused, those who have seen family members killed or taken to prison, and others whose parents were drug dealers, addicts, and alcoholics. We have taught students like Tommy whose parents or guardians moved constantly because they were homeless or were evading either law enforcement or bill collectors.

Like virtually every teacher, we have known countless children who lived in extreme poverty or neglect. We have taught classes where barely half the students were part of a traditional family of two parents living in the same home. On numerous occasions, we have seen children suddenly plunge into academic and emotional turmoil, only to learn shortly afterward that their parents were moving toward divorce, or that there was some other form of domestic chaos in their lives. My wife and I are not unusual. Experienced teachers know all of these children personally, and they know that these students' struggles outside of school affect their academic success.

The assertion that educators are guilty of soft bigotry dishonors both students and educators. It dishonors disadvantaged young people by oversimplifying their plight and deflecting needed attention away from the social problems that affect their lives in and out of school. It dishonors educators by labeling them with a reprehensible personal trait (bigotry) and indicting them for the results of conditions far beyond their control.

When educators call attention to the social problems that affect children's academic achievement, they are not renouncing the challenge to teach disadvantaged students. In fact, Americans should not be surprised that teachers and administrators sometimes explain less than exemplary school performances by citing the difficulties faced by students like Tommy, especially when these educators are being called out for every student who fails to be proficient.

The issues faced by children like Tommy are real and consequential, and teachers confront them every day. When educators are challenged publicly to explain every perceived shortcoming, they may be inclined to mention the social conditions that present obstacles to school success, but they are not conceding defeat. They are simply stating an important relationship that teachers and administrators cannot ignore and that our elected officials should begin to acknowledge and address.

Yes, all young people can learn, and it is right to hold every teacher and child accountable, as I think we always have. Nonetheless, it is foolish to assert that children's lives outside of school do not affect their school performance. I doubt that anyone who read the earlier description of Tommy would suggest that he did not face substantial obstacles to academic success.

If Tommy's family had been able to obtain adequate housing, food, and clothing, perhaps he would have come to school ready to learn. Further, with extra attention and instructional support, his achievement probably would have improved dramatically. Even so, it is not likely that Tommy, who entered my sixth grade classroom barely functioning on a third grade level, would have attained grade-level proficiency by the end of the spring semester.

Most Americans seem to understand the relationship between school achievement and the conditions of young people's lives, even if many of our elected officials will not publicly acknowledge that connection. In the 2005 Phi Delta Kappa/Gallup Poll, 75 percent of the respondents stated that the performance gap between white students and African-American and Hispanic students was mostly related to factors other than quality of schooling (Rose & Gallup, 2005, p. 48).

Unfortunately, this poll did not ask the public about their perceptions of the achievement gap between poor students and more affluent students. As Allington (2002, p. 11) has noted, the performance disparity between various income levels best explains differences in academic achievement among racial and ethnic groups. That is, because average incomes for African-Americans and Hispanics do not match average incomes for whites, it appears that the most important factor in understanding school performance gaps is income level, not race. In America we give a great deal of attention to differences in academic achievement among various races and ethnic groups, when we should probably give far more attention to the issue of poverty and its effects on school success.

In the enactment of NCLB, elected federal officials have acted as if the disparities between poor and affluent schools are meaningless. However, it is clear that schools in wealthier neighborhoods enjoy substantial advantages. For example, it is not unusual for a

suburban district to provide double, or even triple, the local appropriation for each student of an urban or rural system nearby. Not
only do richer districts provide better facilities, materials, and technology, but they are also able to attract the best teachers with their
superior salaries.

Sometimes the challenges of hiring qualified teachers in low-
income schools are daunting. In one of the poorest districts in South
Carolina, the superintendent had to resort to hiring teachers from
other countries because so few American teachers were willing to
work there. Parents complained that their children could not understand verbal instructions from these foreign teachers and sued the
state for its failure to provide an equal opportunity for their children.

In my own area, there are significant salary differences among
systems that are a short commute from each other. As a principal, I
once lost two of our school's most outstanding teachers in one year
because they took positions in nearby districts that paid considerably more. (One of the teachers told me that she was increasing her
salary by 25 percent.)

A few years ago, a local school director commented in a newspaper article that teachers sometimes come into her office in tears
because personal financial circumstances compel them to take
higher paying jobs in other systems. As this administrator explained,
usually these teachers are exemplary educators with a strong sense
of loyalty to the district, but ultimately they have to move so that
they can meet the financial needs of their families.

Because poorer schools serve more students with special needs,
the problems they face are compounded. That is, not only are there
fewer resources in such schools, but there are also more challenges.
Low-income schools are more likely to have higher numbers of
English Language Learner students (like Maria from chapter 7) and
others with special learning challenges, greater numbers of children
who move from one school to another during the year, and young
people who go home each day to neighborhoods with all of the social ills related to poverty.

As noted above, these schools experience significant teacher
turnover, sometimes losing outstanding educators to richer systems,
and often have to scrape the bottom of the barrel just to find suffi-

cient numbers of teachers, including some who are not qualified. Low-income schools are far more likely than more affluent schools to employ teachers who are not certified and lack appropriate content knowledge in the subjects they teach. Politicians and journalists who claim that a lack of teacher knowledge is the explanation for America's educational performance problems—and then call for radical and unproven changes in teacher preparation—rarely mention that poor achievement most often occurs in low-income schools, the same schools that are more likely to hire unqualified teachers.

Even though it should be obvious that poorer schools are generally underfunded and face multiple challenges, we have resisted the idea that these schools should receive substantial infusions of additional support. Even within systems, where there should be an equal distribution of resources, there are often inequities that shortchange children of poverty. These differences may be unintended, but their effects are just as real for the children involved.

I encountered that kind of problem when I was a principal in South Carolina during the late 1980s. The Lowcountry school where I worked at the time was poor, rural, and predominantly African-American. Our student population came from an area of several hundred square miles, and some children rode buses for over an hour each morning and afternoon. Many parents did not have cars and had to call on friends or neighbors to drive them to school conferences with teachers or administrators. Others worked late shifts at the few manufacturing plants in our area and could not attend evening meetings.

The Lowcountry of South Carolina can be extremely hot and humid, and warm temperatures begin as early as April and continue well into September. When I began working as the principal of this school, the classrooms did not have air conditioning, so children and teachers endured intense heat and humidity for approximately the first six weeks and the last six weeks of each year (about one third of the school year). I recall walking into classrooms on days when the outside temperature was 95 degrees or higher and the heat was even more oppressive inside.

Teachers placed fans around the classrooms, but they made little difference in the comfort level and created a substantial noise distraction. Lethargic children struggled to focus on learning activities, and many simply put their heads on their desks. Because teachers had to open windows and doors to let in any available breeze, flies and mosquitoes added to everyone's torment. Obviously, in these conditions, instructional effectiveness was severely limited for a significant part of the year.

As well as I can remember, every other elementary school in the district had air conditioning. However, the students' parents in those schools, not the school system, had purchased the window unit air conditioners that cooled their children's classrooms. When I approached the superintendent to request funding for air conditioning, he told me that the district was treating every school equally, but that the parents in the other schools had gone the extra mile to obtain air conditioning.

Of course, those families were far more capable than the parents in my school of making financial contributions on behalf of their children, and the middle-class parents in some of those schools had the time and organizational background to orchestrate fund-raising efforts. As I saw it, our parents were at a distinct disadvantage in pulling off that kind of accomplishment. Even if one argued that they should have cared more and that they could have tried harder to obtain air conditioning for their children (or that their principal should have done a better job in that regard), the fact remains that the children in our school were at a distinct disadvantage to their peers in other parts of the county for reasons that were beyond their control.

At the end of the year, I made an impassioned plea to the school board during budget hearings and managed to convince them to use system funds to air condition our school. One could argue that we were receiving special treatment and that the district was wrong to abandon its policy of giving equal consideration to every school. However, I would suggest that *equal* does not always mean *fair* in the distribution of school resources.

Clearly, it is time in America that we began to strive for fairness in our approach to children in low-income schools. Although the example provided above is about a particular school system, I believe it is analogous to policy at the state and national level. That is, at every level of school management, we need to rethink the notion that equal treatment under existing funding guidelines results in fair treatment for all of America's children.

Few people would suggest that life would have returned to normal in coastal Mississippi and Louisiana in the aftermath of Hurricane Katrina without massive assistance from the outside. In fact, most Americans seem to agree that it was appropriate for residents of those areas to receive extra help until they could get on their feet again. Similarly, we should recognize that our nation's poorest schools will usually struggle to perform at the level of schools in middle-class neighborhoods without the continuous commitment of substantial additional resources.

We should also acknowledge that the social problems that plague certain segments of our school-age population are more pronounced in America than in virtually any other industrialized nation. According to UNICEF, in 2003 the United States ranked twenty-fifth among the world's richest countries in "maltreatment deaths" of young people under age fifteen, placing us higher than only Mexico and Portugal. Marian Wright Edelman noted in 2003 that American children were twelve times more likely to die as victims of gunfire than children in any other industrialized nation. She also reported that the United States was twenty-eighth in infant mortality and had the highest teen pregnancy rate of any industrialized country.

The child poverty rate in America—which has increased over the last thirty years—ranked next to last in a comparison of twenty-six industrialized nations (UNICEF, 2005). In 2005, 21.9 percent of our children lived in poverty, fewer than only Mexico's 27.7 percent. At the top of this list were Denmark (2.4 percent) and Finland (2.8 percent), two of the nations that typically outperform the rest of the world on international academic assessments.

Of course, it is important to remember that public school educators in America take a beating every time we fail to score at or near the top on international studies of student achievement. Given that America ranks in the middle to top of the industrialized nations on international test scores (as indicated in chapter 2 by Boe and Shin's 2005 analysis), and that we rest near the very bottom on numerous other measures relating to our children's well-being, perhaps we should wonder why our elected officials have focused so much of their rhetoric on education instead of the numerous social issues that so adversely affect our youth and their future.

In chapter 7, I said that the intended purpose of NCLB is to legitimize public school vouchers and that the accomplishment of that aim will undoubtedly increase the disadvantage of poor children compared to their more affluent peers. Hopefully, the privatization of public education will never come. Even so, it is clear that NCLB is already having troubling effects on children in low-income schools.

First, as suggested earlier in this chapter, one of the most serious challenges faced by schools in poor systems or neighborhoods is the difficulty they have in attracting and retaining quality teachers. Aside from the problems their children bring to the classroom, educators in these schools often work in decaying buildings and receive inadequate supplies and materials. It is hard to imagine that giving such schools the designation "in need of improvement" and assessing other penalties will do anything but further erode teacher morale and make them even less desirable places to work.

I recall a conversation I had one afternoon with an acquaintance who teaches in an area high school that had not met one of the adequate yearly progress standards of NCLB. She was clearly demoralized by the label applied to her school and the additional requirements that were placed on her and her colleagues. Educators already have too many external demands on their instructional time, and those who work in low-income schools face additional challenges. Because these schools are more likely to receive penalties under NCLB, they will probably have even more difficulty attracting good teachers in the future than they do now.

A second negative consequence of NCLB for low-income schools is that it will become increasingly difficult for them to maintain positive identities in their communities. Years ago an African-American teacher in the school where I was a principal in South Carolina told me that the black children we served were better off in some ways before schools in our area were racially integrated. I argued with her vehemently, but her words haunted me for a long time.

This teacher's point was that the African-American school that once served her community had an intense pride in its accomplishments and the ability of its people to overcome obstacles. They celebrated their culture and identity and possessed a strong sense of unity and shared purpose. Most important, she said, no one looked down on their children, as she felt some of the less culturally sensitive white teachers now did in our racially integrated school. She was a teacher whom I respected professionally and regarded as a friend, and her comments troubled me deeply because I knew they contained considerable truth.

When white middle-class Americans look at an urban or rural school that serves mostly poor African-American children, they sometimes fail to see the strong sense of pride and community that enables the people there to accomplish all that they do. The same situation can apply to schools that are not predominantly African-American. Having worked in a poor, rural school that served equal numbers of white and black students, I know how effective a school with a strong sense of purpose and community support can be in making a difference in the lives of its children.

We can only hope that the penalties and "failing school" labels dispensed under NCLB do not erode the faith of students, parents, and other citizens in the schools that serve low-income Americans of all races and ethnicities. If young people and community members lose confidence in these institutions and their educators, these schools will have lost perhaps the most important ingredient of the successes they have been able to achieve.

The third negative consequence of NCLB for low-income schools is one I have mentioned in previous chapters, but it should be reiterated here. The history of accountability measures has demonstrated repeatedly that the pressures of high-stakes testing affect schools with predominantly poor students much more negatively than they do wealthier schools. That is, low-income schools are far more likely to adopt the kind of curriculum and instructional approaches that were imposed on Mr. Jackson and his students (as described in chapter 5).

Although these strategies often result in short-term test score improvements, they do not serve children well over the long haul. They increase student boredom and apathy and intensify the disconnect between many young people and school. Even when students use technology in such a test-driven environment, it is typically for "drill and kill" activities.

In addition, the crushing emphasis on basic skills usually leads to a de-emphasizing of everything else, including history and the arts. Young people who might have turned on to school reject classroom instruction as meaningless, and they drop out—if not literally, then at least figuratively. Their reaction seems to say, "If this is what school is all about, you can have it."

In fact, the fourth negative consequence of NCLB for low-income schools is that it will probably increase their numbers of dropouts. As Linda McNeil (2000) reported, dropouts among minority students increased substantially in Texas during the 1990s because of that state's rigid accountability measures, and NCLB already seems to be having that effect on African-American and Hispanic students (Miao & Haney, 2004). We should be especially concerned about the societal consequences of pushing so many young people out of our schools and onto the streets. It should be obvious that we cannot prevent children from being left behind academically if they are not in school.

If the passage of NCLB has accomplished anything, it has called attention to America's most pressing educational and social issue, the failing academic performance of children living in poverty. Unfortunately, NCLB is based on fraudulent assumptions about the causes of that dilemma, draws attention away from real problems, and offers solutions that have no grounding in research or practice. Perhaps NCLB fails in these ways because the law was never really intended to achieve the purpose implied in its title.

America will continue to fail in its ethical obligation to the children left behind until we (1) aggressively address poverty and other social problems that affect our children's achievement, (2) infuse substantial additional resources into low-income schools in a sincere effort to provide all students with a fair chance for success, and (3) enact policies that reflect the expertise and experience of educators who have been effective in teaching children who live in difficult circumstances. There are many outstanding educators in poor urban and rural settings who have helped their students achieve extraordinary success, but we have ignored their voices in developing school policy.

Before we can enact these steps to improve the school performance of children living in poverty, we must first reject two popular political assertions: (1) the notion that there is little connection between the conditions of children's lives and school achievement, and (2) the suggestion that educators have failed our youth through the "soft bigotry of low expectations." It is becoming increasingly clear that elected leaders who criticize schools for their inability to overcome all of the social problems their students inherit are creating a smokescreen to obscure their own failure to improve the conditions of our children's lives. If America has an accountability problem, it is not in our public schools. It is in the White House and the halls of Congress.

Chapter Nine

───────────○───────────

The NAEP
and International
Assessments:
Education's Catch-22

As INDICATED IN CHAPTERS 5–7, high-stakes testing has had profound and unexpected effects on public education. It has created illusions of quality and has actually limited, rather than increased, children's learning. Further, it has begun to strip teachers of the passion and creativity that distinguish exemplary classroom instruction and has started to erode the ethical foundations of the teaching profession. The tests that have produced these results initially grew out of state mandates, but now they are being used to demonstrate compliance with the federal standards of No Child Left Behind (NCLB).

This chapter is about a different set of tests—specifically, the National Assessment of Educational Progress (NAEP), often called the Nation's Report Card, and the various international measures that so frequently capture the attention of politicians, journalists, and the general public. My concern with these instruments is that they are driving the federal politics of education, even though they often misrepresent public school quality and do not provide lawmakers with useful information for developing policy.

Data from the NAEP and international assessments are much more than indicators of educational performance in America. In politics and media coverage at the national level, test scores have been for some time the language of virtually all discourse about public school quality. In fact, even in the era of NCLB and its emphasis on state-developed tests, journalists and elected officials continue to give considerable attention to international measures and the NAEP, so it is essential that we understand them.

To begin our examination of these tests, imagine for a moment that a group of young basketball players was divided into three teams of equal talent, each with a coach of comparable ability and experience. For two months each team practiced under a particular set of rules and did not know that the other two teams were operating under different sets of rules.

Team A was taught to play using contemporary basketball rules. Like most teams in the modern era, a key part of Team A's offensive strategy was to develop long-range shooters and ways to get these players open for three-point shots.

Team B practiced without a three-point line. Therefore, their offensive focus was on short jump shots and getting the ball inside to their tallest players, just as high school, college, and professional teams did before the advent of the three-point line. A shot from what we know today as the three-point area was considered a poor shot by Team B, since it was harder to make and still counted as only two points.

Team C did not have a three-point line for long jump shots but practiced instead with a semicircular line eight feet from the basket—that is, about half the distance between the foul line and the basket. Within the area between this line and the basket, successful shots counted as three points. Therefore, the offensive strategy for Team C was the exact opposite of Team A. There was a strong incentive for Team C to develop a power game close to the basket, less motivation to take midrange jump shots, and no reason at all to venture outside for long shots.

Imagine, then, that after two months of practice, these teams came together for a tournament. Unbeknownst to the players and coaches, officials drew straws right before the first game to decide which of the three sets of rules would govern play. Since the three teams had players and coaches of comparable quality, the rules selected would obviously make all the difference.

If the rules practiced by Team A were chosen, Team B (which learned the older basketball rules and practiced without a three-point line) might have a fighting chance, although it would clearly be at a disadvantage to Team A. Team C, which had been drilled in the power game, would be at a decided disadvantage to Team A. Players on Team C probably would not be able to score from beyond the three-point line, having not practiced shots from that area at all. In fact, the ability of Team C to play defensively on the outside would also be compromised, since the players would not have learned how to defend long-range jump shots. Of course, if one of the other sets of rules were chosen, the advantage would shift to the team most familiar with that set of rules.

I hope this fictional scenario helps to make a point about the varied tests on which our nation's leaders and journalists focus so much of their attention in public discussions about educational quality. Every test is different, and if students are taught a specific set of skills and a certain body of knowledge in preparation for a particular test, they will be at a disadvantage on any other kind of test. The extent to which they will be disadvantaged will depend on the amount of difference between the test for which they prepared and the one they did not expect to take.

If our children are going to be tested on multiple kinds of assessments, and if critics of public schools are going to scour all available data to locate a single score that enables them to argue that our students are failing, they will always be able to find it and proclaim an educational crisis. In the basketball scenario described above, we could safely predict that each team would win the tournament when its set of rules was in play.

Further, if the teams played three tournaments, with each tournament being governed by a different set of rules, the composite records of each of the three teams would be mediocre. Each team would have more or less equal numbers of wins and losses, and none of the three would stand far above the other two in terms of overall success. In that scenario, it would be altogether unfair to suggest that all three teams were failures because not one of them had an outstanding overall record.

Are various standardized tests really that different? In fact, there is compelling evidence that they are. As readers may recall from chapter 2, Boe and Shin (2005) analyzed American students' scores on a number of international assessments to provide a clear picture of how the United States compared educationally with other industrialized nations. Obviously, there were at times significant differences in how our young people ranked worldwide on the various tests used in the analysis.

For example, America's eighth graders may have scored substantially higher on one international assessment of math than on another. Given that variation, we can only infer that the tests were different and that the test on which our young people scored higher was probably a better match to the curriculum they were taught. It's not as if our eighth graders were somehow dumber on the day they took the other test.

When we consider this situation, we have to wonder if international assessments are truly dependable measures for comparing educational quality among nations. Perhaps the only thing they really tell us is the degree to which different countries' curricula match the content assessed on the various tests. If we accept the limitations of each test and analyze all of them (as Boe and Shin did) to construct a fair picture of how our students performed overall, we might gain insights that would help us to improve instruction. However, selectively examining data from international assessments, as politicians and journalists have tended to do, will usually produce an inaccurate picture of public school quality.

The NAEP is sponsored by the U.S. Department of Education and has been given for over thirty years. For this assessment, students in grades four, eight, and twelve take tests in reading, math, writing, science, history, geography, civics, and the arts—although political and media interest in the NAEP has seemed to focus only on math, reading, and science scores. Schools from each of the fifty states are randomly selected for participation in this assessment, and its stated purpose is to provide data that will allow comparisons of states and of the nation's performance over time.

Are NAEP tests really different from the state tests that drive instruction in America's public schools? In fact, even the federal government's education website asserts that they are. Further, educational researchers Nichols, Glass, and Berliner (2005) conducted a study that confirmed these differences. They examined high-stakes testing pressure and NAEP scores in each state to see if more pressure to succeed on state tests led to improvements on the NAEP.

Their data indicated that pressures put on fourth grade students to perform on state math tests correlated "weakly" with score improvements on the fourth grade NAEP math test. In other words, in states where there was a great deal of pressure to perform well on state tests—such as the threat of retention for a failing score—fourth grade students did a little better on the NAEP math assessment.

However, these researchers did not find a correlation between pressures to perform on state tests and the eighth and twelfth grade NAEP math scores or scores on any of the other subjects tested by the NAEP in fourth, eighth, or twelfth grade. As they explained, the math curriculum in the early grades is apparently more standardized across the United States than it is in higher grades.

Since Nichols, Glass, and Berliner (2005) could not establish a correlation on any other subject assessed by the NAEP or in math at the eighth grade or twelfth grade, we can infer that there is a curriculum mismatch between some, or most, of the state tests and the NAEP in all areas except fourth grade math. In brief, with the exception of that one subject and grade level, the NAEP appears to be substantially different from many state tests.

As Gerald Bracey (2003b) noted, discrepancies between students' scores on state-mandated tests and the NAEP are often huge. For example, 91 percent of the eighth graders in Texas scored proficient on their state's math test in 2003, but only 24 percent of Texas's eighth graders scored proficient on the NAEP math assessment. Scholars and test statisticians agree that it is more difficult to achieve a score of proficient on the NAEP than it is on most state tests. Nonetheless, as Bracey suggested, it is incredibly ironic that the home state of President Bush and former Secretary of Education Rod Paige had the greatest discrepancy between a score on its own state test and the corresponding NAEP test of any of the fifty states.

We can understand this huge variation by considering the high stakes associated with performance on state-mandated tests in Texas. As the model for NCLB, Texas has been noted for exerting especially intense pressure on schools to have all students score proficient on its state assessments. If there is a substantial difference between the content and format of the NAEP and the tests used in Texas, we can logically expect large discrepancies in the number of students scoring proficient on the two sets of tests. Moreover, because NCLB now imposes on all states the same kinds of pressures that have characterized public education in Texas, we can only wonder if other states will soon begin to have lower NAEP scores as they try to achieve higher adequate yearly progress (AYP) goals on their own tests.

If that occurs, schools in those states will be caught in a troubling Catch-22. If they do not improve performance on their state tests in accordance with NCLB requirements, they will be labeled as failing schools. However, if they focus solely on their state tests to achieve compliance with AYP targets, they may perform less capably on the NAEP because their students did not learn the content it assesses. In either case, politicians and journalists will be quick to seize the opportunity to proclaim an educational crisis.

Rod Paige engaged in exactly that type of behavior when he was secretary of education. In a 2003 article, he criticized American students' civics achievement on the NAEP, noting that most fourth graders who took that test could not explain the meaning of the phrase "I pledge allegiance to the flag."

The Tennessee curriculum requires me to teach my fourth graders about the freedoms guaranteed by the Bill of Rights, the responsibilities of U.S. citizens, the roles of the three branches of government, the checks and balances in our Constitution, and numerous other civics concepts. However, as important as it is that children be able to explain the text of the Pledge of Allegiance at some point in time—perhaps when they are old enough to articulate abstract concepts such as allegiance—it simply isn't in the fourth grade curriculum in Tennessee, and that makes me wonder how many other states teach it at that grade level.

When we consider that teachers are evaluated on their children's success on state tests, that NCLB requires steady improvement on these state tests toward an ultimate goal of 100 percent proficiency, that students' scores on these tests are sent home each year, and that school results are published annually, it's obvious that teachers are going to focus on their own states' curricula and not the concepts tested by NAEP. And I suspect Rod Paige knew that when he criticized fourth grade civics achievement on the NAEP.

Especially since the passage of NCLB, state-mandated tests have driven classroom instruction in America's public schools. State-mandated tests are the most frequent topic of discussion at faculty meetings, administrative gatherings, and educator workshops. Teachers, principals, and district-level administrators are evaluated on their effectiveness in raising scores on state-mandated tests. Systems select textbooks according to their suitability for helping teachers improve scores on state-mandated tests, and teachers plan their lessons in all subjects with curriculum guides that match the content of state-mandated tests.

Parents purchase homes using scores on state-mandated tests as the primary measure of school quality, and the public decides whether teachers and administrators are doing their jobs on the basis of their scores on state-mandated tests. In some places, educators who do not improve or maintain their students' scores on state-mandated tests can lose their jobs. (I apologize for repeating the phrase "State-mandated tests" so often, but I think the emphasis is important.)

Conversely, I have never heard an administrator or teacher mention student performance on the NAEP or an international assessment in a faculty or grade-level meeting in the more than thirty years I have been an educator. In planning instruction I do not consider concepts that are assessed by the NAEP or any international test and, like most teachers, I know very little about the actual content of these tests. Moreover, to my knowledge, there is no place in America where teachers or administrators are evaluated for their students' performance on the NAEP or international assessments.

In fact, it would be impossible to use the NAEP for that purpose since it does not provide reports for students, teachers, schools, or districts. I suspect that many teachers who can recite by memory objectives from their state curriculum guides do not know what the letters *NAEP* represent and cannot give the name of a single international assessment.

In all my years in education, I have never administered the NAEP or any international assessment to my students, and I do not know of any teacher or school that has in the systems where I have worked in South Carolina, Florida, Indiana, and Tennessee. In other words, while educators must focus their undivided attention on state-mandated tests, the NAEP and international assessments are not even on the radar screen of most teachers and administrators. So why do the NAEP and international assessments play such an important role in our national discourse about public school quality?

For starters, most politicians and journalists seem to be altogether unaware of the differences between various standardized tests. Based on their comments about test scores, it is clear that they believe that a test is a test is a test. Further, most of them do not appear to understand how substantially teaching and learning have changed as a result of high-stakes accountability measures.

Before the 1980s, standardized tests were administered in many locations, but there were rarely any consequences associated with student performance. Teachers taught as well as they could, students took the tests, and most educators briefly examined the scores and filed them away. Most of today's adults, including elected officials and members of the national media, experienced standardized testing in that way, but those days are long gone.

When today's students take the NAEP or an international assessment, they are much like the fictional basketball teams described earlier. They have received rigorous preparation for a game that they believe will be played in a tightly prescribed way. However, when they arrive at the gym, they learn that they will be required to play under a set of unfamiliar rules.

I also suspect that most lawmakers and journalists do not know that schools chosen to participate in the NAEP, the so-called Nation's Report Card, do not receive information indicating how well students, teachers, schools, or even their systems performed. Without such data, it is impossible for educators to know how to improve their scores.

There are compelling reasons why schools must focus their attention on state-mandated tests, but it isn't clear why they would concern themselves at all with the NAEP when (1) the odds are extremely small that they will ever take it, and (2) they do not receive performance data if they do take it. Although I have never administered that test, I can only imagine what it must be like to introduce it to a group of students.

> Teacher: Class, today we're going to take a standardized test called the National Assessment of Educational Progress. It will give you a chance to demonstrate to citizens of our state and nation how much you have learned.
>
> [A few students raise hands.]
>
> Teacher: Yes, Jimmy.
>
> Jimmy: Does this test count?
>
> Teacher: What do you mean, Jimmy?
>
> Jimmy: Will it count on my grades?
>
> Teacher: Well, no, but I hope, nonetheless, that you will do your best.
>
> Jimmy: What happens if I fail this test? Will I be retained?
>
> Teacher: Actually, Jimmy, we will not receive any score reports, so, no, there will not be any consequences associated with your performance on this assessment.
>
> Jimmy: [in a low but discernible voice] So it doesn't really count.
>
> [There is a soft murmur of voices. Some students look to the left or right and make eye contact with classmates. A few roll their eyes or smile.]

As a fourth grade teacher, I find it hard not to envision children reacting in that way, and I can't imagine what it must be like to introduce the NAEP to a group of eighth graders or high school seniors and have to tell them that it doesn't really count. Maybe I'm being a bit cynical. I believe that most of my students would perform to the best of their ability on any assessment that I might give them, but I doubt that all of them would under these circumstances.

At any rate, we have to wonder. Why would national policymakers—who seem to believe so strongly that laws like NCLB must contain substantial consequences for performance—not give students or educators any reason to perform well on the Nation's Report Card other than to know that their scores will be pooled with others to provide a portrait of state and national public school quality?

We might also question the validity of NAEP standards. Gerald Bracey (2003c) noted that American students have at times performed extremely well on international assessments and have simultaneously done very poorly on the NAEP. For example, in 2000 our fourth graders scored second internationally in the study How in the World Do Students Read, but only 32 percent of them scored proficient on the NAEP reading test that year.

So how could there be such an extraordinary discrepancy between these two measures of fourth grade reading achievement? As Bracey (2003c) explains, NAEP proficiency levels were developed in the 1980s to "sustain the sense of crisis" (p. 3) created by *A Nation at Risk*. America's educators and students are indeed caught in a troubling Catch-22 when our fourth graders can score second in the world on one reading measure and still be lambasted by politicians and journalists for what appears to be a failing reading score on the nation's report card.

More recently, Bracey (2007) provided further evidence of the absurdity of NAEP standards. He compared American students' performance on the NAEP to their achievement on some of the most prominent international literacy studies and then compared our students' scores on these international measures to the scores of students from other nations on the same tests. In doing so, he was able to suggest that not one country in the world has more than one third of its students performing at a proficient level in reading—that is, based on the NAEP's definition of proficient.

In other words, if students from other industrialized countries had to measure up to NAEP standards, we could conclude that all of the world's educational systems are failing. Bracey's analysis is worth remembering the next time you hear or read of a politician or journalist citing NAEP scores and saying that our schools are in crisis because so few of our young people are proficient in reading.

As regards international assessments, there are compelling reasons why American students sometimes do not score as well as young people in other countries. The Third International Mathematics and Science Study (TIMMS) is an example of a test in which the deck appeared to be stacked high against America's youth, primarily because there were substantial differences in the student populations from the nations that participated.

The average age of students from Iceland who were compared to American twelfth graders was 21.2, and students in Germany, Norway, Italy, Austria, Sweden, and Switzerland were the age equivalent of college sophomores in the United States. Further, the Norwegian students who ranked first in physics and the Swedish students who ranked second were in their third year of physics study (compared to American students who were in their first or second year).

In addition, every country participating in the TIMMS did not sample students as democratically as the United States did. For example, Russia excluded 43 percent of its eligible students, and some nations included only young people who were enrolled in special math and science programs (Bracey, 1998, p. 687).

I want to emphasize that my point here is not to make excuses for American performance on the TIMMS or any other test, or to argue that we shouldn't try to improve our nation's math and science achievement. However, I am suggesting that we understand the conditions under which any assessment is conducted before we make sweeping generalizations, and especially before we recommend the dismantling of any part of our current educational system. In the past, politicians and journalists have been quick to use studies like the TIMMS to call for massive reforms—such as the total replacement of education classes with subject area courses in the preparation of teachers—based on the unsupported assumption that teachers' lack of content knowledge is the cause of our shortcomings on international assessments.

A thoughtful analysis of TIMMS results would suggest a very different course of action. If we are sincerely worried about our students' performance on this test and believe that it tells us something useful about science and math instruction in our public schools, we might consider adding a year or two to high school so that our students are more comparable in age to those with whom they are competing internationally—or perhaps we could have our children start school at a later age. We might also find ways to accelerate math and science instruction in middle school and the beginning years of high school so that our students could take advanced math and science for two or three years before graduation.

These proposals would be very expensive, and I'm not necessarily advocating any of them—only suggesting that they would be logical responses if we accept the TIMMS findings as valid and believe that they should compel us to action. What is important is that we begin to examine more closely all of the assessments we impose on our students and reevaluate their usefulness. Further, we should be careful not to indict our schools for mediocre or poor performances on every imaginable standardized test. In light of the differences between state-mandated tests and the NAEP and international instruments, it is clear that an overemphasis on state-mandated tests puts our students at a disadvantage on most other kinds of assessments.

In a political context in which every measure of educational achievement brings intense public scrutiny, our children and their teachers are indeed caught in a troubling Catch-22. In effect, they are being chastised by politicians and journalists for doing exactly what those same people have forced them to do: prepare exclusively for state-mandated tests. If the NAEP and other assessment instruments reveal shortcomings in that approach, perhaps we should rethink the use of these various tests, rather than excoriating educators for dutifully following the state and federal mandates we have imposed on them. To do anything less is to continue dishonoring American education, our teachers and administrators, and, most important, our children.

Chapter Ten

─────────○─────────

The Political Process of Educational Reform: How Parents, Educators, and Children Get Left Behind

When educational reform is politically driven, parents and educators are usually excluded from the process, and the real needs of children are ignored. To demonstrate the pitfalls of politicizing educational improvement, I open this chapter by relating a personal experience with a regional school change process.

As noted in chapter 5, I worked in a small rural system in South Carolina when the state implemented the Education Improvement Act (EIA) in 1984. Our district lacked financial resources but enjoyed strong community support and had an impressive record of student achievement. Unfortunately, some nearby systems were far less successful. When South Carolina identified the first set of impaired school districts under the new accountability provisions of the EIA, two of them were in our large, predominantly rural county.

Subsequently, several area business leaders convened representatives (both educators and noneducators) from the county's eight systems to discuss school reform. When my superintendent first told me about the newly formed Committee for Educational Excellence (a pseudonym) and asked me to be our district's representative, he said he believed that the organizers' real intent was to consolidate the eight local systems into one. He also suggested that the group of influential citizens supporting this plan wanted the administrators from the largest of the eight districts to assume leadership of the newly configured system.

145

During early meetings of the Committee for Educational Excellence, the two business and community leaders who were co-
chairing the group stated repeatedly that their purpose was not to
advocate consolidation. In their opening remarks at the first meeting, they said that they simply wanted what was best for the children of the county and would support any solution that achieved
that aim.

They also noted, however, that it had always been difficult to attract industry to our region because of the poor reputation of some
of the schools. The announcement that two local systems were impaired had exacerbated that problem and led to the creation of our
committee. Therefore, they emphasized, it was imperative that we
take steps to enhance public perceptions of our schools so that local leaders could recruit industry more effectively.

In other words, the committee co-chairs had adopted the central theme of the recently published *A Nation at Risk* and were applying it to circumstances in our area. Even as they asserted that
their first concern was our children's education, they clearly implied
that our public schools were failing the business community and
must be improved for the benefit of local commerce and industry.

After providing this introduction, the co-chairs divided the representatives into small groups and asked us to brainstorm solutions
for reforming the region's schools. Although they had stated in their
introductory remarks that the presence of two impaired districts in
our area had been the impetus for the committee's creation, they
did not suggest that our purpose was to target these two systems for
improvement and to address their particular needs. Instead they directed us to consider the open-ended question of how all of our local schools might be reformed.

When my group met, I sat next to the superintendent of the
largest of the eight districts represented on the committee—that is,
the man who was reputed to be the leaders' choice for superintendent of a consolidated system. During our subcommittee meeting, he commented to me in an aside that consolidation would easily solve our county's problems by averaging out the failing test
scores of the weaker systems with the scores of the more successful ones. He did not claim that children in the struggling schools

would learn any more, just that their lower scores would become less visible when pooled with the other districts' higher scores.

Neither he nor anyone else in our small group openly mentioned consolidation as the answer to our region's educational concerns, but, lo and behold, when all the representatives reassembled as a large group, it emerged as a solution. More than twenty years later, I still recall vividly how one of the committee co-chairs emphatically called attention to that one proposal. He noted that we had gone into our separate meetings simply to discuss the open-ended question of how to improve education in the area, and, wonder of wonders, we had emerged with a viable solution—consolidation.

Of course, many committee members, especially those who were educators and parents, were opposed to consolidation, since it was not clear to us how simply merging so many systems into one would favorably affect children in the classroom. Nonetheless, the mere mention of consolidation as a reform strategy during that first meeting appeared to have given the committee leadership the opening they wanted. Even though our brainstorming sessions had generated many other proposals, consolidation continued to emerge as the one solution deemed worthy of discussion at every meeting during the months that followed.

Although neither the co-chairs nor anyone else ever cited any evidence that consolidation would improve student achievement, their advocacy of that reform strategy seemed to be absolute. When I contacted an educational scholar who had a national reputation for research on consolidation, he agreed to assist our group by sending one of his graduate students. I shared that information at a meeting, but the leadership did not comment on this offer of expert guidance and seemed suspicious of my intentions.

I served on the Committee for Educational Excellence for two years before taking a position as a principal in another area of the state. During my membership on the committee, the leaders came to regard me as an adversary to its progress, primarily because I kept posing one very straightforward question that they refused to answer. At the suggestion of my superintendent, I persisted in asking that the group explicitly define its goals. That is, the committee's co-chairs had often professed their desire to achieve educational excellence, but they had never articulated that concept in clear and measurable terms. Consequently, I kept asking them what educational excellence was and how we would be able to know if we were attaining it.

For example, did we want to improve student achievement as measured by state-mandated tests, or did we want to enhance academic performance as indicated by some other measures? Did we want to increase the number of students who attended college, or did we want to improve the skills of our graduates for the industries the committee leaders were hoping to attract to our area? Or did we just want greater administrative efficiency—a benefit that the co-chairs said would result from consolidation—and would that really improve children's learning? In brief, just what did the leaders mean when they said they wanted to achieve educational excellence?

Both my superintendent and I believed that clearly establishing the committee's purposes would enable it to work more effectively. We also suspected that if we did not demand some explicit statement of purpose, the committee's leaders would propose the consolidation of the eight systems in our region without considering how such a move would affect the education of the children we served.

The leaders had seized upon the announcement of the two impaired systems to create a sense of educational crisis in all of our schools and to promote a solution that did not seem to have any real promise for improving the experiences of children in the classroom. Our only hope of forestalling an ill-conceived effort at consolidation was to have the group clearly state its purposes and thoughtfully consider changes that would achieve those aims. Consequently, I persisted in asking the committee to define the term "educational excellence."

Of course, the committee co-chairs had implied at the outset that our goal was to repair the damage in public perceptions that resulted from two of our systems being designated as impaired. However, once they had established a need for the committee's existence, statements of purpose became more and more vague, and meetings were dominated by their lengthy professions of concern for the children of our area. Over time, the problem of having two seriously underperforming systems was forgotten, and consolidation somehow became the only viable reform strategy on the table. Those who questioned it—or the committee's purposes—were portrayed as obstructionists and disingenuous opponents of young people's best interests.

As noted earlier, our small rural system already had a history of educational excellence, including a record of exemplary performance on achievement tests. The town's citizens took pride in their schools, and they appreciated the fact that board members, administrators, and teachers were their neighbors and were easily accessible when they had concerns. Our school district was poor and had few tangible assets, but we possessed all of the intangibles that distinguish the best systems from those that are less effective.

Our teachers worked hard and enjoyed close relationships with each other, their administrators, their students' parents, and community leaders. There was minimal turnover in our schools, and many educators spent their entire careers in the same building. We may have lacked physical resources, but we did not lack enthusiasm and commitment. When something needed to be done, volunteers always stepped forward. In addition, our students were generally well behaved and respectful. Many came from humble circumstances, but their parents genuinely regarded the school as a platform from which their children could reach any level of success they desired.

We feared that consolidation would mean that many of our young people, especially our high school students, would have to attend schools in communities far from home and would have long bus rides every morning and afternoon. After-school extracurricular activities would be prohibitive for students without cars, and those who did have their own vehicles would have to drive considerable distances on lonely country roads. Under these circumstances, it was hard to envision our townspeople supporting their children's education as enthusiastically as they did when the schools "belonged to the community."

Our town would take a very hard hit if we were to lose our two small schools to consolidation. Most of the community's citizens had attended these same schools, and they felt a strong sense of pride in the academic and extracurricular achievements of the system's students. The schools also provided an important social connection for many people, and they certainly contributed to the town's racial harmony.

Without its schools, this economically struggling community
would be a far less attractive place to live, and it was not hard to
imagine the town essentially drying up. As for me, I worked tirelessly for a school district that I valued and loved—the kind of system I envisioned when I first began teaching—and it was frightening to think that something so precious could be so easily
dismantled by a handful of business leaders who seemed altogether
uninterested in our children's education or the perspectives of the
parents and citizens in our small rural community.

Our district's exceptional record of student performance provided a troublesome dilemma for the supporters of consolidation.
When I pressed for a discussion of specific educational aims, the
leadership apparently realized they had to avoid the assertion that
they wanted to improve the same academic indicators that led to
two systems being designated as impaired. If they said better test
scores were their primary goal, our district and a few others with
comparable records of achievement could remind them that we
were already performing at a high level. Why should we submit to
a plan that supposedly solved a problem we did not have, while
likely compromising some of our greatest strengths, particularly the
sense of local control and community support we already enjoyed?

In time, the leadership began to scoff at the issue of local control, suggesting that citizens' voices and community involvement were
trivial considerations in discussions of educational reform. When I
continually asked for clarification of the group's goals, I was characterized as an obstructionist, and on several occasions one of the co-
chairs angrily demanded, "Mr. Smith, just what is your agenda?" He
openly questioned my commitment to the education of the children
in our area, a charge that seemed illogical to me since I worked long
hours in a low-paying school system, and he was not an educator.

However, numerous observers in the audience seemed to be
swayed by his proselytizing. In fact, by publicly repeating the same
positions and professions of sincere concern for the children of our
region, the leaders of the committee had managed to convince
many citizens that the solution to our educational problems was obvious and that educators who did not support the proposal to consolidate were selfishly protecting their own hides.

Although this one leader frequently asserted that my opposition to consolidation was based on self-interest, he never said what interest I was trying to protect. I often wondered what he meant. The only personal loss I stood to suffer was the opportunity to work in a professionally gratifying educational environment—one that was satisfying because it was clearly making a difference in the lives of its students.

Ultimately, this leader resorted to the strategy of simply shouting down attempts to raise concerns about consolidation and repeating the charge that opponents of that approach were protecting their own selfish interests. He often stated that those of us in successful districts were demonstrating our lack of concern for all of the area's children when we questioned the wisdom of the leadership's proposals. As he explained, we should be willing to sacrifice our own systems' successes for the unsubstantiated promise that the overall quality of education in the region would somehow be better if we all consented to consolidate the eight districts.

When it was clear that the committee was making little progress toward a solution, the leadership brought in its version of an outside expert to close the deal. At a widely publicized meeting attended by area journalists and state and local politicians—as well as a larger than usual number of interested citizens—a high-ranking official from the South Carolina State Department of Education appeared with a polished visual presentation to make the case for consolidation.

The data presented by this educational expert appeared to be very compelling and seemed to demonstrate clearly that the smaller school systems in our area were far less financially efficient than the larger ones. In his concluding remarks, he stated that our area could "no longer afford eight separate school districts." As I drove home that evening, I feared that the battle was over and that our unique little school system would soon become part of a single gargantuan unit in which our townspeople would have no voice.

When my superintendent and I met the next morning to discuss the previous night's meeting, he noted that all of the arguments presented by the State Department official were based on one set of misleading statistics. Rather than using valid data that were compiled and published annually by his own agency, such as each system's administrative costs per student, this official had used the South Carolina School Directory—essentially a phone book of the state's school system offices—to establish the number of administrators in each district.

Since our system was so small, we chose to list a bookkeeper, a secretary, and even our one part-time speech therapist in our section of the directory. In contrast, the larger districts did not list people who served in those roles. However, this high-ranking State Department official had simply counted all of the personnel that each system listed in the directory and implied that every district included the same types of positions in its section. Using such skewed comparisons, he was able to suggest that the smaller systems were not nearly as cost effective as the larger ones. The implication was that we spent a disproportionate amount of our budget to pay administrators and office staff, diverting precious resources away from the education of children.

Following the guidance of my superintendent, I prepared for the next meeting by gathering valid data on administrative costs for the systems in our region from a widely used State Department of Education publication. Once again, a substantial crowd gathered to observe the Committee for Educational Excellence, apparently anticipating that we would take decisive steps in response to the "expert" presentation of the previous month.

After receiving permission to speak, I questioned the superintendent of the largest district in our county and revealed that his system's directory listing did not include some of the types of personnel that ours did. I then presented the State Department's own statistics on administrative costs and was able to demonstrate that the larger districts were not necessarily more cost effective than the smaller ones in that regard. In fact, as well as I can recall, several of the smaller systems were more financially efficient than some of the larger ones in terms of administrative costs.

The next few meetings of the Committee for Educational Excellence held less interest for the public, and some of the representatives from the eight systems began to attend less frequently. The school board for the largest of the districts supposedly forbade its superintendent from attending any more meetings. Nonetheless, the Committee for Educational Excellence continued to meet (although I was no longer a member, having since accepted a principal's job in another area of the state). Ultimately there was some consolidation of systems, but fortunately the eight districts were not merged into one.

Every educational change process is unique, and the story above is about a regional initiative, not a state or national effort. Nonetheless, this account of the Committee for Educational Excellence provides an informative lens through which we can examine other educational reforms that are politically driven. There are startlingly clear parallels between the workings of the Committee for Educational Excellence and the development of public school policy at the state and national level, including the enactment of laws such as No Child Left Behind (NCLB). In the passages below, I call attention to some of the characteristics of politically motivated school reforms, with emphasis on the consolidation initiative in South Carolina and the passage of NCLB.

REFORM LEADERS OFTEN CREATE A SENSE OF CRISIS IN ORDER TO JUSTIFY THEIR INVOLVEMENT AND THE CHANGES THEY DESIRE. THEIR PROPOSALS MAY NOT ADDRESS THE REAL PROBLEMS OF SCHOOLS THAT ARE STRUGGLING AND MAY ADVERSELY AFFECT SCHOOLS THAT ARE ALREADY SUCCESSFUL.

The leaders of the Committee for Educational Excellence seized upon the designation of two systems as impaired to promote reform. However, once they had established a reason for the committee's existence and authority, the problems of the two struggling districts took a back seat to the promotion of consolidation, a change that would only disguise the problems of those two systems and would seem to affect others negatively, especially those that were already doing well.

The passage of NCLB took a similar course. The elected officials who promoted the law could not have enacted such a sweeping and punitive act without an intensive political campaign to highlight the academic struggles of children of poverty and to blame that problem

on educators' "soft bigotry of low expectations." The resulting law re-
lies on strategies that have not led to genuine improvement in the
past, especially in struggling schools. Further, because essentially all
schools must comply with the provisions of NCLB, it potentially
compromises the success of those that are already performing well.

**REFORM LEADERS OFTEN CONVEY A COMPLETE LOSS OF
PATIENCE WITH EDUCATORS AND SUGGEST THAT EDUCATORS
HAVE FAILED SO MISERABLY THAT IT IS TIME FOR THEM TO
STEP ASIDE AND LET BUSINESS AND POLITICAL LEADERS TAKE
CHARGE.**

At the first meeting of the Committee for Educational Excellence,
the leadership made it evident that the schools in our region were
failing the business community and that the local economy could
no longer tolerate our schools' shortcomings. I never understood
how the cochairs of the committee were selected or knew what
government entity gave authority to this group to suggest fundamental changes in the education of the county's children. However, it was clear from the start that the co-chairs and their community supporters had decided it was time for them to take
charge, and they were not interested in anyone else's views. Educators and parents who served as representatives had little say in
committee proceedings, and even superintendents had to stand on
the sidelines while the committee deliberated the future of the
systems they administered.

In the passage of NCLB, lawmakers expressed frustration with
educators' inability to completely overcome the academic effects of
poverty and other disadvantages. As James Popham (2004) noted,
Congress was determined in 2002 not to let educators off the hook
when it came to demonstrating universal success in teaching all
children. Officials in Washington believed that educators had
evaded that responsibility in the past, and these lawmakers were going to be sure that there was no way around the accountability provisions of NCLB. The promotion of the belief that educators had
failed to solve the academic problems of the poor helps to explain
why they were uninvolved in the development of the law and why it
seems to be so punitive toward them and their schools.

REFORM LEADERS FURTHER SQUELCH THE VIEWS OF EDUCATORS BY CHARACTERIZING ANYONE WHO QUESTIONS THE LEADERS' PROPOSALS AS OBSTRUCTIONISTIC AND SELF-SERVING.

By taking advantage of their public influence and access to the media, political leaders often claim the moral high ground and define critics of their proposals as obstructionists from the very beginning of the educational change process. Educators who question the soundness of the reforms are usually drowned out by accusations that they are self-serving and do not want what is best for children. With the support of unwitting members of the media—who rarely understand the implications of educational policy—politicians effectively eliminate any educator influence by promoting the view that educators who express concerns are disingenuous opponents of progress.

The leadership of the Committee for Educational Excellence used this strategy very effectively, and President Bush and other supporters of NCLB employed similar methods in their advocacy of that legislation. After expressing their dismay at the achievement gap between poor and middle-class children and suggesting that only they possessed the will to tackle that problem with their tough, no-nonsense approach, they then adopted the mantra "soft bigotry of low expectations" to disarm educators who criticized the law's unyielding accountability measures.

By using their decided advantage in shaping public perceptions, politicians and journalists almost invariably exclude educators from the educational change process. In the end, the people who best understand teaching and learning and who might be able to provide useful insights are rarely involved in major decisions about public school policy.

IN POLITICALLY DRIVEN PROCESSES OF EDUCATIONAL REFORM, IMAGE IS FAR MORE IMPORTANT THAN REALITY.

The leaders of the Committee for Educational Excellence believed that negative perceptions of our area's public schools limited their ability to attract industry to the region. The high-stakes accountability measures of the EIA had severely damaged the reputations of two systems, and committee leaders hoped they could improve the local business climate by erasing these negative images through consolidation. Even though such a move would probably affect some schools and communities adversely, and it was never clear how consolidation would improve student achievement, the leaders knew it would submerge the failing test scores of the impaired systems into a larger pool of scores.

Of course, imagery also played a major role in the passage of NCLB. Instead of addressing the real issues confronting our poorest schools, elected officials wrapped the law in the compelling imagery implied in its title and presented themselves as tough, no-nonsense policymakers who had exhausted their patience with educators who lacked the will to hold struggling students to high standards.

IN POLITICALLY DRIVEN REFORMS, THE CONCERNS OF POLITICIANS AND BUSINESS LEADERS OFTEN TAKE PRIORITY OVER THE INTERESTS OF CHILDREN, PARENTS, AND OTHER CITIZENS.

The leaders of the Committee for Educational Excellence wanted to improve the local economy and seemed unconcerned that consolidation might affect children adversely or that parents and other citizens opposed it. Similarly, NCLB serves the interests of a political ideology by setting in motion a process for legitimizing vouchers that does not reflect any consideration of most parents' perspectives or what is really best for public school students. (As explained further in chapter 14, NCLB contains numerous provisions that parents overwhelmingly oppose but do not realize are the very basis of that law.)

In the committee's efforts to consolidate schools in South Carolina and in the passage of NCLB, reform leaders did not think it was important for the public to understand clearly the potential effects of their initiatives. Unfortunately, the accomplishment of political and economic goals is sometimes far more important to the architects of school reform than whether their policies improve children's learning or reflect parents' and other citizens' wishes.

LOCAL CONTROL OF PUBLIC SCHOOLS IS USUALLY A VERY LOW PRIORITY FOR LEADERS OF EDUCATIONAL REFORM INITIATIVES.

The leaders of the Committee for Educational Excellence openly scoffed at the value of local control, and the lawmakers who supported NCLB passed a law that transfers much of the traditional state and local control of schools to the federal level. Inevitably, efforts to standardize public education increase the centralization of school governance and deprive Americans of decision-making authority in an area of great personal concern—their own children's education. In the end, politicians enacting educational change seem to act on the belief that they—rather than parents and educators—know what is best for America's children.

IN POLITICALLY DRIVEN REFORM EFFORTS, LEADERS TEND TO IGNORE UNDESIRABLE CONSEQUENCES.

Administrators, teachers, and parents in the small South Carolina system where I worked were worried that the education of our children would be compromised if we were consolidated into a larger system. For example, we feared that our high school students would have to travel a considerable distance to participate in sports and other extracurricular activities. However, the leaders of the Committee for Educational Excellence disregarded these concerns in the pursuit of their own goals.

The enormous casualties of NCLB (as outlined in chapters 7 and 8) are too numerous to be recounted here, but suffice it to say that the law's proponents ignored such issues in their push to enact it. They may have been unaware of the potential effects of their proposals, but the results are the same.

In any educational change effort, negative consequences are sure to occur when leaders do not thoughtfully consider all of the possible implications of a reform. Of course, when educators' views are silenced in deliberations about school improvement, consequences that business leaders and politicians do not anticipate are inevitable.

REFORM LEADERS MAY TRY TO VALIDATE THEIR PROPOSALS BY PRESENTING MISLEADING DATA AND ENLISTING THE SUPPORT OF QUESTIONABLE EXPERTS. THEY OFTEN EXCLUDE USEFUL EDUCATIONAL RESEARCH FROM POLICY DISCUSSIONS.

The Committee for Educational Excellence brought in a high-ranking state official, and he presented specious evidence to make the case that the smaller districts in our area were not cost effective. In addition, the committee leaders made no effort to include useful data in our discussions of school improvement, and they even rejected an opportunity to employ the services of a nationally recognized expert on consolidation—apparently fearing that he would not support their position.

The politicians advocating NCLB have often spoken of their reliance on scientifically based research, but educators are still wondering what research validates the use of the act's accountability measures, the inclusion of school choice provisions, and the law's premise that education's biggest problem is the "soft bigotry of low expectations." In the early days of NCLB passage and implementation, Secretary of Education Rod Paige served as the expert who had supposedly transformed a tough Houston school system. Of course, we have since learned that some of the data provided on his success story, particularly dropout statistics, had been manipulated and were not credible.

THE BEHAVIOR OF REFORM LEADERS SOMETIMES REFLECTS A BELIEF THAT THE END RESULTS JUSTIFY ANY MEANS USED TO ACHIEVE THEM.

The officials behind the move to consolidate schools in South Carolina may have genuinely believed that children would benefit in the long run from their initiative, and there are probably some voucher proponents who sincerely believe in the efficacy of that approach. However, the faith of reform leaders in the correctness of their goals does not justify any and all steps they take to achieve their aims.

For example, there is no excuse for suppressing or overlooking useful research and presenting misleading data in the promotion of educational policy. Nor is it ever acceptable to squelch and ignore the views of parents and educators. If we are genuinely concerned about the education of our children, we should be open to thoughtful consideration of every relevant fact and perspective and every implication of the changes we are proposing. In the end, if the policies we advocate are clearly beneficial, we should not have to hide behind imagery or engage in dishonest political behavior to promote them. The truth will speak for itself.

Clearly, one important difference between the work of the Committee for Educational Excellence and the passage of NCLB was that the presentation of valid information to the committee— that is, the debunking of the misleading statistics provided by the State Department official—at least temporarily stalled the move toward consolidation. In the enactment of public school policy, knowledge is power.

An understanding of the political process of educational reform enables parents, educators, and citizens to recognize the patterns revealed in this chapter and to be proactive in other contexts. To be assured that the process of school reform results in policies that are beneficial to our children, we must be vigilant in observing the behavior of elected officials and able to separate political imagery from reality.

We must demand that leaders clearly identify educational problems and articulate reform goals. They should directly involve educators in deliberations and decision making, and they should honestly represent the views of parents and other citizens. They must also thoughtfully consider and openly discuss every implication of policy provisions, and their solutions must be educationally sound and tied directly to reform goals.

Yes, I realize that politics is a slippery business, but I also believe that we should be able to expect elected officials to have our children's best interests in mind when they deliberate educational legislation. In a country that honors public education and its young people, that should not be too much to ask. However, it is clear that we will continue to fall short of that expectation until parents, educators, and other citizens are able to recognize misguided behavior in the educational reform process and demand responsible behavior from our leaders. Only then will we be able to hold elected officials and journalists accountable and demand that public school policies effectively serve our children.

Not only has school legislation in past decades been politicized to the detriment of our children, but it has also been influenced by nostalgic recollections of the "good ole days." Chapter 11 is a brief look at nostalgia and its ineffectiveness as a means for interpreting school quality and developing educational policy.

Chapter Eleven

Why Nostalgia Is a Poor Basis for Educational Policy

ABOUT FIFTEEN YEARS AGO, I was attending an extended family gathering and listening to my uncles reminisce about their youth. One of them recalled a classmate bringing a mule to the rural Depression-era high school that several of them attended and letting the animal loose inside. They laughed about that incident and how much chaos the mule created as it wandered the halls. From what I could gather, letting the mule loose in the school building was what my uncles would characterize as good, clean fun.

The conversation then moved quite seamlessly to a discussion about how badly behaved today's schoolchildren are in comparison to young people of earlier generations. Although I bit my tongue and managed not to comment, two thoughts occurred to me. One, we had all just heard a story about a student from the past who had apparently disrupted learning in his entire high school, but no one had cited any evidence of misbehavior by contemporary schoolchildren. Two, most of the men in that room probably had not walked through the doors of a public school in decades.

I mention this story because it demonstrates something about our perceptions of events from our youth and the dangers of judging present-day schools through the lens of personal memories. It may be true that schoolchildren from the past behaved better than young people do today. However, you couldn't prove it by recounting a story of a student releasing a mule into the halls of a 1930s high school. My uncles' sharing of reminiscences and their comparisons of education past and present were innocent and meaningless, but they suggested to me that nostalgia can trump reality when we attempt to compare twenty-first century schools to the ones we attended years ago.

Our memories of school experiences can be very powerful. When I was an elementary principal in South Carolina, the window from my office afforded an excellent view of the front lawn and sidewalk. I happened to look up one day from my paperwork and noticed a man walking tentatively toward the front door. As he slowly approached the building, his apparent anxiety captured my attention, and I wondered why he was behaving so strangely.

Once inside, he received permission from the secretary to speak to me and cautiously entered my office. He carefully eased into his seat and immediately began to survey the compact room, even turning completely around to glance at the area behind him. His nervous examination of the office appeared to be part curiosity and part inspection for some kind of potential hazard. For those brief, awkward moments, he seemed oblivious to me, even though I was the only other person in the room and seated a mere four feet in front of him.

When his eyes finished searching the office, he looked at me and haltingly recalled how he had attended our school as a youngster and had been paddled by the principal in that very room. Even though two decades or more had passed, the experience remained vivid and alive to him, and his visit to the school seemed to rekindle the emotions he had felt on that day so many years before. As we began to talk casually, he soon relaxed, put that unpleasant memory momentarily aside, and addressed the reason for our conference.

I have long since forgotten the issue that prompted his visit but remember that it involved his young son and that it was quickly and positively resolved. However, I will never forget that parent's demeanor and how one incident still affected his perceptions of school so many years later.

I have come to believe that most adults appraise the quality of the schools they attended primarily on the basis of their personal levels of school success. Those who did well will usually rate their educational experiences highly, even though they may not remember very much about actual classroom practices. Further, they may assume that because they had positive experiences, their classmates did too.

I am one of those people with fond recollections of school. I did well academically and loved going to school. Like all children, I had an egocentric perspective, especially in the elementary years. That is, I naturally focused on my own concerns and gave little thought to whether all of my classmates enjoyed school as much as I did. Clearly, there were students in some—if not all—of my classes who were less successful than they would have liked and perhaps even had unpleasant experiences.

However, I was more or less oblivious to that reality. Like most people, when I am asked today to assess the elementary schools I attended, I do not reflect beyond my own personal perspective. In fact, I really cannot, because I filtered out all but my own narrow views of school events as a child and committed only those to memory.

If you had asked me as a young adult about the quality of my elementary education, I would have had high praise for all of my teachers. However, the truth is, I cannot remember a thing about classroom activities in second grade, and my only vivid memory of first grade is of sitting in a semicircle with about a half dozen other children reading orally about Dick, Jane, and Spot.

I don't believe I recall that experience because the Dick and Jane books were compelling fiction. More likely it was because I knew that learning to read was the primary business of school, and I was nervously looking ahead to anticipate what sentence I would read aloud so that I could practice it mentally and read it perfectly when my turn came. The slight stress of that moment added enough emotion to it to secure its place in my memory. Even though I do not recall that one first grade experience all that fondly, I am convinced, nonetheless, that my teacher that year was excellent.

I recall little about third grade, only a few activities from fourth grade, and progressively more about successive grades—although not substantially more. Because my father was in the Coast Guard, we moved quite often up and down the Atlantic seaboard, and I changed schools ten times by ninth grade. With all those changes, I have always regarded each school I attended as outstanding—although if you asked me to reconstruct a typical class period and how a particular teacher taught, I could only do that successfully with a few teachers, most of them in the upper grades.

Although I have been an educator for thirty years, it is only in the last few years that I have tried to revisit my childhood classrooms in my memory and assess the quality of instruction, just as I might another teacher or student teacher today. When I did, I realized that the few instructional practices I could recall in some of those classrooms were not particularly sound in light of what we now know from current research on teaching and learning.

Nonetheless, until I pushed myself to reflect on those school experiences through the lens of an instructional evaluator, I did not assess those teachers objectively. Even though I have been a professional educator for thirty years, for most of that time nostalgia trumped reality in my appraisals of the schools of my youth. I accepted unconditionally that all of them were excellent.

When we assess the schools we attended based on our individual personal experiences, we tend to dismiss many salient facts. As an avid viewer of *NBC Nightly News*, I became accustomed to hearing Tom Brokaw, the show's longtime anchor, suggest that the quality of America's schools has been in decline in recent years. In fact, in his autobiography, *A Long Way from Home* (2002), he described his own schooling as if that era was the golden age of American education.

Brokaw clearly intended for this book to be a nostalgic look at his personal past, and in it he consistently cast a positive glow on essentially all aspects of his upbringing. Nonetheless, when I read his recollections of his teachers and school experiences in South Dakota, I could not help but wonder if he was cognizant of the problems of urban schools during his youth, such as those in Midwestern cities not so terribly far from his boyhood home. Was he not considering the rampant school failure faced by Native Americans, including those in his home state?

In fairness, Brokaw did discuss issues relating to Native Americans and African-Americans with sensitivity and understanding in

A Long Way from Home, and he has consistently called attention to racial injustice throughout his journalistic career. However, in his autobiography, he seemed to let nostalgia trump reality in the suggestion that schools of his era were superior to schools today. In doing so, this racially sensitive journalist overlooked the fact that African-American children who lived in the South during the 1950s attended segregated and poorly funded public schools, as did many who lived in Northern urban ghettos.

He also ignored the status of handicapped children. The federal law mandating services to the handicapped was not passed until 1975, almost two decades after Brokaw graduated from high school. Parents of the educationally handicapped children who attended schools in the 1950s would probably disagree with the assertion that those schools—which offered no special services for children with disabilities—were superior to schools that work diligently today to provide every child with an appropriate education. Moreover, dropout rates were substantially higher when Brokaw attended school than they are now. Many academically struggling youth—including those with mental handicaps—simply left school in the "good ole days."

Of course, those casualties of that earlier educational era do not muddle the unblemished images of classroom life that their more fortunate classmates carry with them today like so many Norman Rockwell pictures. I admire Tom Brokaw for his career of journalistic integrity, and I devotedly watched his news show until his retirement. However, I believe that when he offered appraisals of public education, he suspended his usual professional objectivity and made his assessments through the rose-colored lens of personal experiences.

We should all be careful not to let nostalgia distort our perceptions of the past. Until I was ten years old, I lived in the historic town of Beaufort, North Carolina, residing the first six years in a house built in the 1770s that overlooked the Atlantic Ocean. I have idyllic memories of that period in my life, including the memory of my first games of sandlot baseball. During the summer my friends and I played for what seemed like hours on an open, grassy area just around the corner from my home. That baseball field seemed to stretch forever, providing more than enough room for us to pitch, hit, field, and run the bases.

My family moved away from Beaufort when my father received a transfer, and I did not return to see that field until my wife and I visited the town in the summer of 2000. We registered at a bed and breakfast just a few houses away from the residence of my youth, and I couldn't wait to put on my walking shoes and revisit my old neighborhood, including the site of my first baseball games.

Imagine my surprise when I arrived at the lot and realized that it was little more than a grassy alley between two large old homes. At first I thought perhaps a house had been built on the spacious field that I remembered, but the houses on each side of my field had clearly been there for a hundred years or more. As I assessed the lot through the lens of adulthood, I wondered if maybe a garage or shed of some kind had once filled that small space. There was no wonder the lot was still vacant. Not even the narrowest of homes could fit in that tiny area.

I am sure every reader has similar memories. The point, of course, is that my image of that "field" was formed through the eyes of a little boy and frozen in my memory until the moment I revisited it and saw it through a different lens. The day I returned to that vacant lot I suspected it would be smaller than I recalled, but I was stunned by the difference between my memory and reality.

I would suggest that our recollections of the classrooms of our youth are similarly skewed in varying degrees. When we were school-age children, we interpreted classroom events through youthful eyes and filed them away in that condition. Although we may attempt to revisit them mentally as adults—and they may appear vivid and real—our visual images are not a reproduction of the actual event. The child in each of us filtered out much and retained only what seemed relevant from our youthful and egocentric perspectives.

If we could return to our past and relive our school experiences through the wiser and more mature eyes of adults, we would commit to memory pictures of events that would appear very different from those frozen in time from our youth. Those images from an adult perspective would probably reflect an understanding of the complexity of classroom life and teaching that we as youngsters could not appreciate.

I would also like to suggest very gently that our memories might tell us that we were more accomplished as children than we actually were. In my first year of Little League baseball at age nine, I was the youngest and smallest member of my team. The coach put me in right field where I could do the least amount of damage defensively, and when it was time for me to bat, he encouraged me to crouch low and take as many pitches as possible in hopes of getting a walk.

For years my memory of my first hit pitch was of a solid drive that left the bat with a sharp crack and me racing like the wind to first base, my quick feet barely touching the ground. When I viewed that momentous event on home video years later, I saw instead a slowly looping ball come off the end of the bat and a gangly little boy trudging down the base path with steps so heavy he appears to be stomping ants. (If you look closely, you can see one of the ants escape death by beating me to first base.)

The tendency to remember our own accomplishments as greater than they were may help to explain our willingness to believe that today's children are not doing as well in school as previous generations. Anyone who pays close attention to the news has heard from time to time of surveys that supposedly demonstrate how little our young people know about history and civics. After these surveys, critics of education almost always announce that we are facing a national crisis and warn us about the imminent demise of our democracy.

If history is any indication, we can breathe a sigh of relief that such predictions have been issued frequently in the past and have invariably proven false. Educational scholar Richard J. Paxton (2003) analyzed historical surveys from the last ninety years and decided that today's youth know as much history, and probably more, than any previous generation dating back to the early 1900s.

Paxton noted that researchers conducting historical surveys throughout the twentieth century consistently concluded that students from the middle grades through college did not know much history. Further, critics of education responded to these survey results time and again with dire warnings that our children's lack of history and civics knowledge constituted a national crisis and a threat to America's future.

Curiously, one of the worst performances on a history survey was the average score of 24 percent correct by undergraduate freshmen in 1943. In writing about that finding in *Bail Me Out!* Gerald Bracey (2000) noted that the abysmal score by those college freshmen is even more startling when we consider that there was a high school graduation rate of approximately 45 percent in 1943 and that only about 15 percent of those students attended college. In other words, the college freshmen who could not name the president of the United States during the Civil War or list the contributions of George Washington, Thomas Jefferson, Abraham Lincoln, and Andrew Jackson represented an academic elite of the best-educated 7 percent of young people their age in 1943 (p. 33).

As Paxton (2003) noted, members of the Greatest Generation may not have done well on that history survey, but they went on to sacrifice and accomplish much for our nation. Nonetheless, critics of the time had a field day suggesting that the shift away from history instruction to a broader social studies focus was the culprit responsible for young people's alleged lack of history knowledge.

Apparently, there were even suggestions that "social studies extremists" in the teaching ranks included some communists and socialists. Paxton concluded his analysis of history surveys by warning that the assumption that today's students know less history than their predecessors can only lead to the simplistic conclusion that we can fix our history problem by simply teaching more history or going back to the good ole days of teaching more historical facts.

I believe we should extend Paxton's warning about revamping history instruction to educational reform in general. That is, the mistaken assumption that schools were once better can only lead us to the faulty conclusion that we should try to return our educational system to the good ole days.

If we are going to insist on reforming today's schools to recapture our educational past, we should base that decision on data that clearly indicate the superiority of schools from previous generations. The problem is, as Gerald Bracey (2000) has noted, we really don't have very much information to use in comparing today's schools with those before 1960. We know that today's graduation rate of 83 percent is better than the graduation rate of 70 percent in 1959, although we certainly should not be content with today's rate and should work to improve it.

The National Assessment of Educational Progress didn't exist in the 1950s, and the SAT was taken by too small a percentage of high school graduates to allow for valid comparisons with today. The only measures that were used across both time periods are the Iowa Tests of Basic Skills and the Iowa Tests of Educational Development, and the young people who take those tests today are performing better than their predecessors in 1959 (Bracey, 2000, pp. 202, 203). In brief, the scant data that we have to compare today's schools with those from forty to fifty years ago suggest that today's schools are superior.

When all is said and done—although we may not want to admit it—perhaps the real reason that nostalgia plays such a strong role in adult thinking about public education policy is that there is in most of us some small desire to believe that we're a little bit smarter than the generations that have followed us. Richard Paxton said it best in his summary of history surveys: "Let's face it: mocking youthful ignorance rarely fails to satisfy" (2003, p. 265).

There is absolutely nothing wrong with being nostalgic about our personal school experiences. However, nostalgia can skew our appraisals of the schools we attended and form a very poor basis for making decisions about the education of today's youth. Nostalgic recollections of the past may lead us to believe that the best way to reform education is simply to turn back the clock.

In my view, that kind of thinking has influenced much of the school reform legislation of the last few decades. Believing that standards and performance have slipped, and that patriotism, morality, and discipline are rapidly diminishing public school values, elected officials have tried to return our schools to an image of an educational past that is at best fuzzy and probably did not exist as they remember it. These lawmakers have confused nostalgia with vision. Looking nostalgically toward the past will never provide us with a useful vision of education for the future.

Earlier in this chapter I suggested that most people appraise the quality of the schools they attended based on their personal levels of school success. If we assume that individual school success is necessary—at least to some degree—for adult achievement, we can conclude that most people elected to high office had generally positive educational experiences. Therefore, they probably have pleasant memories of schools and likely perceive that those schools were of high quality, whether they were or not.

Increasingly, elected officials at the state and national level determine the direction of public education in America. Unfortunately, if these men and women have not been educators or studied education extensively, they have little on which to base their assumptions about school improvement other than their nostalgic perceptions of the schools they attended and straightforward, logical thinking—or common sense. In this chapter, I examined the inadequacy of personal memories as a way of understanding education and devising school policy. Next, I consider the limits of common sense when applied to educational decision-making.

Chapter Twelve

——————————O——————————

The Shortcomings of Common Sense as a Basis for Educational Policy

THE SUMMER OF 2002 WAS A DIFFICULT TIME for nontenured teachers in Tennessee. In late spring the legislature in Nashville finally confronted the reality that our state's revenues were inadequate for funding existing programs and targeted public education for major cuts. By June some systems had already released teachers, including a few award-winning faculty members, and it was predicted that 8,000 additional teachers would lose their jobs statewide before the summer was over.

Recent graduates of the state's teacher preparation programs recognized the futility of seeking positions in Tennessee and began actively applying in neighboring states. An outstanding teacher candidate I knew from a local university transferred to another state to complete her final year of study, saying she was doubtful she would ever be able to find employment in Tennessee. I suspect she also questioned the commitment of our legislators to education, so she chose to pursue her career in a state that she thought was more supportive of its public schools.

I had changed systems two years earlier and had returned to classroom teaching, so I was still nontenured in 2002 and spent most of that spring and summer wondering if I would have a job when school resumed in August. Although friends and colleagues reminded me that the state legislature had engaged in such antics before and that everything usually worked out, I knew there weren't any guarantees.

Some of the legislators were clearly running scared—concerned that they would have to raise taxes and would feel the wrath of voters—so I knew that anything was possible. In fact, the legislature very nearly deadlocked without any funding solutions before finally increasing the sales tax, engaging in a few other budget manipulations, and bailing out the state's public schools at the eleventh hour.

Before they took those steps, however, it seemed that the legislature was dangling my job on a string right in front of me—always in full view, but just beyond my reach. Each day I sought every fragment of information I could about the proceedings in Nashville. Some days the news sounded promising, and state lawmakers seemed to be nudging my job closer to me as if to say, "Here. Here's your position. You can have it back." But whenever it seemed to be almost within my grasp, legislative negotiations broke down and they pulled it away again.

In one of our more desperate moments, my wife and I began looking at openings in other states. However, we had so much invested financially and emotionally in our present location that we decided to take our chances that the legislature would ultimately restore basic funding to Tennessee's public schools.

Administrators could not complete schedules that summer without knowing for sure how many faculty and staff they would have. Even veteran teachers, whose jobs were presumably safe, were concerned about the impact of cuts affecting materials and programs, as well as the welfare of colleagues whose jobs were threatened.

I cannot speak for other teachers whose positions were in question, but I was angry, disappointed, and frustrated for most of that spring and summer. It did not help that our state's lawmakers waited until the last possible moment to do what they must have known was inevitable from the very beginning of this budget crisis.

For these reasons, I wondered how educators in our system would respond when school resumed in August. At a kickoff ceremony each year, all teachers, administrators, and staff members convene at a local college auditorium the week before the students' first day. The basic program for these gatherings rarely changes. The superintendent and school board chairperson welcome the assembled educators, principals introduce new hires, and a speaker provides a motivational address. In recent years, a highlight of these meetings has been the presentation of "unsung hero" awards. One obvious purpose of this annual program is to give everyone in the system an inspirational boost for facing the challenges of the coming year.

To my surprise, spirits were especially high at the opening meeting of 2002. Principals elicited even more rousing applause than usual with their introductions of new faculty and staff and their commendations to returning employees. Each school presented an unsung hero award to a secretary, custodian, maintenance worker, or teaching assistant. There were several standing ovations and occasional tears and embraces. One district administrator preparing to address the crowd briefly lost her composure in response to an especially poignant story by the previous speaker.

Most teachers sat with building colleagues and celebrated the accomplishments of coworkers and their schools with exuberant cheers. Even so, a sense of shared purpose transcended school boundaries, and a powerful synergy pervaded the entire gathering. If there was any mention of the difficult summer we had just endured, I do not recall it. Soon after the program began, any negative emotions I retained from the difficult summer disappeared, and I was swept up in the celebratory spirit that washed over everyone in the auditorium.

Although I had attended many opening-of-school meetings, I had never experienced one quite like this. It certainly was not what I anticipated after the disappointing summer of legislative wrangling over whether or not to fund basic educational programs. I expected some evidence of lowered morale, but instead the tone was one of joyful celebration.

Some of the emotions described above had been present in previous opening-day meetings, but not nearly at the level of this gathering. When I went home that evening, I went directly to my study and tried to capture some impressions of the day's event in my journal. The best description I could manage was to call it a combination love-in, political convention, pep rally, and tent meeting revival.

That day our system's teachers and administrators closed the curtain emphatically on the legislative debacle of the previous months.

It was as if the hundreds of educators present shared an unspoken desire: "Just give us our students, get out of the way, and let us teach."

By no means do I want to suggest that the behavior of the Tennessee legislature that summer was acceptable or that it was quickly forgotten. Collectively, that group of elected officials egregiously dishonored education, our state's schools, and its educators and students. However, even though they were able to hold Tennessee's educational system under siege for several months, once the school year began, nothing could distract the teachers in our system from fulfilling their professional commitment to their students.

My concern in this chapter is with "common sense" approaches to public school policy. I recounted the story above to make a point about teachers' values, because I believe that one of the primary reasons why common sense reforms fail is that they do not reflect an understanding of these values. That is, no matter how successful a strategy might be in business or any other professional domain, and no matter how logical that initiative might seem to lawmakers, it will not succeed in education if it doesn't account for the primary reason why people choose to teach: to make a difference in the lives of children.

Having spent all but one year of my adult work life in education, I cannot presume to understand the values of people in other fields. However, I suspect that every professional group has its own unique set of values, and those cultural beliefs, motivations, and mores undoubtedly have a strong influence on how people in that environment work and interact. Hopefully, the brief reflections in the following paragraphs illustrate the significance and impact of different value systems on people's behaviors.

Growing up in the South during the 1950s and 1960s, I was surrounded by very conservative political thinking and heard and participated in quite a few discussions about capital punishment. Almost invariably, someone who favored that approach would say, "If you thought you were going to die in the electric chair for murdering someone, you know you'd think twice about it." In my youth, that common sense argument seemed very compelling, as I could not imagine anything worse than dying prematurely in such a shameful and violent manner.

However, as I matured and reflected more deeply on the issue of capital punishment, I began to question this popular line of thinking. Like most people, the real reason I could never commit murder is that the idea of physically hurting anyone is completely repugnant to my nature. In other words, I like to think that I have fundamentally different values from most criminals.

If murderers thought like law-abiding citizens, they might be deterred by capital punishment. Clearly, however, most murderers don't think like the rest of us, because, if they did, they wouldn't murder people. In brief, there may be many compelling reasons why we should have capital punishment (and better reasons than this one why we should question its effectiveness), but one fact remains: we cannot be sure that most potential murderers fear that horrible consequence simply because most of the rest of us do.

I hope this little diversion helps to demonstrate a point about values. We will not always be successful in understanding the behavior of violent criminals by trying to put ourselves in their shoes, simply because we have such different core values from them. Similarly, anyone who has never taught will always have difficulty predicting the professional behavior of teachers without understanding the unique value system of that group of people.

Every teacher has heard the comment, "I don't know how you do it. There's no way I'd be able to put up with kids all day long." Of course, we teachers like to think that we do more than just put up with kids. We welcome the opportunity to work with young people and shape their lives. We may even celebrate their little foibles and the developmental idiosyncrasies that are maddening to most adults. In brief, we have very different values from the people who wonder why we teach, and the fact that they so frequently question us about our career choice clearly affirms the distinctiveness of our values and professional culture.

Educational reforms have often failed to achieve their desired results because they have not accounted for the unique value system of teachers. That shortcoming has been most evident in the accountability measures of the last twenty or thirty years. Perhaps the biggest problem with these laws is that they have been based on the false assumption that teachers will not do their best to serve their students without incentives or the threat of embarrassment or punishment. The elected leaders who have repeatedly imposed on education the common sense strategy of high-stakes accountability have ignored the reality that most teachers have always had a strong sense of accountability to their students.

If we could travel back to the days of the one-room schoolhouse, we would see that teachers of that era were clearly accountable to their students and communities. When a group of farmers pooled their resources to build a small log or frame structure on the corner of one of their farms and hired a teacher to serve their children, everyone knew quite well to whom the teacher was accountable.

Whether state performance standards existed or not, no one really needed them. Those teachers provided a direct service to their students and did it to the satisfaction of the children's parents (often living in the homes of the families they served). As times have changed, so has the nature of teacher-parent relationships, but one constant has remained over the years. True teacher accountability is, and always will be, to children in the classroom—and, by extension, to their parents and the community—and it is the only kind of accountability that has ever motivated teacher performance. At the end of the day, teachers have to be able to look in the mirror and know that they served their students as well as they could.

If you would, please think for a moment about the teachers who had the greatest influence on your life. As you reflect on their contributions, ask yourself if their motivations for making a difference in the lives of students came from within, or if their exceptional day-to-day performance was merely a response to externally imposed pressures, standards, and expectations.

I simply cannot imagine an excellent teacher whose motivation is not intrinsic. Teaching is physically demanding, emotionally challenging, and intellectually rigorous work. Those who are able to provide inspired teaching over a career could not sustain that commitment without the energy that comes from a desire to serve and make a difference in children's lives.

Accountability laws that ignore that fundamental truth about the culture of teaching will never be completely successful, and they can be counterproductive. If externally imposed expectations conflict with what teachers believe is best for children, they will work around the accountability measures to do what they believe is ethical. Consequently, most standards of accountability are not only ineffective; they are obstacles to good teaching. High-stakes accountability laws ignore the real, innate motivations of teachers and demonstrate that what counts as common sense in some professional domains may not be common sense at all in the culture of teaching.

Performance pay incentives are an especially good example of a common sense strategy that has little chance of sustained, meaningful success in improving public education. Teachers would like to receive better salaries, and they should. However, monetary incentives will simply never be an effective device for manipulating the behavior and work habits of teachers, no matter how compelling and logical that strategy may seem to some politicians and corporate leaders.

The vast majority of teachers already work very hard because of their commitment to making a difference in children's lives. Most extend themselves each year to their absolute physical, mental, and emotional limits. When I hear a campaign promise to give extra pay to teachers for exceptional performance, I wonder immediately how many people hearing that message actually perceive that teachers are coasting along, just waiting for a compelling reason to expend some effort in the classroom. In general, teachers work hard, and I think most people already know that. No incentive will increase the effort of someone who is already giving full effort.

The people who choose teaching as their life's work regard it as a calling, not as a way to earn monetary rewards. If given the opportunity to earn a pay incentive, teachers may focus their efforts to achieve the requirements of the incentive, but in the end they will serve their students in the manner that they believe is most ethical. In other words, they will play the game to earn an incentive so long as they do not believe that it demands a compromise of their fundamental principles. If they perceive that it does, then they won't play the game at all. Either way, the incentive will not achieve the goals of the policymakers who devised it.

Pay incentives for teachers are not only ineffective, but they clearly dishonor teachers and teaching. When politicians advocate monetary incentives for teachers (rather than across-the-board, meaningful pay increases), they imply that a desire to earn money is one of our primary motivations. If that were true, it would clearly indicate our lack of intellect, because no one ever got rich teaching school.

As a teacher, I sometimes wonder if people who measure success primarily in terms of financial gain regard teachers as either foolish or simply incapable of performing "better" jobs—that is, jobs with a higher pay scale. No, we are not foolish or incompetent. We chose the noble profession of teaching because we believe it is important.

There is one other compelling reason why the common sense approach of paying performance incentives to educators is seriously flawed. To thoughtful, informed observers of education, one of the most obvious dilemmas in trying to discriminate between one teacher and another is that good teaching is very difficult to measure. If you think about your best teacher, chances are that the qualities that distinguished that professional are difficult to assess, perhaps even to define.

I will not presume to understand the world of business, but I suspect it is much easier to measure standards of performance in most businesses than it is in teaching. Giving salespeople bonuses for selling more than their colleagues seems fairly straightforward. But what single criterion should we use to discriminate between the performance levels of different teachers? Accountability advocates have chosen test scores as the only measure of importance, and we have seen the inadequacy of that approach and the problems it causes.

Accountability measures and pay incentives are just two examples of common sense approaches that will always fail because they ignore the cultural values of teachers. I suspect that the tendency of educators to subvert such reforms is maddening to the elected officials who advocate these legislative initiatives. Increasingly, frustration is evident in the tone of their comments about education. It is as if they are throwing up their arms in disgust and screaming, "Why can't these educators get this right?"

In response, I would like to suggest that it might make more sense for lawmakers to gain an understanding of the culture of teachers and schools and to rethink legislative approaches accordingly than to imply that the vast majority of public school educators are hopelessly intractable (as Rod Paige did with his "terrorist" remark). In the end, that more rational approach might not be as politically advantageous, but it would reflect better common sense.

Some educational approaches defy basic common sense because their effects seem illogical to people who have not studied schools or worked in them. Although research and experience usually provide clarity about these confounding dilemmas, elected officials often choose to trust their own common sense instead of the knowledge of educational scholars or the practical insights of seasoned teachers and administrators.

Sometimes pundits, journalists, and writers for popular publications are also guilty of disregarding established educational wisdom, and they can be very critical of educators as they assert their claims to superior common sense. For example, in an article dripping with sarcasm and derision toward the educational community, Michael Crowley (2004) lambasted school systems for abolishing awards and other approaches that make distinctions among students. As he referred to a decision by a New Hampshire school board to eliminate tracking, he concluded that educators' "Kumbaya attitude" had clouded their judgment about this issue. As Crowley explained, "Tracking students makes good academic sense" (p. 36).

If Mr. Crowley had any knowledge of educational research, he would realize that tracking—also called ability grouping or homogeneous grouping—is an example of a common sense approach that is not in children's best interests academically. As educational scholar Robert Slavin (1995) has noted, decades of research on tracking have not revealed any evidence that it benefits students in general.

Although ability grouping has a very compelling logic to noneducators—and some educators too—it actually limits learning. When students are tracked into groups for instruction throughout the day, overall achievement suffers. Lower achieving students learn substantially less because teachers' expectations for them are lower, and, as illogical as it may seem, higher achieving students do not learn more.

In contrast, when students perform in mixed ability groups, the teachers' expectations for all students remain high. High-achieving students do just as well as when they are tracked with other high achievers. The normally low-achieving students learn much more, apparently because they benefit from their interactions with more successful students and from teachers' higher expectations. In addition, teachers tend to use a variety of approaches to help struggling students attain high standards when children are in mixed ability groups.

These conclusions about grouping may seem counterintuitive to most people, but the research findings on this issue have been so consistent over the years that it is hard to find educational scholars who will argue in favor of grouping children by ability throughout the school day. The reason educators oppose tracking is not because they are disregarding its compelling common sense in a misguided effort to protect students' feelings—as Mr. Crowley suggested in his article—but simply because students learn less when they are taught that way.

My most memorable experience with ability grouping was as a teacher of sixth grade social studies and reading in a system that grouped children from the time they entered school. In every grade through the sixth, students were grouped in sections A through D. My approximately twenty students in Section 6D knew exactly how the school perceived them, and they worked hard to live up to that expectation. Most of them had been in a low section since they began school, and almost all of them had been retained at least once, some of them twice. A number of the boys (there were only two girls) had already determined that they would drop out of school as soon as possible, and they often reminded me of that fact.

Academically and behaviorally they were one of the most challenging classes I have ever taught. So few of them were models of good behavior that negative behavior was more the norm than the exception. My next seven years of teaching were in a school that did not use ability grouping, and children's academic achievement and social behavior were far superior to those in the school that used tracking.

When I became a principal in a different South Carolina community in 1986, I entered another system that used the common sense approach of ability grouping students in sections A through D. I began my first year as principal after class rosters had already been established and did not challenge that arrangement—a mistake I have regretted ever since. Once school began, I immediately noticed that most of the white students were clustered in the A and B sections, and most of the C and D sections were entirely African-American. Further, the majority of the teachers for sections A and B were white.

The next summer I quietly and deliberately went about the work of using every available piece of information about student achievement to set up class rosters of mixed (or heterogeneous) ability. I also worked to attain racial balance in all sections. Knowing that someone would approach our elected superintendent to express dissatisfaction with these changes, I kept my plan under wraps until the beginning of school.

About a week of school went by, and I was in the district office one afternoon. As I tried to walk unnoticed past the superintendent's open office door, his sonorous voice called out to me, "Mr. Smith, could you please come in here?" Once I had taken a seat across from his desk, he proceeded to chastise me soundly for using an instructional approach that made such little common sense. Although I pointed to the research indicating higher achievement on standardized tests when children are grouped heterogeneously, as well as the district's focus on improved test scores, he remained unconvinced. At the end of our conversation, he conceded that it was too late to change class rosters and said he hoped my plan would have favorable results. He also made it very clear that I had better not attempt to go against established district practices again.

Although I saw many indications of an improved learning environment throughout the year, I knew that test scores were the only measures that would convince my boss to let me continue using mixed ability groups. Sure enough, our test performance improved substantially in every area that spring. In fact, when I dug into past school records, I could not find a single year when our scores had been nearly as high or a year in which they had increased so significantly from the previous year.

More important, our school's collective self-image seemed to have changed dramatically. We were no longer the poor, rural, underachieving school at the edge of the county. We were educators who were beginning to see that we could make a real difference in the lives of our children, and our building possessed a new spirit of pride and efficacy.

One day shortly after the arrival of statewide testing data, I was once again trying to slip unnoticed past the superintendent's door at the district office when he called me in to talk. This time our conference was quite brief. He congratulated me on our school's performance for the year and concluded by saying, "Well, I still don't like what you're doing, but since it seemed to work, I'll leave you alone." Obviously, heterogeneous grouping of students for instruction still did not qualify as good common sense in the eyes of our elected superintendent.

Common sense may have been the culprit when California decided that the state's poor reading performance in the early 1990s was due to a shift to "whole language." Apparently, policymakers did not think that the draconian cuts in funding that resulted in larger class sizes, reduced student access to books, and more teachers on emergency permits affected reading performance. Instead, the common sense approach was to mandate intensive phonics instruction. Unfortunately, as educational scholar Stephen Krashen (2003/2004) noted, California's reading scores have not improved in the decade since and remain at the bottom of the ranks for the whole country.

If policymakers in California had sought the advice of teachers, administrators, and educational researchers in their own state and genuinely listened to what these real experts had to say, the reading performance—and thus, the life chances—of millions of their young people might have been improved. As this example demonstrates, the problem with noneducators employing common sense to reform schools is that only educators can fully understand the complexity of some educational dilemmas—just as only businesspeople completely understand certain aspects of the business world.

However, as noted often in this book, educators are usually not a part of decisions about state and national policies affecting schools. Perhaps one of the reasons is that the effects of many educational approaches are so counterintuitive—that is, they do not meet the common sense litmus test. For example, if you suggest to acquaintances in casual conversation that grouping children by ability decreases academic achievement, some of your listeners will probably conclude that you are not thinking very clearly.

Educators who make that assertion will most likely be perceived as ideologically bound to a position that is kindhearted but not intellectually sound. That is, "It's nice that you teachers want all children to feel good about themselves, but the real issue here is improved performance." Sadly, that perspective about educators seems to be the one taken by many of the tough-talking, common sense politicians who have been trying to "fix" education for the last twenty or thirty years. When educators provide insights that do not pass the common sense test, they are dismissed as intellectually mushy and not to be trusted with policy decisions in their own area of expertise.

Conversely, most Americans seem to regard professionals in other fields, such as medicine, with deference to their specialized knowledge. If someone who was suffering from a life-threatening disease rejected the advice of expert physicians at a prestigious medical school and instead sought guidance from a witch doctor, we would question that person's sanity.

However, such irresponsible behavior is really not so different from the approach elected officials have often taken in developing public school policy. They have typically disregarded educational research and the perspectives of teachers and administrators in the field and then acted on their own, apparently believing they possess common sense that educators do not.

They were clearly wrong. We adults can employ common sense in making decisions about our own lives because we have acquired practical knowledge and experience over the years. The lessons we have learned are so familiar that we have internalized our insights,

and we can easily draw upon them to make common sense appli-
cations. Similarly, each of us who has worked in a particular field
for a substantial period of time has acquired wisdom and understanding about that professional culture, and we are able to make
common sense decisions within that domain. However, we should
all be careful not to suggest that we possess the knowledge and understanding to exercise common sense in fields in which we have
never worked or studied.

Unfortunately, education suffers from a unique burden—an almost universal perception that any intelligent person can devise
common sense solutions to improve it. Perhaps that is because
most people spend such a substantial part of their youth in schools
that they feel completely familiar with that context. However, as I
hope I demonstrated in chapter 11, having attended school as a
child does not necessarily provide any of us with genuine understanding about teaching and learning, the professional culture of
schools, or educational change.

Before closing this chapter about common sense, I would like
to ask a question that begs a common sense response. That is, if the
repeated application of a set of ideas has not worked for more than
twenty years, wouldn't common sense suggest that it is time to try
a different approach?

HONORING TEACHERS AND THE PROCESS OF EDUCATIONAL CHANGE: MAKING A COMMITMENT TO SOUND PRINCIPLES

Chapter Thirteen

———————O———————

Honoring Teachers and Teaching

WHEN I WAS AN ELEMENTARY PRINCIPAL in South Carolina, I spent about a week each summer analyzing student achievement data in an effort to construct mixed ability classes at every grade level. I wanted each teacher to start the year with a group of children whose overall academic performance was as equivalent as possible to every other class in that grade.

By the end of the year, certain teachers would have created classroom communities of happy, disciplined, and high-performing children. In varying degrees, other teachers would have attained less success, some of them considerably less. My purpose in balancing classes was to improve student achievement, and it did, with particularly dramatic results on standardized tests, but this experience also reinforced my most fundamental belief about education. Simply stated, teachers make all the difference.

As I argued in chapter 8, the obstacles some students face outside of school can make it very difficult for them to achieve academic success. Nonetheless, schools can have a powerful influence on young people, even in the most challenging circumstances. This is especially true when those schools have outstanding teachers.

Teaching is a complex endeavor. The best teachers exhibit a deep sense of caring and sensitivity to students' needs, as well as

187

an ethical commitment to helping young people succeed both in and beyond the classroom. They have a sophisticated knowledge of children's development and behavior and the judgment to apply that understanding wisely in diverse and changing circumstances. Good teachers are intellectually curious and possess competence in the subjects they teach and a repertoire of effective instructional strategies. In brief, teaching is both an art and a science, and the talented people who are able to orchestrate effectively the many and varied skills of that complex act deserve our respect and support.

There is now a solid consensus among educators at all levels that teacher quality is the most important factor in student achievement. Clearly, if we want the best for our children, we must (1) attract outstanding people to teaching and (2) give teachers every opportunity for continued professional growth and classroom success.

In this chapter, I suggest four approaches for achieving these two related goals. Before considering these proposals, however, it is important that we examine certain myths about teachers and teaching. Some of the misconceptions discussed below seem to be widely accepted, perhaps even by a majority of Americans, while others are endorsed by smaller, but very vocal, well-organized, and focused groups of citizens. In spite of their popularity, all of these beliefs are inaccurate, and they provide obstacles to thoughtful consideration of ways to enhance the profession of teaching. In the following section, I address nine erroneous perceptions about teachers and their work.

THE TRUTH ABOUT TEACHERS AND TEACHING

On the Whole, Teachers Just Aren't Very Smart.

I believe we have heard this suggestion more in the last few years than at any time in the past, perhaps because of an inaccurate claim that has since been exposed by Richard Allington. According to Allington (2002), Martin Gross stated in *A Conspiracy of Ignorance* that teachers come from the bottom third of their high school graduating classes and that they are the "dregs" of the college-educated population. Former Secretary of Education William Bennett also made this assertion in a *Washington Post* editorial on the basis of the "evidence" used by Gross. When questioned about the source of his information, Gross said that he drew his conclusions from research done by the Pennsylvania Department of Education. However, as Allington noted, officials from that agency reported that they never conducted such a study and suggested that doing so would be prohibitively expensive and difficult.

In contrast to the false pronouncements of Gross and Bennett, research by Bruschi and Coley (as cited in Allington, 2002) indicated that teachers on average perform intellectually as well as other college-educated adults. In fact, the teachers in Bruschi and Coley's study outscored administrators and managers in the area of "prose literacy" and had scores similar to professionals such as lawyers, physicians, and electrical engineers (p. 26). Claims that teachers aren't very smart may sell books and newspapers, and they may justify holding teachers in low esteem, but such statements are simply false and unethical.

Courses in Teacher Education have no Bearing on a Person's Effectiveness in the Classroom and May Actually be Counterproductive.

The evidence clearly contradicts this myth. Educational scholar Linda Darling-Hammond (2004) concluded on the basis of extensive research she conducted in California that teacher certification was the most important factor in student success in mathematics and reading. In addition, Darling-Hammond found that 40 percent of the teachers on emergency certificates in that state (that is, teachers who had not taken all required education classes) quit within one year, a startling figure of attrition that suggests that college graduates without full teacher preparation are not prepared for the rigors and challenges of the classroom.

There is currently a strong political push to eliminate or dramatically reduce the number of education courses required for teachers and to enable graduates in other fields to become teachers without having to go through teacher certification programs. As Allington (2002) suggested, perhaps the impetus for these proposals is the desire to hire teachers for lower salaries. Whatever the reason, adopting such policies would exacerbate the problems of all schools, especially those serving the children historically left behind.

The Primary Reason that Many Students Aren't Successful Academically is that Their Teachers Do Not Know the Subjects They are Teaching.

This too has become a popular political myth in recent years. As Gerald Bracey noted in 2000, only 8 percent of the teachers in schools that are not low income did not major or minor in the subject areas they teach. I suspect that most of these teachers were providing instruction in mathematics and science, because people with majors in these academic areas have always been able to make substantially higher salaries in private enterprise than in the classroom.

Of course, the percentage of teachers without appropriate content knowledge has been much higher in low-income schools, driving up the proportion of out-of-field teachers to 23 percent overall (Bracey, 2000, p. 121). My greatest concern about the myth of teachers not knowing their subject matter is a problem that was mentioned under the above bulleted item. That is, some politicians and journalists are now suggesting that we eliminate or severely reduce the number of education courses teachers take and require them to take more subject area courses instead.

Again, we have a proposal that is based on a misrepresentation of the issue. The problem is not that properly credentialed teachers are not knowledgeable. The evidence indicates that these teachers know the subjects they teach and that their understanding of best instructional practices enables them to make a greater difference in young people's lives than teachers without certification. The real problem is that we do not have enough properly credentialed teachers, especially in low-income schools.

The politicians and journalists who confidently assert that we should eliminate or reduce the amount of preparation that teachers receive in colleges of education are proposing a change that will seriously erode teaching quality. Instead, we should take steps to improve the supply of fully certified teachers, especially for our low-income schools. We must also address the problem of teacher retention. It is simply unacceptable that nearly half of the nation's new teachers leave the field within five years. Solving that one problem would go a long way toward resolving many other educational dilemmas.

Public Schools are Filled with Incompetent Teachers, and It's Impossible to Fire Those Who Have Tenure.

I have yet to hear or read a claim of widespread teacher incompetence that was supported with data. As noted above, we do know that the teachers who lack credentials are the ones who have the least success helping students achieve, and they most often receive positions in low-income schools.

The suggestion that tenured teachers cannot be fired ignores several realities. First of all, yes, they can. (In fact, I've had to do it.) Second, teachers undergo continuing evaluation throughout their careers. It is simply false to assert that there are no safeguards in place to protect against teacher incompetence. Third, there's a very good reason why the teaching profession has fought to retain tenure. Without it, teachers in many states can be dismissed summarily and without cause. In Tennessee, for example, an untenured teacher can have excellent evaluations and still be fired without any explanation. Achieving tenure does not guarantee a teacher a free ride until the end of a career. Its only assurance is that the teacher cannot be dismissed without a good reason.

In brief, no matter how persistent the myth, tenure does not guarantee job security for incompetent teachers. In most systems it would be very difficult for an incompetent teacher to receive tenure, and abolishing that protection would make teaching a very precarious and unattractive career choice. It is frightening to imagine how severe the problem of teacher supply would be if teachers did not have any job security at all.

Teacher Organizations and Unions Only Care about Improving Teacher Salaries and Conditions, Even at the Expense of What's Best for Children.

When teachers are clearly underpaid, resulting in teacher shortages that compromise the education of our young people, it is hard to understand how anyone could suggest that teacher salaries and educational quality are unrelated. Moreover, the National Education Association (NEA), America's largest teacher organization, has long been more than just an advocate for improved teacher pay.

For many years, the NEA has been this country's most persistent proponent of quality public education. Its affiliates have aggressively lobbied and promoted policies that benefit our young people at the state and federal levels. The NEA may not be a popular group in the White House, the halls of Congress, or in state legislatures, but perhaps that is because it has been uncompromising in its demands that elected officials enact thoughtful, well-designed educational policy, rather than laws that simply satisfy political motives.

The Way to Improve Teaching is to Increase Oversight and Regulation.

Teaching is already highly controlled and regulated, perhaps more so than any other profession or vocation. Teachers follow prescribed state and local curricula in every subject level and grade, and they are evaluated annually during their beginning years and intermittently afterward. In addition, it is standard practice in many schools for teachers to submit lesson plans to the principal every week. (How many people in other fields have to give their supervisors a written description of everything they will do during the week?)

As noted in chapter 6, my colleagues and I must conduct periodic assessments in mathematics and provide summaries of the results to our supervisors. In systems throughout the country, teachers submit similar reports in reading and other subjects to demonstrate their adherence to local and state curriculum guidelines.

Politicians and journalists who continually argue that we need to increase the standardization and regulation of teaching are ignoring the fact that teachers' work is already highly regulated. They also fail to see that the standardization of instruction eliminates teaching that truly matters in the lives of students, as suggested by the contrast between Mrs. Elkins and Mr. Jackson in chapter 6.

Moreover, if greater regulation is really the answer to education's problems, supporters of that approach need to explain why a low-income school might perform poorly when a nearby suburban school with the same federal, state, and local regulations is doing much better. In other words, maybe regulations are not the issue. Perhaps the reason that so many politicians and journalists continue to call for more and more standardization, regulation, and control of teaching is that they don't understand education well enough to generate any other proposals. They just continue to re-circulate the same flawed ideas.

Teachers Just Aren't as Committed or Hardworking as They Once Were.

As I suggested in chapter 2, my personal experience indicates just the opposite. In fact, according to an NEA study, teachers on average spend over fifty hours each week on all teaching duties, and that amount is the highest since the NEA started researching teacher workload in 1961. This survey also revealed that 15 percent of teachers work more than sixty hours each week. Further, even though teachers' salaries are much lower than those of professionals in other fields with a similar amount of training and responsibility, teachers on average spend $443 of their own money on their students, and 8 percent spend more than $1,000 per year (O'Neil, 2003, pp. 27, 28). The evidence clearly contradicts the notion that teacher commitment has slipped over time.

We Cannot Count on Today's Teachers to Provide Appropriate Moral Guidance to Our Children.

According to a Gallup poll, teachers top the list for trustworthiness among all vocations, rating higher in the American public's opinion than doctors, clergy, judges, police officers, and the president

(Flannery, 2004). In my view, the perception by some citizens that teachers are not as ethical as they once were is at least partly the result of the relentless repetition of the assertion—particularly by leaders of the religious right—that "God has been taken out of the public schools."

Of course, we know what these critics really mean. Their concern is that the courts have consistently affirmed that a school representative saying an oral prayer in school violates the Constitution. However, these people do not say, "I would like for educators to recite in the presence of all students prayers that reflect *my* religious beliefs, no matter how different they might be from the beliefs of some children and their parents." Most Christians realize that such a demand is unfair.

Unfortunately, the refrain that "God has been taken out of the public schools" has been repeated so often that some people, particularly evangelical Christians, have accepted its literal interpretation: that is, if God has been removed from public schools, then they are now godless. I apologize for delving into this sensitive issue, but it has strong implications for the future of our nation's schools, and the public clamor about it has only seemed to intensify in recent years.

If the goal of the religious right is to have our government institute vouchers so that Christians can receive tax dollars to attend church schools, its leaders should pronounce that position openly and clearly, rather than continually disparaging our nation's public education system and implicating everyone who is a part of it. Further, it is important to note that no profession or occupational group provides as many Sunday school teachers for America's Christian churches as our country's public school educators (Troy, 2004). If the religious right is really worried about public institutions becoming godless, education should probably be that group's lowest priority.

Caregiving is One of Teaching's Most Important Roles.

A few years ago, I was named Teacher of the Year for my system. At the time, my daughter, who brags about her dad almost as much as he brags about her, was a college senior. When Meaghan proudly told one of her university advisors about my recent honor, this professor said, "Well, he deserves it for all of those years of wiping snotty noses." After my daughter related this response to me, I searched my memory and could not recall in thirty years of educational service ever having wiped a dirty nose except for my own.

Hopefully, Meaghan's professor intended the phrase "wiping snotty noses" as a metaphor, not a description of the one of the primary functions of teachers. Even so, her comment illustrates a common myth: that caregiving is one of teaching's most important roles. The truth is, teachers spend the majority of their time planning, delivering, and assessing instruction, as well as learning how to be more effective in these pursuits.

I have a bachelor's degree in history, a master of arts in teaching degree, and a PhD in education, as well as numerous credit hours in education courses outside of these degree programs. I have been an educator for thirty years, and I continue to read avidly about teaching and learning and to seek ideas from other teachers. Even so, I enter the classroom every day with a sense that I do not know nearly as much as I would like to know about my craft, and I have never been bored with the challenge of helping every student achieve high standards in every academic discipline. Caregiving is certainly one small dimension of teaching, but, first and foremost, teaching is challenging intellectual work.

ELEVATING THE PROFESSIONAL IMAGE OF TEACHING

My first proposal for honoring teachers and their work is that we take steps to elevate the professional image of teaching so that we can recruit and retain the best and the brightest for our children's classrooms. As suggested by the discussion of caregiving above, it is essential that we start by eliminating as much as possible those roles that diminish the professional image of teaching and do not relate directly to children's academic achievement.

Over time society has imposed on education an increasing number of caregiving responsibilities. About twenty-five years ago, I took a position as a sixth grade teacher in a community in the upstate region of South Carolina. For reasons that I never fully understood, this town apparently used little or no fluoride in its water system, and children in the area had an unusually high incidence of tooth decay. Consequently, the school district instituted a program called Swish and Spit.

At the beginning of my one year in this system, a woman who was apparently affiliated with a local public health agency brought to my classroom a plastic jug of concentrated liquid (presumably some form of fluoride) and a substantial supply of cups, napkins, and clear plastic bags. She also provided a chart for recording the weekly administration of Swish and Spit, as well as copies of a permission form, since children had to obtain written parental consent to participate in the program.

I sent home the permission forms, collected them as students returned them in the coming days, and early one morning shortly thereafter I conducted Swish and Spit. Dutifully following the directions provided, I mixed the concentrated liquid with the correct volume of water and poured precise amounts into cups for each of the eligible children. I then dispensed the cups and napkins, directing my students to wait before gargling so they could all begin at the same time.

On cue, the children swished for the prescribed amount of time (30 seconds, I think). As you might imagine, there was a fair amount of silliness, and some mouthwash ended up on desks, the fronts of shirts, and the floor. When I announced that the gargling period was over, the children spit the liquid back into their cups, wiped their mouths with their napkins, and stuffed the napkins into the cups, which I then collected in one of the clear plastic bags.

I was supposed to document this effort on the form provided by the woman from the local agency, but I never did. Nor did I ever repeat the administration of Swish and Spit. It seemed to me that the morning we engaged in that program was compromised academically. Sure, the whole Swish and Spit operation only lasted a few minutes, but it took much longer that morning than usual to get the students settled down and prepared for learning.

As most teachers will attest, a disruption at the beginning of the day can have a lingering effect for many children, and it was my perception that Swish and Spit had that consequence for most of my students that morning. In addition, it troubled me that I was being asked as an educational professional to mix and dispense mouthwash, oversee an activity that took me away from teaching, and collect liquid that students had gargled and spit.

For years, I have seen Swish and Spit as a metaphor for things that teachers really should not do—roles that devalue teaching, compromise academic achievement, and should be performed by someone else in our society. Perhaps I was wrong to abandon Swish and Spit, and I certainly do not want to suggest that schools should not serve any function other than to provide core academic instruction.

Nonetheless, I hope the example of Swish and Spit encourages readers to consider whether teachers ought to be expected to fulfill the wide range of social responsibilities they sometimes perform. Educators usually carry out these jobs without complaint because they care about the welfare of their students, and they recognize that some student needs (such as hunger or pain) must be addressed before children will able to learn.

Still, such roles reinforce the view that teachers are primarily caregivers, and that perception diminishes the image of teaching, thus making it more difficult to attract the best and the brightest to the profession. To some degree, caregiving will always be an educational role, but we should guard against the automatic assignment of such functions to schools. Two questions should guide decisions regarding caregiving in public education. First, is this caregiving service necessary for children's learning? Second, could someone else do this job?

We should also remember that criticisms of education do not usually relate to Swish and Spit, after-school programs, prevention of obesity and drug and alcohol usage, character education, sun safety, or any of the many other noninstructional roles educators often fulfill. Local, state, and federal entities may impose these responsibilities on public school people without considering the time taken away from academic learning, but, in the end, academics and academics alone are most often the subject of discussions about school effectiveness.

In other words, if educators are going to be consistently called out for student performance on measures of math, science, social studies, and language proficiency, let's give them the opportunity to focus on that mission. Otherwise, let's acknowledge that we as a society expect schools to do much more and honor all of those varied contributions.

Even if we choose the latter path, we should carefully consider whether teachers should have to collect student spit. "Wiping snotty noses" and collecting spent mouthwash are not roles that suggest a high degree of professionalism. We should do all that we can to replace that image of teaching and enable teachers to spend their time fully engaged in the intellectually challenging work of academic instruction. After all, in most public discourse about education, we have emphasized their accountability for that result and that result alone.

There are other steps we can take to enhance public perceptions of teaching. As I have argued from the beginning of this book, our society has dishonored the image of teaching by rewarding politicians and journalists who present negative and unsubstantiated portrayals of public school educators. Politicians know they can win elections by suggesting that teachers are not doing their jobs and need to be held accountable, and journalists know that these perspectives sell the news.

If we have learned anything about public perceptions in the last few decades, we have seen that a misleading message can take on the appearance of reality if repeated often enough—especially if the people promoting it can condense it to a catchy and memorable phrase. (The Republican and Democratic parties affirm this Madison Avenue principle every time there's an election.) It appears that neither evidence nor truthfulness is necessary when promoting an image to the public. All that really matters are persuasiveness, persistence, and access to a medium for reaching most citizens. Of course, that last requirement gives politicians and journalists a decided advantage in shaping public perceptions.

In any society, the prestige of a particular profession depends on the accumulated cultural messages people receive about it. A single disparaging public statement about teachers will not affect the way most Americans perceive them, but the ceaseless repetition of such statements undoubtedly damages the image of teaching—

especially in the impressionable minds of young people who are deciding their futures. As citizens, we need to be vigilant in recogniz-
ing assertions by public figures that misrepresent teachers and their
work.

As I explain in greater detail in chapter 14, a red flag should go
up whenever a politician or journalist discredits educators without
offering valid evidence, and we should hold such critics accountable by supporting political candidates and media representatives
whose public statements are accurate and responsible. If we don't
reverse our culture's unjust denigration of educators, it is hard to
imagine that we will ever be able to attract the best and the brightest to the profession.

We educators also need to take some responsibility for revers-
ing the negativism in public discourse about America's schools. No,
we did not create this problem, but if we do not take an active role
in solving it, it will surely persist. Although we do not have the kind
of access to the public that politicians and journalists enjoy, each of
us has the power to reach a small audience: the parents of the students we teach.

Most of the elementary teachers I know periodically send home
newsletters, some as often as every week. There's absolutely no reason why we could not include in each newsletter a column providing some positive indicators of school quality to counter the negativism people read and hear elsewhere—for example, the finding
reported in chapter 2 that an analysis of international assessments
shows American students number one in the world in civics, or the
annual Phi Delta Kappa/Gallup Poll findings regarding the public's
true perceptions of school quality. Teachers within a school or district could easily create a system for sharing information of that nature. Collectively, we could make a powerful impact on public perceptions and begin to reverse the negative consequences of
unwarranted criticisms of teachers and schools.

In addition, we educators need to become less timid about confronting elected officials and members of the media who mislead
the public about school quality. The truth is, we have allowed ourselves to be easy targets for detractors simply because we do not
fight back. Apparently we have become inured to the kind of unjust

denigration education receives, or perhaps we have concluded that the onslaught of attacks on our profession is so overwhelming that our voices will not matter.

Most teachers I know simply shrug off public criticism of education and insulate themselves in their classroom work. Maybe our reluctance to speak out is a cultural legacy of the days of the one-room schoolhouse, when teachers were expected to remain single (if they were female), submissive, and out of public view. Or perhaps it is because we are naturally disposed to introspection when faced with the suggestion that we have failed. After all, the best teachers first reflect on what they might have done differently when their children are not successful, so it's natural that we would do the same when a public figure blames us for every real and perceived shortcoming of our schools.

Whatever the reasons, our reluctance to stand up and confront our attackers is no longer just an issue of protecting our own dignity. As I have argued throughout this book, negative public perceptions have driven educational reform efforts for two or more decades, and these laws have had real consequences for America's youth. Simply stated, this fight is not just about us anymore. It's about our children.

By confronting misinformation and working to enhance the image of teaching, we can not only begin to reverse destructive policies that have been based on an illusion of school failure, but we can also make teaching a more attractive career choice and thus ensure a brighter future for tomorrow's students. In the end, promoting appropriately positive images of schools and educators is no longer a political act that we can leave in the hands of a select few of our colleagues, such as NEA representatives. It has become a professional imperative for every educator.

IMPROVING THE CONDITIONS OF TEACHING

My second proposal is that we improve the conditions of teaching. At present many teachers toil under conditions that other professionals would find unacceptable. In low-income areas, teachers often work in drab, uncomfortable, and even unsafe buildings. In some schools, elementary teachers are still required to eat lunch with their students, meaning that they are on the job even during lunch.

A typical lunch period is thirty minutes in most schools and for all practical purposes can be less than twenty minutes, since teachers must either walk their students to and from the cafeteria (especially in elementary schools) or must serve hall duty at the beginning and end of the lunch period (in some middle and high schools). Most educators accept the reality of lunch on the run, and nothing short of large increases in personnel would enable schools to schedule longer teacher breaks for lunch. However, every teacher should have an unencumbered lunch—that is, a lunch free of students. If for no other reason, teachers need that opportunity to visit a bathroom, something they often have to wait several hours to do.

As part of the effort to improve the conditions of teaching, we also need to examine the instructional workloads of America's teachers. Of all developed countries, our teachers are directly responsible for students for the longest hours. For example, Japanese elementary teachers are in the classroom 617 hours per year, compared to 1,139 hours for America's elementary teachers, and the differences for America's middle and high school teachers, as compared to those in Japan and other industrialized nations, are just as dramatic ("Time Out," 2005).

Reducing the workload of America's teachers would certainly make the profession a more attractive career choice, but that change would also have other positive implications. For example, one of the strengths of Japanese schools is that their teachers spend substantially more time outside of class planning and perfecting their lessons with colleagues. As noted in chapter 2, American teachers plan collaboratively when they have the opportunity, but the amount of time they have for that activity is very limited.

If there has been one inexorable trend over the thirty years I have been in education, it is that teachers' noninstructional duties (in addition to those related to caregiving) have increased steadily. For example, accountability laws have spawned record-keeping jobs that once did not exist. When policy and societal changes continually compel our educators to take on responsibilities that are not related to classroom instruction, teaching quality always suffers.

I would also like to propose some in-house workplace reforms that would not require substantial additional funding. Just as university professors do, teachers in public schools should play a major role in hiring colleagues, mentoring beginning faculty, and evaluating their peers. These changes would enhance the professional culture of teaching and have great potential for reducing the number of teachers who leave the classroom in their beginning years.

In my experience, when teachers assist in the hiring of new faculty, they feel a greater sense of responsibility for the success of those new hires. Having played a role in bringing new teachers into the school, the veteran teachers are more likely to go the extra mile to ensure the newcomers' success. Perhaps just as important, new teachers begin the school year believing that the colleagues who hired them are their supporters and can be consulted for assistance. In these circumstances, beginning teachers are far less likely to perceive that they have to face alone the daunting challenges of the first years.

Most schools attempt to mentor beginning teachers by assigning a veteran teacher to each new one. However, without the support of funding, experienced teachers usually cannot meet during the day with the inexperienced teachers they mentor. Consequently, they rarely develop close, working relationships or have the time to solve dilemmas the rookie teachers are experiencing.

A program in Ohio has demonstrated how a small budget appropriation can make a substantial difference in the success and retention of beginning teachers ("Major Mentoring," 2004). In this system, substitutes are provided for eight days so that the mentor and beginning teacher can observe each other in their classrooms. That one provision seems to enable the two to develop a strong camaraderie and gives the new teacher a chance to learn from a master teacher. In the system where this program has been in effect, 96 percent of beginning teachers return for a second year. By comparison, one in every five American public school teachers leaves the profession after one year.

As I learned in my four years of university teaching, faculty members who evaluate each other's work performance also possess a heightened sense of responsibility for their colleagues' success. Through that process, they become aware of areas for improvement and approach their colleagues with ideas and support. Principals and other supervisors could still be the final arbiters in this evaluation process, just as department chairs and deans are in colleges and universities, but beginning teachers would receive a level of support that they presently do not have in most schools.

These proposals for involving teachers more actively in hiring, mentoring, and evaluation are based on the idea that professionals are people who exercise some control over their work and are accountable not only for their personal success, but for the success of colleagues too. We need to confer upon teaching these important dimensions of professionalism. Like many other educators who have expressed these views, I believe these proposals would improve teacher morale, bring more talented people to the profession, and increase teacher retention.

INVOLVING EDUCATORS IN POLICY DEVELOPMENT

My third proposal is that we honor educators' knowledge by involving them in decision making at all levels. Throughout this book, I have criticized the exclusion of educators from policymaking decisions. As important as education is to the health of our nation (as often expressed in public surveys), I have never known of congressional hearings to examine in depth the views of teachers, administrators, or educational scholars.

If such hearings have occurred, they were certainly inadequate, because the legislation that has shaped public school policy over the last few decades has usually ignored the views of practitioners and researchers. Instead, most school policy has either been politically motivated or based on common sense and nostalgic views of the past. When educators have been involved in decision making, they have often been token representatives whose views were known to support the ideological positions already placed on the table by politicians.

In chapter 3, I discussed the statement by former Secretary of Education Rod Paige characterizing the NEA as a "terrorist organization."

As noted, Paige explained that his remark was a reaction to the opposition of NEA officials to certain requirements of No Child Left Behind (NCLB). I will not burden readers here with a rehashing of my perspectives on Paige's comment. In the earlier discussion, I said that this incident was an indication of how low we have sunk in our public discourse about education in America and how accepting we have become of unjust criticisms of schools and educators.

However, Secretary Paige's behavior also revealed the low regard our leaders have for educators' knowledge and perspectives. By lashing out at educators who were advocating for needed changes to NCLB, Paige said to America's entire educational community, "Shut up, sit down, and do what you're told. We really don't care what you think." Not only did he address millions of committed educators as if they were wayward children who should be ignored, but he also made it very clear that they would be condemned in the strongest terms possible if they dared to offer informed opinions to our leaders.

If ever there was an affirmation of the need to involve educators in policymaking, it is revealed in the wide discrepancy between the reactions of educators and noneducators to NCLB. As noted in chapter 7, many educators had doubts about the viability of NCLB and the motives of its authors when they first learned about the law's requirements.

However, most politicians, journalists, and interested members of the public seemed to perceive the law as a genuine expression of the noble sentiments implied by its title. Even those who do not support President Bush on most issues (such as Senator Kennedy from Massachusetts) seemed to think that he was exactly the kind of no-nonsense leader to dispense strong medicine to America's educators and tough love to America's students in the interest of improving academic learning. In brief, almost all noneducators seemed to believe that the law was exactly what it purported to be, while many (if not most) educators immediately knew something was amiss.

In fact, I suspect that one reason why leaders from the political left have not been more critical of NCLB is that these elected officials were taken in by the rhetoric of NCLB and did not realize what they had endorsed. Having been deceived by the imagery surrounding the law, now it is too late for them to say NCLB was a bad idea, much less to suggest that its intended purpose was to do something other than improve the achievement of disadvantaged children. To criticize NCLB now, they would have to concede that they either did not examine the act carefully or that they do not understand education well enough to have recognized the law's implications.

If Americans sincerely want our schools to be the best they can—and I believe they do—we clearly have to honor educators and affirm their professional status by involving them in legislative and policy decisions at all levels. Politicians should not be solely responsible for generating educational legislation any more than bus drivers or insurance adjusters should develop guidelines for NASA.

Elected leaders have chastised teachers and students for alleged failures in academics, including history and science, but they themselves are apparently unaware of the history of failure associated with high-stakes accountability measures, and they have ignored the science of educational research. Public school policy should result from extended study and discussion by diverse groups of citizens, but teachers, educational researchers, and school, district, and state-level administrators should always be at the center of such decisions, just as all other professionals are trusted with decision making in their own areas of expertise.

INCREASED PREPARATION AND PAY

My fourth proposal for honoring America's teachers involves both teacher preparation and pay. In chapter 2, I noted that the educational level of teachers has risen over the years and that approximately half of today's public school teachers hold advanced degrees. As a way of promoting the professional image of teaching and improving overall teacher quality, I recommend that we phase in a requirement that every public school teacher in America hold at least a master's degree.

There are quite a few colleges of teacher education in which the master's is already the standard path to certification, and they are among the nation's most respected programs. With this advanced degree as an established expectation, the level of education required of teachers would be equivalent to that of most other professions. Further, the master's would accommodate the increased demands of preparing teachers for today's schools. It would go far in ensuring that all teachers have both the content and pedagogical knowledge needed to be successful in twenty-first-century classrooms.

The fact that steadily growing numbers of teachers are already obtaining advanced degrees suggests that this move would simply be a way of codifying a trend that has been evolving for some time. Please recall that it wasn't so many years ago that only two years of college were needed for teacher certification, and we moved from there to the requirement of a bachelor's degree. It is time to take the next step in the evolution of teacher preparation standards.

Obviously, we cannot ask prospective teachers to spend an additional year or more in college acquiring understandings of their craft and the subjects they teach and not pay them for that commitment. In fact, it is clear that teacher salaries are already grossly inadequate for the amount of training teachers receive, the skills they possess, and the responsibilities they assume.

According to one study, inflation-adjusted teacher wages rose just 0.8 percent between 1996 and 2003, while the wages of other college graduates rose 11.8 percent (Winans, 2004, p. 38). Further, low salaries undoubtedly contribute to the problem of teacher retention. According to an NEA study, the reason teachers most often give for leaving the field (37 percent of survey respondents) is low pay (O'Neil, 2003, p. 28).

The American public seems to believe that teachers deserve higher pay. In the 2003 Phi Delta Kappa/Gallup Poll, 59 percent of the people surveyed (including 60 percent of parents) said that teacher salaries in their communities were too low. Interestingly, only 33 percent expressed that opinion in 1969, and the percentage has steadily increased in the years since (Rose & Gallup, 2003). This change appears to reflect either the public's belief that teacher salaries have declined relative to other jobs or that today's citizens are more likely than before to acknowledge the difficulty and importance of good teaching. Either way, it is clear that we need to increase teacher salaries substantially.

In this chapter about honoring teachers and their work I have proposed the creation of conditions that I believe will foster exemplary teaching. For some readers, especially those seeking the kind of can't-miss, cause-and-effect policies we have tried over the last twenty or thirty years, the ideas in this chapter may be disappointing. These readers may wonder why I have not included a provision—some kind of silver bullet—that will cause good teaching to occur.

The truth is, there are no such remedies, and the reason is quite simple. Teaching, especially teaching that matters, is as much art and craft as it is science. If we have learned anything from accountability legislation, we have seen that we cannot cause artistry to occur, but we can extinguish it by removing the conditions it needs for survival. Therefore, I have tried to suggest in this chapter an educational context that will attract to the profession the creative, intelligent people who have the potential for changing children's lives.

I have also proposed changes that will nurture artistry and will give the classroom artists who are our best teachers the opportunity to develop and practice their craft. Educational research and history have demonstrated how imperative it is that we provide such a context. Similarly, the history of the last few decades has shown us that the standardization of teaching squelches artistry and fosters mediocrity.

In the final chapter I suggest strategies for elevating our nation's public discourse about education. Like this chapter, chapter 14 includes no quick and easy remedies for fixing our schools. Instead it provides proposals for establishing the political conditions needed for continuous and meaningful educational improvement. Its only promise is that America's public schools will fulfill our expectations when we give them a fair chance.

Chapter Fourteen

─────────○─────────

Elevating Our Nation's Public Discourse about Education

MAGGIE'S MOTHER COMPLAINED LOUDLY, vehemently, and often that I gave too much homework and that my academic expectations were unreasonably high. From August until spring, I lived with the specter of answering the telephone—or greeting this parent at the classroom door—and hearing a torrent of vitriol about my outrageously high standards, the harm I was causing her daughter, and the discord I was creating in their household.

Near the end of the year, Maggie's father set up an after-school conference with the principal and me. As the three of us sat in the principal's office for almost an hour, the father lambasted my teaching on the grounds that I did not give enough homework, was not challenging his daughter academically, and was thus compromising her chances for future success.

The tragedy in this situation is not that two adults had such unreasonable criticism of a teacher. The real misfortune is that these parents unwittingly victimized their daughter. It should surprise no one that a child whose mother and father expressed such negative opinions of her teacher and such conflicting expectations for her performance would be an unreceptive and unenthusiastic student. Maggie gave minimal effort throughout the year and achieved far below her capabilities—in my opinion, because she understood that her parents did not support her teacher and could not reach agreement about their own expectations for her.

209

As bizarre as the behavior of these parents may seem, it is not really so different from the conduct of some of the politicians, journalists, and pundits who have dominated our nation's public discourse about education. For example, some of the most outspoken advocates of No Child Left Behind (NCLB)—a law that emphasizes math, English, and science performance to the exclusion of all other subjects—have disparaged public schools since its implementation for alleged shortcomings in civics and history.

As noted in chapter 9, former Secretary of Education Rod Paige (2003) pointedly criticized fourth graders' performance on the civics test of the National Assessment of Educational Progress (NAEP) roughly one year after the passage of NCLB. Paige did not concede that the state tests used to demonstrate achievement of NCLB standards might not assess the same civics concepts as the NAEP and that the fear induced by NCLB was narrowing school curricula across the country to only the competencies measured by these state tests. Nor did he acknowledge that most systems have responded to the demands of NCLB by decreasing the amount of time elementary teachers spend on social studies instruction.

Similarly, in 2003, as implementation of NCLB was beginning its second full year, Senator Lamar Alexander was giving speeches in which he suggested that schools no longer teach American history or civics. Had he stated instead that the emphasis on history and civics had diminished (not disappeared) as a result of NCLB and that we should make policy changes to resolve that dilemma, his criticism would have been constructive. However, making that assertion would require that he take responsibility for a result of the law that he and its other supporters apparently did not anticipate or did not want to acknowledge publicly.

Both of these former secretaries of education engaged in a disturbing political hypocrisy. They enacted a law that predictably resulted in educators giving less attention to subjects other than math, English, and science, and then they denounced schools for doing exactly that.

My concern is not simply that these officials were critical of public education. We should have a rigorous and ongoing discussion about educational priorities in America, and leaders such as

Paige and Alexander should raise questions about public school performance.

However, when they aggressively criticize our nation's public schools for failing to achieve goals that so clearly contradict each other, they are being just as unreasonable as Maggie's mother and father were when they demanded that I simultaneously raise and lower my academic standards. In fact, just as these two parents diminished their daughter's chances for success by eroding her faith in her teacher and failing to reach agreement about their own expectations for her, Paige, Alexander, and other politicians have diminished the effectiveness of our nation's schools by undermining the public's confidence in them and making it difficult for them to sustain a focus on meaningful educational goals.

Of course, the difference between the behavior of Maggie's parents (whose complaints only affected their child and her teacher) and the conduct of Paige and Alexander is that the pronouncements of such prominent leaders have real consequences for our educational system. The most frightening result of the unending political clamor about American education is that many citizens are beginning to question whether our public schools can continue to serve the nation's interests—just as Maggie concluded that there was no reason for her to buy into my teaching as long as her parents could not agree on their own expectations for her or me.

Many of the politicians and journalists who have engaged in this continuous verbal assault on our schools probably did not realize that they were placing public education in such a quandary. However, observers of Paige and Alexander do not have to be terribly cynical to wonder if perhaps their behavior was deliberate and purposeful. After all, their political allegiance was to an administration that has sought to promote vouchers—apparently by first convincing Americans that our educational system is hopelessly beyond repair. In the end, like so many public figures before them, Paige and Alexander transformed the discussion and development of educational policy into a political game in which our children are invariably the losers.

Throughout this book, I have been careful not to suggest that such political conduct has been primarily Republican or Democratic.

The truth is, placing blame exclusively at the feet of one party or the other would completely miss the point. Conservative Republicans—and the journalists and pundits who share their perspectives—have more clearly aligned themselves with the goal of privatizing public education and have therefore been more conspicuous in their attempts to disparage public schools.

However, neither party has taken a thoughtful approach to the development of educational policy, and both have been guilty of using education for political purposes. In order to win elections and bolster their reputations by fixing education, elected leaders from both parties have misrepresented public school quality and posed as saviors of an institution that they clearly do not understand—but have nonetheless presumed to understand better than the educators who work in it and the parents whose children are served by it.

Another reason I have not made a clear distinction between Republicans and Democrats is that their educational policy positions have not varied substantially in recent years. For example, Congress passed NCLB in 2001 with strong bipartisan support. Further, as we approach the time for reauthorizing, revising, or rescinding that act, the views expressed by the leaders of the two parties are not significantly different.

On the whole, Republicans seem to support the law as it is. A few Democrats have spoken in favor of abolishing NCLB, and others have argued for fuller funding or for modifications in the evaluation of students who are in special education or are still learning to speak English. In general, however, most Democratic and Republican leaders seem to agree that the key accountability provisions of NCLB should be retained. Republicans and Democrats may be as deeply divided on most issues today as they have ever been in our nation's history, but there really isn't much to separate them when it comes to educational policy.

Their collective position on NCLB is especially disappointing. Many of them appear to be unable to move beyond the imagery invoked by the law's title to assess it thoughtfully and offer well-reasoned alternatives. Those who raise questions about its effectiveness know that they expose themselves to charges that they are ignoring the academic struggles of poor and minority children, that they lack the toughness and resolve to address this persistent problem, and that they are pandering to the selfish desires of educators who refuse to be held accountable. The truth is, NCLB has become so synonymous with educational accountability that its critics assume a considerable political risk—the perception that they oppose accountability in any form.

Although it appears that NCLB will probably be reauthorized with few, if any, substantive changes, I believe that we should completely overhaul its accountability provisions. As illustrated in chapters 6–8, NCLB encourages questionable instructional practices, squelches teacher creativity and student interest, and fails miserably in its promise to lift up the children traditionally left behind. Moreover, it is hard to imagine how an act that was designed to dismantle our educational system could somehow improve that system without undergoing fundamental revisions.

However, no matter what Congress does about NCLB, we must recognize that no single change in policy will ever ensure the long-term success of America's public schools. It is time that we ended our search for educational silver bullets and quit supporting politicians who claim to have found them. Instead we need to work to establish the kind of political climate in America that will foster meaningful and continuous educational improvement. That begins with our acceptance of a simple but inescapable truth: As long as our leaders politicize the process of educational change, we will never achieve educational excellence.

To create the schools that our children deserve, we have to abandon the politically driven processes that have influenced educational policymaking in recent decades. If we do not, elected officials will continue to enact misguided reforms, and our children will continue to suffer the consequences. In other words, we can alter current policies, including NCLB, but we will be at best only partially and temporarily successful in improving our schools if we do not change the politics of education in America.

As part of that effort, we must consistently reject exaggerated claims of public school failure and legislative proposals that are not supported by research and knowledge from the field. Instead, we must demand informed appraisals of educational quality, thoughtful consideration of what our children should know and be able to do, and proven strategies for accomplishing our aims.

It is imperative that we no longer view the need for educational reform as evidence of past failure. Instead, we must acknowledge that school improvement is a continuous process and the responsibility of every adult generation to its children. In today's world, social and economic conditions change constantly, and such changes require that we periodically reexamine our vision for the future and rethink the ways we will achieve it. If change is a constant, so too is the need for educational improvement.

Perhaps most important, we must forever disabuse ourselves of the belief that excoriating public education is a necessary impetus for reform. In the past, many of us have not been more outspoken in countering false political and media claims about educational quality because we hoped that criticisms of schools would somehow bring them increased attention and resources. However, for the first time in our history, American education is facing a challenge to its very existence. Voucher advocates show no signs of relenting in their efforts to denigrate public schools in order to promote privatization. Now more than ever, it is incumbent upon the rest of us to confront misrepresentations of educational quality with accurate information.

There simply is no need to startle Americans with claims of impending doom in order to gain their commitment to educational reform. When parents and citizens come to recognize that school change is a continuous process, and when they become accustomed to hearing appropriately positive and critical messages about our nation's schools—accompanied by thoughtful appraisals of problems and solutions—they will approach challenges to educational quality with optimism and resolve.

I realize that I am presenting a lofty vision of educational politics and that many readers will suggest that it is impossible to change the culture of American politics. However, I believe we can achieve a more principled politics of school improvement if we act purposefully to elevate our nation's public discourse about education. Further, I believe that the four actions described below will help us to accomplish that aim.

BECOMING ASTUTE CONSUMERS OF POLITICAL
AND MEDIA STATEMENTS ABOUT EDUCATION

As a first step, educators, parents, and other citizens must be able to see through the fog of political and media rhetoric about education so that they can demand more responsible behavior from elected officials and journalists. Throughout this book, I have called attention to misleading statements about education. Below, I codify my concerns by suggesting some red flags that will help readers to recognize misrepresentations of school issues and will enable them to participate actively in public discourse about education.

BEWARE OF PROMISES OF QUICK, EASY SOLUTIONS.

When it comes to school improvement, there are no silver bullets. America has several million public school teachers, hundreds of thousands of administrators, and tens of thousands of educational scholars. If there were a quick, easy fix for all of public education's problems, one of these professionals would have figured it out by now. Business leaders, politicians, and journalists who claim to have discovered panaceas may be sincere in that belief, but they are deluding themselves, and they should not delude others.

We need to hold elected officials and the media accountable for presenting well-informed, responsible proposals for improving schools. I would suggest that we only support measures that receive the endorsement of respected educational groups. It is hard to imagine Congress enacting a law to require doctors to employ a particular medical procedure if the American Medical Association was overwhelmingly opposed to its use. Similarly, we should not allow elected officials to enact educational policies unless these initiatives meet the approval of respected organizations such as the National Education Association, the American Association of School Administrators, and the American Educational Research Association.

BEWARE OF INFLAMMATORY RHETORIC.

We should be concerned about the intentions of anyone who announces an educational position with a statement such as, "Public education in America is a mess" (Scheiber, 2005, p. 120), especially if that person provides no evidence to support such a bold claim. If someone you just met at a social gathering initiated a discussion of the medical profession by stating, "Every doctor I've ever known is a quack," would you suspect that person had an ax to grind? We should be no less skeptical of "experts" who carelessly proclaim the existence of an educational crisis (a definite red flag). Our schools have their problems, but past pronouncements that they are in crisis have not held true, and such statements have not contributed to improvement.

IN PARTICULAR, BEWARE OF ANYONE WHO SAYS, "IT'S JUST ANOTHER EXAMPLE OF OUR FAILING EDUCATIONAL SYSTEM."

The most disturbing use of this statement that I have witnessed was by Bill O'Reilly of the Fox News Network. In commenting on the 2005 abduction and murder of a child near her home in Florida, O'Reilly went so far as to blame this horrific crime on public school administrators. As it happened, the convicted sex offender accused of the crime was working for a contractor employed by the school that the victim attended. Even so, there was no evidence that the child was abducted near the school or that the man accused of the crime identified her as a potential victim while working there.

In fact, he lived near her family's home, and law enforcement officials believed he kidnapped her in that area. However, O'Reilly argued that the school should have reviewed the personnel records of the contractor's employees and identified this man as a sex offender. O'Reilly ended his story of this heinous crime by stating that it was further evidence of our failing educational system.

Though his delivery of that conclusion made it seem convincing, a moment's reflection reveals how irresponsible it really was. Although it would be appropriate to expect the contractor to screen personnel records before working at a school, it is unlikely that education officials could legally demand the personnel records of a vendor in order to review them. At best, the school system might be able to compel any company providing a service to the school to take that precaution.

In fact, according to a statement by a school district administrator (in the March 22, 2005, edition of the St. Petersburg Times), the system did require the contractor to sign a bid document verifying that no one convicted of a sex offense would work at the construction site. However, O'Reilly did not mention this fact or imply any responsibility on the part of the contractor. Instead, he blamed the horrific murder of an innocent child on our "failing educational system."

When journalists can play on the emotions of outraged audiences and direct such egregious and irresponsible charges toward our nation's schools, citizens have a responsibility to view those reports critically. We should be able to expect members of the media to behave more professionally, but until they do, we should recognize such desperate attempts to arouse emotions against public education for what they are. In fact, we should probably regard with skepticism any political or media statement that includes the words "another example of our failing educational system." No one who uses those words is genuinely interested in offering useful criticism or guidance for our schools.

BEWARE OF APPEALS TO NOSTALGIA.

As noted in chapter 11, a fundamental problem with nostalgic appeals to return our schools to their former glory is that the available evidence simply does not support the assertion that schools were once better. More to the point, it should be clear that we cannot meet the challenges of preparing our young people for the future by continually looking backward.

SIMILARLY, BEWARE OF APPEALS TO COMMON SENSE.

As suggested in chapter 12, there is an extensive history of failed common sense solutions to educational problems. I would suggest that politicians and journalists who use the words *common sense* to advance their arguments are revealing their ignorance of the complexity of public school issues and their inability to offer any other form of support for their ideas. In discussions of educational policy, no two words should throw up a bigger red flag than *common sense*.

BEWARE OF CAUSAL LEAPS—THAT IS, CLAIMS THAT ONE EDUCATIONAL CONDITION CAUSES ANOTHER, ESPECIALLY WHEN NO REAL EVIDENCE IS PROVIDED TO SUBSTANTI-ATE THE CONNECTION BETWEEN THE TWO CONDITIONS.

On his CNN show one evening, Lou Dobbs executed a succession of some of the most enormous leaps I have ever witnessed. Of course, he began by suggesting that schools are in crisis. He then leaped to the conclusion that shortcomings in student achievement are due to teachers' lack of knowledge about their subjects—although he did not provide any evidence for such a connection.

Having bounded forward so impressively, he seemed emboldened by his success and began to advocate for the replacement of teacher education courses in college with more subject area study. Of course, he ignored the research indicating that students taught by teachers fully certified in education courses are the ones who perform most successfully and that schools that are forced to hire teachers without educational credentials are the ones most seriously underperforming.

As he shook his head in disgust at the obviously obstructionist educators who continue to cling to the belief that teachers should really know how to teach, Dobbs looked into the camera and asked how teachers could teach subjects that they do not know. (As he did, I could not help but wonder: if it were true that teachers know how to teach but know little about their subjects, wouldn't that be analogous to journalists who know how to play to an audience but do not understand the topics they are covering?)

The reason that journalists, politicians, and pundits make such leaps is that they simply do not understand the issues over which they have bounded so carelessly. It is not necessary that a person know educational research to recognize most leaps. For example, in Dobbs's case, we just have to ask whether there might be reasons for mediocre student performance other than the one he suggested, especially when he fails to provide any data to substantiate his arguments.

Simply stated, journalists and politicians who try to establish cause-and-effect relationships without providing any evidence are making leaps, and we should ignore their comments or take them to task for being so careless and irresponsible. We cannot continue to allow educational policy in America to be influenced by the musings of armchair experts.

BEWARE OF THE USE OF SELECTIVE DATA.

In particular, be wary of the use of one test score to assert that schools are in crisis. As explained in chapter 9, there are good reasons why American students sometimes score well on one test in a particular subject (such as reading, for example) and then do not perform as well on another assessment in that same subject. If a politician or journalist employs one score to suggest that schools are failing, we should immediately wonder why other scores are not included. With all of the state, national, and international testing we impose on our children, it should not be hard to find numerous indications of academic deficiencies if they actually exist.

BEWARE OF POLITICIANS AND JOURNALISTS WHO REFER TO "A TEST" OR "A STUDY" AND NEVER GIVE ANY IDENTIFYING INFORMATION ABOUT THE SOURCE OF THE TEST OR STUDY.

As suggested in chapter 3, we should ignore those who employ this strategy. There have been too many misrepresentations of educational data in the past for us to trust a politician or member of the media who will not identify the assessment instrument or research used to support a position. There simply is no reason for a politician or journalist not to state clearly the source of a test or study.

BEWARE OF POLITICIANS AND JOURNALISTS SUGGESTING THAT EDUCATORS HAVE AN AGENDA AND DON'T WANT WHAT'S BEST FOR OUR YOUNG PEOPLE.

As noted in chapter 13, Americans regard teachers as the most trustworthy group of people in our country. Politicians and journalists may find it advantageous to make statements about the "agendas" of teachers, administrators, and researchers, but citizens hearing these pronouncements should stop and ask themselves: do most educators really have any agenda other than to educate our children?

We should be especially skeptical when advocates of unproven reforms employ terms such as "the educational establishment" to characterize teachers, administrators, and scholars who are opposed to their initiatives. After more than thirty years of work and study as a teacher, administrator, and assistant professor, I still have no idea who the educational establishment is. I can only infer that this shadowy phantom group is anyone in the field of education who finds fault with the simplistic solutions of armchair experts. Ultimately, if most teachers, administrators, and educational researchers oppose an idea, maybe we should accept that they do—not because of some selfish agenda—but because it's a really bad idea.

LAST, EXAMINE CAREFULLY THE MOTIVES OF REFORM ADVOCATES.

As I said in chapter 7, I am not a person who is quick to impute sinister motives. However, after years of observing educational reform initiatives, I have had to accept the hard truth that the leaders of many of these efforts have more on their minds than what is best for our children. Although many politicians have been well intentioned in their support of educational reforms, some have not.

We should be especially careful to examine the motives of corporate leaders who become involved in school change initiatives, particularly when they exclude educators from their deliberations. Public education in America is an enormous enterprise, and there is money to be made from transportation to textbooks to tutoring children in "failing" schools. Many of these folks may mean well, but the fact remains that the primary business of business is making money.

In the end, we should never assume that what is in the best interests of the corporate world will necessarily be in our children's best interests. Business leaders who support educational changes that they believe will benefit them financially without hurting our children are fooling themselves. As I have suggested throughout this book, the effects of educational initiatives are often unexpected—especially when these reforms are designed by noneducators. When our children's best interests are a secondary consideration in the development of educational policy, our children always suffer.

DEMANDING IMPROVED MEDIA COVERAGE OF EDUCATIONAL ISSUES

There is a second essential action that educators and citizens can advocate in the interests of improving the quality of our nation's public discourse about education. To demonstrate the need for this change, I list below some findings from the 2006 Phi Delta Kappa/Gallup Poll of the Public's Attitudes toward the Public Schools (Rose & Gallup,

2006). All of the following data reveal the public's lack of knowledge about NCLB, the act that is fundamentally changing the educational experience of essentially every public school student in America.

- In 2006, four years after NCLB was signed into law, 55 percent of the Phi Delta Kappa/Gallup Poll respondents, including 50 percent of parents, said they knew "very little" or "nothing at all" about the law. That percentage was an improvement from the 59 percent who said they knew very little or nothing about NCLB in 2005, the 68 percent who said the same in 2004, and the 76 percent who had that response in 2003. We can only imagine how few Americans knew anything about NCLB when it was enacted in 2002.[1]
- In 2006, 88 percent of survey respondents said that it was important to close the achievement gap between white students and black and Hispanic students. However, only 19 percent said that the differences in achievement between these groups were related to the quality of schooling students received, and 77 percent said that factors other than schooling explained the achievement gap.
- In that poll, 69 percent of respondents said that a single test cannot determine whether or not a school is in need of improvement, and 81 percent said that we should not evaluate schools by assessing only English and math proficiency. Also, 78 percent said that a singular focus on English and math scores would reduce the attention given to other subjects.
- The majority of respondents (54 percent) opposed the reporting of student test scores for each of the eight separate subpopulations identified by NCLB.
- Seventy-five percent opposed requiring special education students to meet the same standards as all other students. (In the 2005 poll, 48 percent said that a school should not be designated as needing to improve if its special education students are the only ones who do not meet NCLB standards. The 2006 poll did not ask respondents about that provision of NCLB.)

[1] In 2007, 46 percent of respondents said they knew very little or nothing about NCLB—still a shockingly low proportion of the public, given the significance of NCLB and the fact that citizens were being asked about it six years after its passage. In the 2007 poll, respondents were not asked questions about their perceptions of the various provisions of NCLB as they were in 2006—thus the focus on the 2006 poll numbers in this discussion.

- Eighty percent of respondents said they did not support the idea of having children transfer out of a school that has not achieved NCLB standards to a school that has.
- Sixty percent of respondents said they were opposed to allowing children to attend private schools at public expense.
- When respondents were asked if they favored reforming the existing public school system or finding an alternative system, 71 percent said they preferred making changes to the present system.

These data are startling evidence of the failure of our news media to provide the American public with accurate reporting and thoughtful analysis of important educational issues. NCLB is fundamentally changing teaching and learning in American classrooms and may be an instrument for dismantling our educational system as we know it. Yet most parents and citizens said they knew very little or nothing about this far-reaching educational act more than five years after its passage.

As someone who cares about the health of our nation and believes that informed citizen participation is essential to our democratic way of life, I find it very disturbing that most Americans have apparently given their implicit approval to NCLB, even though they clearly disagree with almost everything about it. For example, according to the poll results cited above, three out of four Americans reject one of the act's most basic premises, the suggestion that quality of schooling is the reason why African-American and Hispanic students do not score as well on standardized tests as white students.

The vast majority of Americans do not believe that a single test is a valid measure of a school's effectiveness, disagree with the use of English and math tests as the sole determinants of school quality, and are concerned that attention to other subjects will suffer when only English and math test scores count. The public does not agree with the idea of reporting test data for various subpopulations, the feature of NCLB that most clearly distinguishes it from other accountability measures.

Most citizens do not believe that special education students should be held to the same standards as other students, and about half do not think it is fair to single out schools whose special education students are the only ones who do not achieve standards.

Eight in ten Americans disapprove of one of the most fundamental sanctions of NCLB, the practice of allowing students to transfer out of schools labeled as failing.

Moreover, most Americans do not want our present educational system to be replaced with an alternative and do not support the use of private school vouchers, even though the adoption of that strategy appears to be the goal of the architects of NCLB. In brief, Americans oppose virtually everything about the landmark act that is fundamentally changing their children's education—but apparently do not know that the very basis of that law is a set of provisions with which they strongly disagree.

So how did President Bush and Congress enact an educational reform that so flagrantly contradicts the wishes of most public school parents and other citizens, and why don't the majority of Americans even know that it happened? Simply stated, the proponents of NCLB very cleverly wrapped that legislation in the compelling imagery of "no child left behind," and our news media were unable to penetrate the law's illusions and report the truth.

Rather than explaining the accountability provisions of NCLB to the public with the kind of detail that would enable citizens to make intelligent decisions about whether or not to support it, the elected officials who devised the law sold it as a tough-minded, common sense proposal that would finally hold educators responsible for "the soft bigotry of low expectations." America's print and television journalists could not resist the political sales job and jumped on board without conducting the inquiry needed to separate the law's imagery from its reality. As a result, a tragically deleterious educational act is being imposed on our children, even though the educational community and most American citizens oppose its most basic provisions.

Americans care about the quality of their public schools, and they should receive accurate information about them. In fact, our educational system is one of the foundations of our democratic way of life, and citizens cannot actively participate in decisions about that institution if they are not adequately informed. When journalists fail to provide accurate reporting and thoughtful analysis of educational issues, they fail in one of their most basic responsibilities to our democracy.

As I have stated elsewhere in this book, most journalists simply do not understand education well enough to provide useful reporting and analysis about our schools. They cannot comment insightfully about the educational news that emerges, and they do not know how to uncover and illuminate the issues that are hidden from most citizens.

Clearly, the quality of media coverage of education will not improve until major news outlets employ educational consultants, in much the same manner that television networks now hire medical and legal experts to report the news in their fields and offer analysis and commentary. In the absence of these qualified educator-journalists, the American public will remain in the dark about policies affecting their children, and politicians will continue to enact laws that are more likely to be damaging than beneficial to our youth.

By employing knowledgeable, experienced educators to report and interpret educational news, America's media organizations can elevate our nation's discourse about matters that are important to our citizens and fundamental to our democracy. When major news outlets hired doctors and lawyers as reporters and analysts, they acknowledged that medicine and law had become too complex in twenty-first-century America for average journalists to cover effectively. The media should also recognize that most educational issues are beyond the grasp of journalists who have not been educators. Having once been a child does not make an adult an authority on child rearing. Similarly, having once been a student does not make a journalist or commentator an educational expert.

The employment of educator-journalists would ensure that educational issues are more thoroughly reported than they are now. Surely the academic preparation of tens of millions of American school children deserves as much attention from our media as the legal woes of Michael Jackson. As tragic as it is that a young woman was apparently murdered on a graduation trip to Aruba, or that a philandering husband in California killed both his wife and unborn child, the time committed by our news media to sordid and sensational crimes should not be exponentially greater than the attention focused on important issues affecting millions of our public school children.

News networks with qualified educator-journalists would be able to probe and report issues that are currently untouched by today's media. In addition, the news agencies that hired such experts could examine the educational platforms of politicians with a level of depth and clarity that are sadly missing in today's coverage of election campaigns. Ultimately, the work of these educator-journalists would empower average American citizens to make prudent choices among political candidates based on their positions on educational issues.

Educator-journalists could inform the public of findings that are published in professional journals, such as the study indicating that improvements in test scores by minority students appear to be the result of an increase in African-American and Hispanic dropouts—not proof that NCLB is working (Miao & Haney, 2004).

They would also be able to report that states are struggling to provide the resources mandated by NCLB to help schools in trouble and that very few students are choosing the two primary interventions provided by NCLB—supplemental services and transfer to other schools. These educator-journalists would enable citizens to evaluate the effectiveness of NCLB knowing that the Public Education Network and the Center on Education Policy concluded that the exclusive focus on English and math test score improvement has narrowed the curriculum in most schools (Lewis, 2005). In brief, well-informed educator-journalists would empower citizens to assess more effectively the success of laws such as NCLB and to participate actively in democratic decisions affecting their children's education.

If our news media had previously retained people with experience in education and knowledge of educational research, these journalists would have been able to report incisively in 2000 and 2001 about the "Texas miracle" that was the model for NCLB. The public would have learned before the passage of NCLB that overall graduation rates dropped dramatically in Texas during the 1990s and that the graduation rate for African-Americans and Hispanics dipped below 50 percent. American citizens would have known that the gap between these two groups and white students increased so dramatically that Linda McNeil characterized education policies in Texas as "a creative new form of discrimination" (2000, p. 732).

Had the public been aware of data and perspectives about the Texas miracle other than those provided by the politicians promoting it, perhaps more people would have questioned the effectiveness of a federal law based on the Texas experience and wrapped in the imagery of racial equality and accountability. In addition, Americans would probably have scrutinized more carefully the appointment of a Texas school administrator to the office of secretary of education in 2001 on the basis of his alleged success in solving the dropout problem in his Houston school district.

Apparently the elected leaders who endorsed Rod Paige readily accepted the assertion that he essentially eliminated dropouts in a large urban area with massive social problems. The media eventually discovered that officials in Paige's system had manipulated data to disguise the actual number of dropouts in his district, but that startling revelation did not benefit America's children. Mr. Paige served as our highest ranking education official for more than four years of their lives, apparently because he was the person the Bush administration thought was the best advocate for promoting the ideological agenda of NCLB.

APPOINTING QUALIFIED EDUCATORS AS SECRETARIES OF EDUCATION

The office of secretary of education is too important to our children to be assigned to anyone for purely political or ideological reasons. Therefore, the third action we must advocate in the interests of changing our nation's discourse about education involves the selection and length of office of the secretary of education.

As I watched and read news reports of the federal government's response to Hurricane Katrina in September 2005 and heard citizens react with outrage to the revelation that FEMA Secretary Brown had little or no previous experience in emergency management, I wondered how many citizens knew that Secretary of Education Margaret

Spellings has never been an educator and does not hold a degree in education. As suggested in chapter 4, Spellings has neither the background nor the knowledge about education to offer leadership to our schools and universities.

She cannot possibly possess the understanding needed to provide useful guidance in the dissemination of educational grants, and she clearly lacks the insight to render informed opinions about educational policy. Sadly, she is little more than a political appointee, charged with overseeing an institution that most Americans and President Bush himself consistently identify as one of the most important to our nation's health.

In the end, it appears that she was chosen not for her knowledge of education, but rather for her lack of it. I would suggest that her role is not to provide Bush administration officials with understanding about education, but simply to promote their predetermined ideological positions—that is, the views of leaders like her who have no personal experience in public education and little or no knowledge of educational research.

In fact, it appears that most of the presidents who have been entrusted with the responsibility for naming the secretary of education have based their selections on reasons other than their appointees' expertise. Beginning with Jimmy Carter's choice of Shirley Hufstedler in 1979, we have had eight secretaries of education. Four of them had law degrees and backgrounds in politics or the legal profession.

Only two, Terrell Bell (appointed by Ronald Reagan) and Rod Paige (appointed by George W. Bush) had experience in public schools. Curiously, their selections were perhaps the most ideologically driven of the eight. It was during Terrell Bell's tenure that the Reagan administration released the inflammatory *A Nation at Risk*. Rod Paige became the spokesperson for NCLB and consistently attacked educators who dared to express disapproval of any portion of the law, culminating with his characterization of the National Education Association as a terrorist organization.

If the improvement of public education is one of the most important issues facing our society—and elected officials and citizens continue to assert that it is—we must give more thoughtful consideration to the selection of our nation's secretary of education. The person in that position can elevate the quality of public discourse by serving as a spokesperson for our schools, enhancing our citizens' understanding of key issues, generating increased interest in education, and stimulating a thoughtful national discussion about public school reform.

Only a person who is knowledgeable about education and respected by public school educators and researchers can fulfill these roles. To identify this leader, our elected officials could consult major educational organizations for possible candidates.

As noted earlier, the National Education Association represents more than half of our nation's public school teachers and many of its administrators. There are a number of established organizations representing administrators, including the American Association of School Administrators, the National Association of Elementary School Principals, the National Association of Secondary School Principals, and the Association for Supervision and Curriculum Development.

The American Educational Research Association is perhaps the most respected and inclusive organization of educational scholars and often acts as a voice for that group of professionals. A secretary of education with the endorsement of each of these groups would be able to lead teachers, administrators, and academics, and that person would be capable of presenting the views of these diverse educational groups to the general public.

Of course, the appointment of the secretary of education is ultimately the responsibility of the president of the United States, and the people elected to that office are not obligated to acknowledge the perspectives of the educational community, as past Democratic and Republican presidents have clearly demonstrated. However, by the same token, the American public should not be deceived by any president who says that improving public education is one of the most important issues facing our nation and then names as the secretary of education a politician with no educational background or an extreme ideologue who lacks the support of the majority of our nation's educators.

America's children deserve better than patronage appointees to the offices that oversee their education. In recent decades, candidates for president have been quick to say that they are going to hold teachers to higher standards. Similarly, I believe we should hold our presidents to a higher standard in the selection of secretaries of education. When they name noneducators or ideologues to the highest educational office in the land, they not only make it clear that they are uninterested in having their perspectives challenged by people who actually understand education, but they dishonor our children and suggest that they are not very important.

We might also consider increasing the length of office for the secretary of education—to perhaps ten years—and appointing this person at a midpoint between presidential elections. What's best for the education of our children does not change with every four-year election cycle and should not be influenced by election politics. Having a secretary of education whose length of office spans more than one presidential term would lend continuity to school policy at the national level and would go far in depoliticizing our nation's discourse on education.

Again, I realize that I am questioning a presidential prerogative. However, we should all remember how passionately presidential candidates from both parties have proclaimed their desire to improve our schools. If they are sincere in these statements, they should be willing to support a change that so clearly benefits our children.

RETHINKING TESTING AND ACCOUNTABILITY

My fourth and final suggestion for elevating America's public discourse about education is that we examine carefully the effectiveness and uses of standardized tests and that we make long-overdue revisions to these state and national assessments. Readers might wonder why I am suggesting a relationship between changes in testing and the quality of our nation's public discourse about education. As a reminder, I noted in chapter 9 that test scores have become the language of the politics of education in America. As long as we use standardized tests as the primary way to assess school performance, it is clear that they will dominate discussions about education and will drive reform.

Many educators would simply like to eliminate these tests altogether. However, because they offer quantitative evidence of student performance, they have a compelling logic to most lawmakers and citizens. Since they will probably be with us for a very long time, it is imperative that we begin to administer tests that tell us what we really need to know about our schools, encourage the kinds of educational practices that are best for our children, and stimulate a more thoughtful national discussion about public school improvement.

Clearly, the tests we use now are the proverbial tail wagging the dog. As much as we might like to believe that the purpose of these tests is simply to measure what students have learned, they actually play a much bigger role in determining what students will learn. That is, accountability legislation has placed so much emphasis on test performance that educators in most schools now focus their instruction almost exclusively on the tested curriculum. Teachers are painfully aware of this reality, but it appears that the majority of the American public is not.

When most citizens hear that a school has had a less than acceptable performance on a standardized test, they logically assume that the educators in that building did a mediocre or poor job, and sometimes that is true. However, when teachers receive a report showing lower test scores than they expected, they usually do not conclude that they taught badly, but that they did not put enough emphasis on the right material.

That is, they assume that they gave too much attention to facts, concepts, or skills that were not assessed by the test and too little attention to those that were. They then adjust their curriculum to try to achieve a more perfect match with the test. In brief, test scores are not so much a reflection of instructional quality or teacher effort as they are an indication of how well teachers taught to the test. Therefore, it is imperative that we develop instruments that measure academic competencies that truly matter.

As noted earlier, today's standardized tests often assess content of questionable value, do not measure creativity, rarely evaluate higher levels of understanding, and tell us little or nothing about how students think or solve complex problems. More to the point, even though they dominate our nation's public discourse about education, no one has yet established a correlation between a student's performance on any standardized test and that person's future success or ability to contribute to society.

Of course, that fact doesn't keep politicians, pundits, and journalists from predicting America's demise every time a mediocre test score is announced. In response to such statements, the pressure on educators to improve test scores invariably increases, and they ratchet up their efforts to teach exclusively the tested curriculum, whether it has any genuine value for students or not.

Because it is clear that standardized tests are not going away, it is imperative that we take some time away from the relentless pursuit of higher scores to ask if what we're assessing—and therefore teaching—really matters to the future of our children and the health of our nation. To clarify this issue, I believe it would be helpful to consider for a moment two related issues that are on the minds of many Americans today: science achievement in our public schools and the ability of our country to maintain its international preeminence in science and technology.

Over the last few years, citizen concern about student performance in science has seemed to explode. Hardly a week passes without a major news outlet, politician, or pundit commenting on the allegedly disastrous state of science achievement in our schools and the frightening consequences for our future. The connection that the public is making between our students' science knowledge and the ability of our nation to compete scientifically and technologically is logical and appropriate.

We do need to consider carefully what our students learn about science today and how that will affect America's future. However, if we allow public discourse about this topic to be characterized by the kind of simplistic political and media analyses that have dominated such discussions in the past, our educational system will be caught in the worst kind of Catch-22, and our nation will ultimately feel the effects.

Perhaps the most popular line of thought promoted by today's politicians and pundits is that student shortcomings on standardized science tests foreshadow a future deficit of scientists and engineers. There are two problems with this reasoning. One, there simply isn't any evidence that test scores are good predictors of adult success in the fields of science and engineering. Two, we should really question the assumption that a mediocre score by a student on a single test is a reliable indication that this young person will decide not to pursue science or engineering as a career (or, for that matter, that an exceptional score will catapult a student into one of these careers).

It seems far more likely that young people will choose these vocations because they perceive that the work will provide the financial and emotional benefits they hope to enjoy professionally. To the extent that students examine their past performance in a given field before deciding whether or not to make it their life's work (and they certainly should), it seems doubtful that they would weigh standardized test scores more heavily than coursework success or other factors.

Although there may not be any relationship at all between standardized test performance and the number of young people choosing science and engineering as careers, our nation's purveyors of common sense educational solutions will probably continue to insist that there is. Consequently, the pressure to improve science test scores will continue to grow, and classroom teaching will continue to change in undesirable ways, just as it already has in response to the pressures of NCLB and earlier accountability measures.

Because most of the multiple-choice tests we now use require students to regurgitate information rather than demonstrate genuine understanding, science teachers will use experimentation and other intellectually engaging strategies less frequently and will increase drill and memorization. Subsequent improvements in science test scores will validate these academically stifling approaches and further affirm their use—even though they squelch student interest in science.

As our schools take on the challenge of improving science test scores to meet the demands of NCLB, we need to be especially concerned about extricating ourselves from this cycle. At the beginning of this discussion, I said that we need to consider carefully what our students learn about science. The problem with science performance in America today is not that too few students have memorized geological facts such as the three types of rock—which is exactly the kind of rote learning assessed by most of our state-mandated science tests.

The real problem is that most science instruction does not light a scientific fire in our children, and it does not allow them to get a taste of the kind of work that scientists such as geologists do. Consequently, our young people do not discover that geologists, for example, go to fascinating places to study the earth and its layers, to monitor and predict earthquakes and volcanoes, to explore for mineral wealth, or to assist construction engineers by determining the stability of certain soils and rock strata for supporting bridges, dams, and buildings.

In other words, the problem is that our students are not learning that science can be an exciting subject and career choice. They do not learn from skill and drill that science is simply the study of the world around us—the same world that enthralls young children when they play outdoors or explore a toy to determine how it works. They do not learn from skill and drill that scientists are interesting people doing fascinating, engaging work to improve other people's lives and increase our understanding of the universe. Instead, students attending school in the era of accountability see science as a collection of meaningless facts that they must memorize in order to pass a test.

Our children will not know how science can enrich their lives as long as we continue to pressure teachers to generate improved scores on today's standardized tests. In the public debate about science, some attention has appropriately focused on the number of young people who are choosing science as a career. However, too few voices in this discussion have been prescient enough to suggest that schools involve students in science learning that nurtures and sustains a lifelong interest in the subject.

In a thoughtful and in-depth examination of the challenge of keeping America preeminent in the world of science, Michael D. Lemonick (2006) of *Time* magazine called attention to a variety of problems with our nation's science performance, including concerns about the quality of public school science instruction. The cover of that issue of *Time* posed the question, "Is America Flunking Science?" Unfortunately, the answer will continue to be yes if we do not soon recognize that few of our high school graduates will ever want to be scientists as long as we pressure teachers to improve scores on the kinds of standardized tests we use today.

This dilemma illustrates one of the fundamental concerns educators have about high-stakes testing and our children's future. Standardized tests have been very seductive to policymakers because of their ability to quantify results. However, these assessments simply do not tell us everything we need to know about public school performance, particularly our students' love of learning, and young people who are not passionate about a subject are not very likely to choose careers related to that subject.

Unfortunately, our schools are presently engaged in a struggle to improve science test scores, and the instructional methods employed in that pursuit are more likely to squelch than to nurture our children's interest in science. At the same time, the politicians and journalists who endlessly clamor about the allegedly declining numbers of students choosing science and engineering careers are also demanding higher test performance—apparently never realizing the inherent contradiction they are expressing, the Catch-22 they have created for our schools, or the fact that they (not educators) are the real problem.

If, in fact, the number of young people choosing science-related careers is decreasing to troubling levels, it isn't because of our students' inability to score high on standardized science tests. It is because they think science is boring. If America is facing a crisis in science instruction, it isn't because of poor test performance. It is because the drive for improved test scores on today's standardized tests invariably results in academically stultifying instructional practices.

Ideally, a single assessment should simply be one indicator of quality, and we should employ a variety of instruments to determine student success in any subject. However, as a result of high-stakes accountability laws, state-mandated tests have become the only measure of importance in most school systems. As stated often in this book, these tests now drive instruction in America's public school classrooms. Because the tail is clearly wagging the dog, we must change the instruments we use to assess school quality so that they provide a more meaningful portrait of student performance and are more likely to encourage desirable instructional practices.

To address this challenge, I suggest that we convene genuine experts in the field of educational assessment to examine current practices and make general recommendations for the future. The participants in this study should include educational researchers who understand multiple performance measures, teacher representatives and school administrators who are sensitive to the impact of high-stakes testing at the classroom level, district and state administrators, commercial producers of standardized tests, curriculum scholars, and educators who have been successful in working with poor children from both rural and urban areas.

Parents and other citizens should also be involved, as should the secretary of education. I do not suggest that elected leaders be a part of this study, partly because most of them do not understand the issues involved in educational assessment, but also because this important examination of the measures that drive teaching and learning in our children's classrooms should not be a political process. We know that lawmakers will ultimately have the final say, and we can only hope that the laws they pass will reflect the expertise of the educators and citizens who provide them with a thoughtful plan for assessing learning in America's public schools.

The people charged with the responsibility to develop assessment guidelines will know better than I what questions to ask, but I would like to suggest a few—not for this gathering of experts, but rather to demonstrate to readers the direction and potential of such a comprehensive study. The questions addressed by this group might include the following:

1. What do we want our children to know, understand, and be able to do when they complete their schooling? Are these competencies that will help them succeed in life and contribute to our democratic society?

2. How can we measure these achievements in ways that foster advanced levels of learning and best classroom practices?
3. How can we fairly measure the achievements of all students, including those with disabilities?
4. In addition to academic learning, what academic dispositions (such as a love of learning) do we want our students to have, and how can we effectively measure these? What kinds of assessments will lead to increased achievement without compromising these academic dispositions?
5. Should we try to measure academic growth from one year to the next (that is, calculate how much students have improved over the previous year), or do we simply want to provide snapshots of how different grade levels of students are performing at given points in time?
6. Do we need both national and state tests? If we have both, how can we be sure that attention to one set of standards does not compromise the other?
7. In what grades should students take standardized tests, and should all students in these grades take them, or should we randomly select students for testing? Of course, the answer to this question might depend in part on the answer to question 5.

Again, these are just some examples of the questions that could be addressed in an assessment summit. Before closing, I would like to discuss briefly a few of the issues they raise, especially those suggested by the first two questions and the last one.

Over the years educators have developed assessments that measure more than rote learning and basic skills and provide a more authentic portrait of student achievement than most of the standardized tests we currently use. These instruments are usually more expensive to grade because they require students to write extended responses rather than simply filling in answer bubbles, but there are ways to mitigate the costs of grading.

One solution would be to test randomly selected students and assess fewer grades than we currently do. After all, that is exactly what the National Assessment of Educational Progress (NAEP) does: it tests students in grades four, eight, and twelve and randomly selects schools in each state to provide a representative sample. Further, it is worth remembering that standardized testing began as a means of furnishing information to the public about the quality of schools and systems, not the performance of individual teachers and students.

To assure citizens that schools are doing their jobs, it simply isn't necessary that we test as many grade levels as we do now or that we test every child in the grades assessed. Most standardized tests provide very little useful information to help teachers instruct individual children. At best, they just confirm what good teachers already know from their own classroom assessments and daily interactions with students. Further, parents already receive information about their children's academic performance from many sources throughout the year. Test scores really don't tell them very much either.

Hopefully, this comprehensive study by assessment experts will be able to resolve the troubling Catch-22 discussed in chapter 9. If there continue to be state tests and a national test such as the NAEP, it is essential that these instruments not be so different that efforts to succeed on one measure result in mediocre performance on the other. To the extent that it is possible, we also need to be sure that American students are not at an unfair disadvantage when they participate in international assessments. No matter what we do to elevate our nation's discourse about education (such as taking the three steps discussed earlier in this chapter), it is clear that there will always be politicians and journalists eager to create a sense of crisis by citing a single discouraging test score, even if it is not meaningful, valid, or useful.

Near the beginning of this chapter, I expressed confidence in the ability of parents, educators, and other citizens to elevate the quality of America's public discourse about education. Each of the actions described here is essential to the achievement of this ambitious aim.

One, we must hold elected officials and journalists accountable for making responsible statements about education. Two, we must demand that the media employ qualified people to report on educational issues so that Americans will be better informed about public school quality and policy. Three, we must insist that our secretaries of education be qualified for that position. It is not asking too much of our presidents to require that they name educators to the most important educational position in America. Four, we must revise our standardized tests so that they measure competencies that are important to our children's success in life.

I believe that this last step is imperative. We will not be able to elevate our nation's discourse about education until we change the language of that discourse. If we cannot discuss public schools using any language other than scores on multiple-choice tests that measure basic levels of learning, we will continue to be deceived by the illusions they create, and our children's experience of schooling will continue to be influenced negatively by the drive to raise scores on these faulty measures. Conversely, when we begin to use meaningful assessments of educational performance, teaching and learning will improve, and we can have a thoughtful and ongoing national discussion about how we can most capably equip each generation of our children for the future.

Afterword

EARLY IN CHAPTER 5, I COMMENTED briefly on the performance of educators in the South during the racial desegregation of that region's public schools. Their contributions serve as a powerful reminder that education does much more than simply impart a discrete set of academic skills to our children. In fact, the impact of public school integration on life in the South demonstrates how imperative it is to our nation's continued health that we maintain the integrity of our educational system.

Public education is the glue for our society. Despite its imperfections, it is the one context in America where young people from every imaginable background learn to live and work together, and it is the democratic institution with the greatest potential for providing equal opportunity for all citizens. Inequalities and cultural divisions still exist in America, but the fact remains that public schools have been an effective instrument for unifying our diverse society and preparing our youth for participation in democratic life. Our dissatisfaction with the success of public education in eliminating all social inequalities is not an indication that we should abandon that institution, but rather that we should increase our resolve to improve its effectiveness.

When we honor our public schools, we honor America and its noblest democratic ideals. We also honor our children, and in doing so we empower them to secure our nation's future.

References

Alexander, L. (2003). Senate floor remarks of Senator Lamar Alexander regarding the American History and Civics Education Act of 2003. Retrieved June 21, 2004, from http://alexander.senate.gov/news/205169.html.

Allington, R. L. (2002). *Big brother and the national reading curriculum: How ideology trumped evidence.* Portsmouth, NH: Heinemann.

Asimov, N. (2003, August 16). Schools miss mark on new U.S. rules. *San Francisco Chronicle.* Retrieved June 22, 2004, from http://www.sfgate.com.

Berliner, D. C., & Biddle, B. J. (1995). *The manufactured crisis: Myths, fraud, and the attack on America's public schools.* Reading, MA: Addison-Wesley.

Boe, E. E., & Shin, S. (2005). Is the United States really losing the international horse race in academic achievement? *Phi Delta Kappan, 86,* 688–695.

Bracey, G. W. (1998). TIMMS, rhymes with "dims," as in "witted." *Phi Delta Kappan, 79,* 686-687.

Bracey, G. W. (2000). *Bail me out! Handling difficult data and tough questions about public schools.* Thousand Oaks, CA: Corwin Press.

Bracey, G. W. (2003a). Those misleading SAT and NAEP trends: Simpson's paradox at work. Education Disinformation Detection and Reporting Agency. Retrieved June 17, 2004, from http://www.america-to-morrow.com.

Bracey, G. W. (2003b). The 13th Bracey report on the condition of education. *Phi Delta Kappan, 85,* 148–164.

Bracey, G. W. (2003c). The No Child Left Behind Act, a plan for the destruction of public education: Just say no. Education Disinformation Detection and Reporting Agency. Retrieved June 17, 2004, from http://www.america-tomorrow.com.

Bracey, G. W. (2007). The first time everything changed: The 17th Bracey report on the condition of public education. *Phi Delta Kappan, 89,* 119–136.

Brokaw, T. (2002). *A long way from home: Growing up in the American heartland.* New York: Random House.

Campbell, P. (2007). Edison is the symptom, NCLB is the disease. *Phi Delta Kappan, 88,* 438–443.

Congress adds issues to No Child law, rather than aiding education (Guest Commentary from *The New York Times*). (2006, May 16). *Johnson City Press,* p. 10A.

Crowley, M. (2004, November). A is for average. *Reader's Digest,* 33–36.

Darling-Hammond, L. (2004). Inequality and the right to learn: Access to qualified teachers in California's public schools. *Teachers' College Record, 106,* 1936–1966.

Edelman, M. W. (2003, October 19). We still have far to go. *Parade Magazine,* 12–13.

Elam, S. M., & Rose, L. C. (1995). The 27th annual Phi Delta Kappa/Gallup poll of the public's attitudes toward the public schools. *Phi Delta Kappan, 77,* 41–59.

Elam, S. M., Rose, L. C., & Gallup, A. M. (1991). The 23rd annual Gallup poll of the public's attitudes toward the public schools. *Phi Delta Kappan, 73,* 41–56.

Elam, S. M., Rose, L. C., & Gallup, A. M. (1992). The 24th annual Gallup/Phi Delta Kappa poll of the public's attitudes toward the public schools. *Phi Delta Kappan, 74,* 41–53.

Elam, S. M., Rose, L. C., & Gallup, A. M. (1994). The 26th annual Phi Delta Kappa/Gallup poll of the public's attitudes toward the public schools. *Phi Delta Kappan, 76,* 41–64.

Elam, S. M., Rose, L. C., & Gallup, A. M. (1996). The 28th annual Phi Delta Kappa/Gallup poll of the public's attitudes toward the public schools. *Phi Delta Kappan, 78,* 41–59.

Flannery, M. E. (2004, October). Who me? An activist? *neatoday,* 28.

Flannery, M. E., Holcomb, S., & Jehlen, A. (2004, October). Respect. *neatoday,* 22–24.

Gallup, A. M. (1986). The 18th annual Gallup poll of the public's attitudes toward the public schools. *Phi Delta Kappan, 68,* 43–59.

Gallup, A. M., & Elam, S. M. (1988). The 20th annual Gallup poll of the public's attitudes toward the public schools. *Phi Delta Kappan, 70,* 33–46.

Goldberg, M. (2005). Test mess 2: Are we doing better a year later? *Phi Delta Kappan,* 389–395.

Gundersen, A. (2004, February). For the love of kids. *neatoday,* 64.

Houk, R. (2003, September 27). Alexander: Drama tied to values of Americans. *Johnson City Press,* p. 1A.

Kaufman, D. (2005). NEA study reveals teacher salaries stagnant for last decade. National Education Association. Retrieved June 27, 2005, from http://www.nea.org/newsreleases/2005/nr050623.html.

Krashen, S. (2003/2004, December–January). Whole language was not the problem; phonics was not the cure. *Reading Today,* 15.

Lemonick, M. D. (2006, February 13). Are we losing our edge? *Time, 167,* 22–33.

Lewis, A. C. (2005). Sound and fury. *Phi Delta Kappan, 86,* 643–644.

Major mentoring. (2004, November). *neatoday,* 15.

McClellan, M. (1994, March). *Why blame schools?* (Research Bulletin No. 12). Bloomington, IN: Phi Delta Kappa Center for Evaluation, Development, and Research.

McNeil, L. M. (2000). Creating new inequalities: Contradictions of reform. *Phi Delta Kappan, 86,* 729–734.

Miao, J., & Haney, W. (2004, October 15). High school graduation rates: Alternative methods and implications. *Education Policy Analysis Archives, 12*(55). Retrieved June 23, 2005, from http://epaa.asu.edu/epaa/v12n55/.

Mixed messages. (2005, February). *neatoday,* 15.

National Commission on Excellence in Education. (1983). *A nation at risk: The imperative of educational reform.* Washington, DC: Author.

Newkirk, T. (2004, March 8). False positives. *Education Week: On the Web.* Retrieved April 8, 2004, from http://www.heinemann.com/Thomas Newkirk3_5_04.asp.

Nichols, S. L., Glass, G. V., & Berliner, D. C. (2005). *High stakes testing and student achievement: Problems for the No Child Left Behind Act (Executive Summary).* Tempe, AZ: Education Policy Studies Laboratory. Retrieved October 26, 2005, from http://edpolicylab.org.

"No Child" loophole leaves 2M ignored. (2006, April 17). Associated Press. Retrieved May 21, 2006, from http://www.cbsnews.com.

O'Neil, John. (2003, September). Who we are, why we teach. *neatoday,* 26–32.

Paige, R. (2003). Civics education in America. *Phi Delta Kappan, 84,* 59.

Paxton, R. J. (2003). Don't know much about history—never did. *Phi Delta Kappan, 85,* 264–273.

Pons, M. (2002). School vouchers: The emerging track record. National Education Association. Retrieved September 5, 2004, from http://www.nea.org/vouchers/02voutrack.html.

Popham, W. J. (2004). *America's "failing" schools: How parents and teachers can cope with No Child Left Behind.* New York: RoutledgeFalmer.

Rebora, A. (2004). No Child Left Behind. *Education Week: On the Web.* Retrieved October 12, 2004, from http://www.edweek.org/context/topics/issuespage.cfm?id=59.

Report card shows where state falls short. (2003, November 8). *Johnson City Press,* p. 2B.

Rose, L. C., & Gallup, A. M. (1998). The 30th annual Phi Delta Kappa/Gallup poll of the public's attitudes toward the public schools. *Phi Delta Kappan, 80,* 41–58.

Rose, L. C., & Gallup, A. M. (1999). The 31st annual Phi Delta Kappa/Gallup poll of the public's attitudes toward the public schools. *Phi Delta Kappan, 81,* 41–56.

Rose, L. C., & Gallup, A. M. (2000). The 32nd annual Phi Delta Kappa/Gallup poll of the public's attitudes toward the public schools. *Phi Delta Kappan, 82,* 41–66.

Rose, L. C., & Gallup, A. M. (2001). The 33rd annual Phi Delta Kappa/Gallup poll of the public's attitudes toward the public schools. *Phi Delta Kappan, 83,* 41–58.

Rose, L. C., & Gallup, A. M. (2002). The 34th annual Phi Delta Kappa/Gallup poll of the public's attitudes toward the public schools. *Phi Delta Kappan, 84,* 41–56.

Rose, L. C., & Gallup, A. M. (2003). The 35th annual Phi Delta Kappa/Gallup poll of the public's attitudes toward the public schools. *Phi Delta Kappan, 85,* 41–52.

Rose, L. C., & Gallup, A. M. (2004). The 36th annual Phi Delta Kappa/Gallup poll of the public's attitudes toward the public schools. *Phi Delta Kappan, 86,* 41–56.

Rose, L. C., & Gallup, A. M. (2005). The 37th annual Phi Delta Kappa/Gallup poll of the public's attitudes toward the public schools. *Phi Delta Kappan, 87,* 41–57.

Rose, L. C., & Gallup, A. M. (2006). The 38th annual Phi Delta Kappa/Gallup poll of the public's attitudes toward the public schools. *Phi Delta Kappan, 88,* 41–56.

Rose, L. C., & Gallup, A. M. (2007). The 39th annual Phi Delta Kappa/Gallup poll of the public's attitudes toward the public schools. *Phi Delta Kappan,* 89, 33–48.

Rose, L. C., Gallup, A. M., & Elam, S. M. (1997). The 29th annual Phi Delta Kappa/Gallup poll of the public's attitudes toward the public schools. *Phi Delta Kappan,* 79, 41–58.

Scheiber, N. (2005, May). 2 schools, 1 big idea. *Readers' Digest,* 120–125.

Sharma, R. (2006, January). Go figure. *neatoday,* 12.

Slavin, R. E. (1995). Detracking and its detractors. *Phi Delta Kappan,* 77, 220–221.

State's shameful secret: Raising illiterate children. (2005, June 4). *Johnson City Press,* p. 6A.

Teacher demographics. (April/May, 2004). *Reading Today,* p. 36.

Time out. (2005, February). *neatoday,* 10.

Toppo, G. (2004, February 23). Education chief calls teachers union "terrorist organization." *USA Today.* Retrieved December 31, 2006, from http://www.usatoday.com.

Troy, F. (2004, November). I am your public school. *TEAch,* 4.

UNICEF. (2003). *A league table of child maltreatment deaths in rich nations, Innocenti report card no. 5.* Florence, Italy: Innocenti Research Centre. Retrieved June 6, 2006, from http://www.unicef-icdc.org/publications/ pdf/repcard5e.pdf.

UNICEF. (2005). *Child poverty in rich countries, 2005, Innocenti report card no. 6.* Florence, Italy: Innocenti Research Centre. Retrieved June 6, 2006, from http://www.unicef-icdc.org/publications/pdf/repcard6e.pdf.

Watson, J. (2002, September 14). Politicians create new-flag foundation. *Johnson City Press.* Retrieved July 2, 2006, from http://www.johnson citypress.com.

Watson, S. (2003, April 24). Alexander lauds eighth-graders for local history book. *Johnson City Press,* pp. 1A, 8A.

Winans, D. (2004, October). A teacher's worth. *neatoday,* 38–41.

About the Author

William E. (Bill) Smith began his career in public education as a high school English teacher in South Carolina in 1974. Over the next fourteen years, he taught in the middle and elementary grades and served as an assistant principal, a district administrator, and an elementary school principal before pursuing a PhD at the University of Florida. He then worked in the Department of Elementary Education at Indiana State University, teaching courses in reading and language arts methods, supervising preservice teachers, and conducting research in local professional development schools. From 1996 through 2000 he was director of University School, a K–12 laboratory school at East Tennessee State University. Since that time he has been a fourth grade teacher in Johnson City, Tennessee. In 2005 he was Teacher of the Year for East Tennessee and one of three finalists for the state Teacher of the Year Award.

Bill's wife Pat has been a teacher for more than thirty years and often serves as his mentor and adviser. Their daughter Meaghan is a television news reporter in Fort Myers, Florida.